Praise for
The Relational Judaism Handbook

"A dazzling array of fail-proof methods on how to engage people through personal relationships, strong shared experiences, and community leadership interactions. Includes the secrets of some of the most consumer-attractive businesses in the world, translated into Jewish community-building techniques. The processes outlined here are not only exciting; they actually work. Use this handbook to rebuild the vitality of American Jewry: the community you save may be your own."

 —Yitz and Blu Greenberg

"At a time when new ideas are desperately needed, this complementary handbook to [the] important book *Relational Judaism* is filled with examples of how congregations have built relational communities. Starting with the simple but profound principle that Judaism must start by putting people before programs, this new book is the guide to creating a true Beit Knesset, a House of Meeting."

 —Rabbi Sid Schwarz, senior fellow, Hazon; author, *Finding a Spiritual*
 Home: How a New Generation of Jews Can Transform the American Synagogue

"Provides a clear, compelling road map for how we create transformative Jewish communities built on relationships. Both a practical, step-by-step guidebook and an inspirational vision of the future, this book should be required reading for everyone engaged in building Jewish life."

 —Rabbi Angela Warnick Buchdahl, senior rabbi, Central Synagogue,
 New York City

"A must-read primer for those of us who think deeply about institutional transformation. *The Relational Judaism Handbook* is the long-awaited playbook giving us the tools we need to champion the art of deepening relationships in our communities. Read this book and learn from our most discerning teachers."

 —Rabbi Peter Berg, senior rabbi, The Temple, Atlanta

"Synagogue professionals and lay leadership are on a quest to help their communities find greater purpose and meaning, and this remarkable book is an invaluable road map toward a holistic approach to do so through the power of Relational Judaism and small-groups engagement. For those of us working with congregations or in congregations, this book provides the tools we need to deepen the lives of so many in a straightforward, easy to follow, and concise style."

—**Livia D. Thompson,** synagogue consultant and past president, National Association for Temple Administration

THE
Relational
Judaism
HANDBOOK

How to Create a Relational Engagement
Campaign to Build and Deepen
Relationships in Your Community

Dr. Ron Wolfson
Rabbi Nicole Auerbach
Rabbi Lydia Medwin

The Center for Relational Judaism
Dorothy K. and Myer S. Kripke
Institute for Jewish Family Literacy

The Relational Judaism Handbook:
How to Create a Relational Engagement Campaign to Build and Deepen Relationships
in Your Community

2018 Quality Paperback Edition, Second Printing
© 2018 by the Dorothy K. and Myer S. Kripke Institute for Jewish Family Literacy

Scripture translations are from *Tanakh: The Holy Scripture*, © 1985, published by The Jewish Publication Society.

For information regarding permission to reprint material from this book, please send your request in writing to the Kripke Institute, Center for Relational Judaism, at the address / email address below.

The Kripke Institute
Center for Relational Judaism
5110 Densmore Avenue
Encino, CA 91436
ronwolfson1234@gmail.com

Additional copies of this book may be ordered by mail prepaid by check only directly from the Kripke Institute at the address above or from our distributor prepaid by check or credit card sent to:
LongHill Partners, Inc., PO Box 237, Woodstock, VT 05091
tel: 802 457 4000   fax: 802 457 4004   email: awilson@longhillpartners.com

1–10 copies: $19.99 per copy
11–29 copies: $17.99 per copy
30+ copies: $16.99 per copy
Shipping & Handling: Within the continental U.S. add $3.95 for the first book, $2.00 for each additional book

If you would like to explore site visits, individualized consulting, or other presentations for help in taking the next steps toward your own Relational Engagement Campaign, email us at rjhandbook@gmail.com.

For additional materials, please visit relationaljudaismhandbook.com.

For
Ellie and Mark Lainer
Inquisitive learners, visionary philanthropists, and beloved friends

A Tribute from Ron

"It's all about relationships."

In 1978, Mark Lainer was in line to become chair of the Los Angeles Bureau of Jewish Education and he wanted to meet me, a young professor at the then University of Judaism (now American Jewish University). He invited me for lunch to discuss ideas about strengthening Jewish education. Within weeks, Susie and I met Ellie, and thus began a forty-year relationship, filled with love and a shared passion for serving the Jewish community.

Our friendship is the stuff of a Jewish communal professional's dreams. We belong to the same wonderful synagogue (Valley Beth Shalom), our children attended the same terrific Jewish school (Heschel Day School), and we enjoy sharing holidays, celebrating lifecycle moments, and traveling together. With no family of our own in Los Angeles, the Lainers have adopted us into their remarkable family, widely considered the First Family of Jewish Education in our community.

When *Relational Judaism* was published, it was Ellie and Mark who enthusiastically shared it with their broad network of movers and shakers in the Jewish community, not only in Los Angeles but also throughout North America. Their generous support for this transformative work has enabled the publication of this volume with their fervent hope that it will empower Jewish communal organizations to continue the sacred work of relational engagement.

On behalf of myself, Nicole, Lydia, and all the readers of *The Relational Judaism Handbook, todah rabbah!*

Contents

Online Resources: www.relationaljudaismhandbook.com

Index of Contributors

These wonderful diverse contributors represent Conservative and Reform synagogues and independent minyanim of various sizes and geographies (urban, suburban), JCCs, Hillels and millennial engagement initiatives. We encourage you to focus on the *principles* underlying their best practices.

Foreword

Rabbi Rick Jacobs

In plain language, the paradigm of congregations and Jewish life is transforming right before our eyes. Until recently, affiliation with synagogues happened almost automatically. Today congregations must find people where they are—often outside the walls of synagogues—and engage them deeply in real spiritual community. There are many names for this frontline holy work; at the Union for Reform Judaism (URJ) we call this "audacious hospitality" while Ron Wolfson has powerfully named it "Relational Judaism." Whatever you call it, the key is learning to practice it.

Relational Judaism is arguably at the core of Jewish religious life from its very beginning. Early in Genesis, Abraham and Sarah set the standard. On a blisteringly hot day, Abraham runs after three desert wanderers, insisting they come inside for nourishment. What makes his act so memorable is that he doesn't wait for the wanderers to knock on his door; instead, he goes out to meet them where they are and invites them in. Abraham and Sarah had no idea who they were welcoming into their tent, but they quickly discover their visitors are none other than three messengers of the Most High. One brings healing to an ailing Abraham, another shares news that Sarah will finally give birth, and a third warns that God intends to wipe out the towns of Sodom and Gomorrah, sweeping away the righteous with the wicked. The first Jewish couple's life is transformed by this holy encounter, a glimpse of what Relational Judaism can mean.

Too often in our history, Relational Judaism has been drained of its vitality, leaving behind ossified religious bureaucracies. We Jews have created a variety of institutions to sustain our devotion to God's intended path for us. Sometimes, though, we forget that our institutions are means, not ends. We need to be reminded that we are called to do something bigger and grander than simply be caretakers of Jewish institutions. What is that something? Our Jewish job is to build a more vibrant, richer Jewish life for our people and communities, so that we can live up to our responsibility to partner with the Holy One to create a world of wholeness, compassion, joy, and justice.

When religious communities strip away the busyness and organizational layers that often keep us from the heart of Jewish life, a new type of community is born. The Hasidic master Rabbi Nachman of Breslov illustrates how powerfully transformative this reframe can be: "a person reaches in three directions—inward, to oneself; up to God; out to others. The miracle of life is that in truly reaching in any one direction, one embraces all three."

Sounds easy, right? But like all artforms, it's crucial to find the right mentors and guides. I'm blessed to work every day at the Union for Reform Judaism with brilliant colleagues who are reimagining Jewish life and seeing the power of tools, including small-group engagement, and true audacious hospitality taking root within our congregations. And with this new book, Ron Wolfson, Rabbi Lydia Medwin, and Rabbi Nicole Auerbach give us so many of the tools and practices we need to build the kind of communities we just can't live without. Such communities often start as small, intimate groups that come together for primary Jewish acts of learning, spiritual practice, acts of kindness, and justice. The authors are master practitioners themselves so they don't get stuck in lofty theoretical reflections on the state of Jewish life. Rather, they take us by the hand and walk us into a more engaging, enduring, and compelling Jewish future. These reimagined congregations and communities are "not in the heavens" (Deuteronomy 30:12) but rather within our grasp.

Preface

Rabbi Ed Feinstein

"The modern temple suffers from a severe cold!" declared Abraham Joshua Heschel in 1953. But as with most prophetic words, no one listened. Through the 1960s and 1970s, membership was booming, new synagogues sprouted up across the suburban landscape, a baby boom filled Hebrew schools and Sunday schools. Heschel's words went unheeded. Then things changed. Membership fell, congregations began disappearing, vast sanctuaries lay empty. Anxious synagogue leaders went looking for solutions—younger, hipper rabbis; trendier music; new programs. Somewhere, they believed, there must be a secret way to the successful synagogue.

It takes a special sensibility to resist the temptation to seek secrets to success. There are problems that are amenable to simple technical adjustments, teaches leadership guru Ronald Heifetz. But the truly vexing problems of human organization require something deeper. These problems demand what Heifetz calls "adaptive change"—change that transforms the organization; reimagines its mission, reinvents its structure, refashions its operation.

It is Ron Wolfson's genius to grasp that what the contemporary synagogue needs is not a set of technical adjustments—not a menu of new programming—but rather transformational change, a revolution in the synagogue's mission, structure, and operation. That insight, coupled with his deep faith in the eternal relevance of Judaism, his deep love of the Jewish people, and his sunny, midwestern optimism, is the foundation of this remarkable book. Rabbi Nicole Auerbach and Rabbi Lydia Medwin, coauthors with Ron, attest to the energy generated when a synagogue turns to small groups as its organizing principle.

Don't look to this book to find the secrets to a successful synagogue. Although this book is chock-full of tips, recommendations, and portraits of best practices, what we find here is not technique. What we find here is a compelling interpretation of Jewish life and a vision of the synagogue this interpretation entails. It is a Judaism in the best tradition of Martin Buber's dictum "All real life is meeting." In response to the ferocious centrifugal forces of contemporary life driving human beings apart from one another, the synagogue can become the center of connection. This is a synagogue ready to respond when we tire of social media "friends" and seek genuine relationship and solidarity. It is a synagogue offering the deep spirituality of sharing and caring, the deep existential meaning to be found when we step beyond the tight boundaries of the individual sovereign self to reach toward another.

In truth, there is nothing that is genuinely new here. Community, *kehillah*, relationship has always been a core element of Jewish life. What is revolutionary is the imperative to reorganize all the functions of the synagogue around this principle. We will pray, but in a new way. We will learn, but in a new way. We will celebrate and mourn and mark the passages of life, but in a way that connects us, so that we share our joys and our tears, our stories and our wisdom.

Make no mistake, this is a massive undertaking. Few institutions are as resistant to change as the American synagogue. A Relational Engagement Campaign is no easy task. It demands that we reevaluate and reimagine every function of synagogue life. It calls into question much of what we do. We must learn to think small, not big—success is no longer big crowds but small groups that offer intimate friendships and moments of genuine personal connection. It works. And it can be done. Even in your synagogue.

Together, Rabbi Auerbach, Rabbi Medwin, and Dr. Wolfson provide a vision of a Judaism for the twenty-first century; a Judaism that is inspirational, engaging, spiritual, and joyful. They offer a vision of the synagogue our children will join and cherish.

Acknowledgments

Lydia Medwin (LM)

Modah ani l'fanecha, I am so grateful: To my partner and best friend Rabbi Dan Medwin, for his unwavering support and confidence in me and for sharing his passion for our people's future; to our children, Zimra, Gavi, and Jasmine, for all they teach me every day, for their unbridled joy, and for the motivation to reinvigorate Jewish life for them and their children. To my parents, who gave me this precious gift of Torah.

To my incomparable clergy team and Temple staff: Rabbi Loren Filson Lapidus, Rabbi David Spinrad, Rabbi Steven Rau, Cantor Deborah Hartman, executive director Mark Jacobson, Summer Jacobs, Laurie Simon, Jacqueline Morris, Elizabeth Foster, Joya Schmidt, Tena Drew, and everyone else at The Temple who make it all possible, for having the vision and creating the support and going along for the ride and trying new things and being very fun to work with every single day. Special thanks to Rabbi Peter Berg, who inspires me with his vision and from whom I learn every day; Ronnie Van Gelder, on whose shoulders I stand; and Bernie Marcus and the Marcus Foundation for supporting this vision of congregational engagement and for funding The Temple's Department of Engagement.

To my incredible Temple community, especially Jon Amsler, Lauren Grien, Janet Lavine, Hank Kimmel, those who've served on the Core Team, those who've been small-group leaders, and those who have participated and believed in our synagogue's future, for their commitment and creativity in Jewish life and their willingness to *lech l'cha* with me into the unknown wilderness.

To my coauthors, Ron and Nicole, for their commitment to Jewish life and to joy within this process. RW, you've taught us so much; I'm so humbled at all you've given us. NA, I'd write a book with you any time. You guys are the absolute best!

Nicole Auerbach (NA)

I am deeply grateful to my rabbis and mentors at Central Synagogue: Rabbi Angela Warnick Buchdahl; Rabbi Ari Lorge; our president, Abigail Pogrebin; and our executive directors (first) Livia Thompson (and now) Marcia Caban, whose visionary leadership has allowed me to spend the past several years experimenting with how to bring the small-groups model to a Jewish congregation. Their deep belief that building relationships is the key to sustaining and enriching a Jewish community, and their willingness to try new ways to do so, has been an inspiration. I am also indebted to my colleagues: Rabbi Stephanie Kolin, who has taught me how to think strategically and build a team; Rabbi Mo Salth, whose compassionate presence reminds me why I got into this in the first place; and Cantors Dan Mutlu and Julia Cadrain, who regularly demonstrate how to engage our members on a deep spiritual level. I am so lucky to be on their team. I have also been tremendously fortunate to work with talented lay leaders who jumped in with both feet to make our small groups a reality.

Another sustaining source of support has been the Union for Reform Judaism's Small Groups Community of Practice (CoP). The sense of teamwork and camaraderie from our fellow URJ congregations who are experimenting with this form of engagement has been invaluable. I am particularly indebted to Lila Foldes, who took me under her wing as an intern and allowed me the opportunity to learn at the feet of incredible leaders. I owe deep gratitude to Rabbi Esther Lederman, director of congregational innovation at the Union for Reform Judaism and who now heads CoP, for her guidance, as well as to Rabbi Asher Knight, Rabbi Bethie Miller, Rabbi Jill Perlman, Rabbi Benjamin Spratt, and Cantor Shayna DeLowe for being my thought partners and teachers and for always being generous with their time and resources. I never would have been a rabbi in the first place had it not been for the friendship and guidance of Rabbi Leora Kaye, Rabbi Sari Laufer, and Cantor Jennifer Frost, who introduced me to the power of Jewish tradition to transform lives and cheered me on as I made my way along this path. I had the great fortune to take part in the Daniel and Bonnie Tisch Rabbinical Student Fellowship, which showed me what transformational leadership could look like. Deepest thanks to Rabbi Larry Hoffman for pushing us to ask big questions and to "write new sentences," and to Bonnie Tisch for her faith and investment in our growth as spiritual leaders.

Thanks also, of course, to my husband, Josh Auerbach, for staying married to me when I decided to leave the law for rabbinical school and for always allowing me to say yes to wonderful opportunities to grow and learn, even when it is horribly inconvenient. The love and support I have received from him and from our girls, Catherine and Vivian, have allowed me to live the best life I can imagine.

Finally, a huge thanks to LM, who for the past several years has been my relational engagement *hevruta*, and who convinced me we needed to write a book together. And to RW, who took a chance on two people he didn't know from Adam and whose experience, enthusiasm, and generous heart have made this project a reality.

Ron Wolfson (RW)

Thanks, Lydia and Nicole, for cold-calling me from the Central Conference of American Rabbis convention to ask if I was writing a book about small groups. Little did they know, I had proposed a handbook for organizational leaders who wanted to develop a Relational Engagement Campaign based on the principles I outlined in *Relational Judaism*. I am so grateful that you two brilliant pioneers in the development of small groups invited me to collaborate with you in the creation of this book. As always, I am deeply thankful for my beloved partner, Susie Kukawka Wolfson, for her ongoing support of my travels and work with communities across the globe, and our small group family—Havi and Dave Hall, Ellie Brooklyn and Gabriel Elijah Hall, and Michael Wolfson—who teach me every day about the importance of relationships.

From All Three of Us

To our case study and Spotlight on Best Practices contributors: Rabbi Elie Spitz, Rabbi K'vod Wieder, Rabbi Mike Uram, Melissa Balaban, Rachel

Gildiner, Rabbi Angela Buchdahl, Rabbi Asher Knight, Rabbi Peter Berg, Rabbi Susan Leider, Fred Ezekiel, Rabbi Esther Lederman, Rabbi Ken Chasen, Rabbi Lisa Berney, Rabbi Benjamin Ross, Cantor Linda Kates, Rabbi Jill Perlman, and Havi Wolfson Hall.

To Rabbi Asher Knight, for his sacred agitation and his original vision of how small groups could change congregational life. Asher, you and your team first created so many of the documents from which we benefit today. Thank you for letting us learn from you as we continue to do every day.

To Rabbi Esther Lederman and the Union for Reform Judaism, for beautifully facilitating a Community of Practice that has allowed us the benefit of peers in a new field.

To Pastors Rick Warren and Steve Gladen for their warm accessibility and advice to us and our colleagues on the practice of small groups in congregations.

To Rabbi Rick Jacobs and Rabbi Ed Feinstein, for gracing this work with their always supportive words and deeds.

To Stuart M. Matlins, a wonderful friend and visionary educator, for taking a break from publishing retirement to shepherd this volume to publication. Thanks to his team—Emily Wichland, gifted editor, and Tim Holtz, talented designer—for helping us make this book so inviting and accessible in content and style.

A Word about the Kripke Institute

One day in 1953, Susie Buffett, the wife of the famous Warren Buffett, walked into a bookstore and discovered a thin volume titled *Let's Talk about God* by Dorothy K. Kripke, the wife of Rabbi Myer S. Kripke, the rabbi of Beth El Synagogue in Omaha, Nebraska. She brought it home and read it to her daughter Susie, who loved the book. Noticing that the author was local, Mrs. Buffett called Mrs. Kripke to invite her for a cup of coffee. (Today we would call their meeting a "one-to-one.") The two women immediately hit it off and hatched a plan to get together again, this time with their husbands. They explored their interests and passions to see if there was one they shared. Their common ground: bridge. And so the Kripkes and the Buffetts—who, it turns out, lived within a few blocks of each other—began to play bridge together on a regular basis.

Over those bridge games, they became close friends, even sharing annual Thanksgiving dinners together at the Buffetts, Susie making tuna fish casseroles in lieu of turkey for the kashrut-observant rabbi and his wife.

When Warren established his investment groups, Dorothy encouraged the rabbi to invest a modest inheritance with his friend. The rabbi resisted, not wishing to mix business with friendship. Warren, too, would say that he was leery of having his friends in the investment group ... in case things went bad. They didn't go bad. Finally the rabbi asked Warren to invest his savings, converting his stake into shares of Berkshire Hathaway, Buffett's holding company. The small investment turned into millions of unexpected dollars, which the Kripkes began generously giving away in 1997.

On one of my (RW) visits to Omaha, I suggested to Rabbi Kripke that he consider funding an institute to honor Dorothy's extraordinary contributions to Jewish children's and family literature. He readily agreed, and we created the Dorothy K. and Myer S. Kripke Institute for Jewish Family Literacy, which I have the honor to lead. We established a National Jewish Book Award in Dorothy's memory. We fund the Omaha branch of the outstanding PJ Library program of building Jewish family libraries. Most recently, the Center for Relational Judaism was founded to support the research that resulted in the publication of *Relational Judaism* and to be a resource hub for those doing the important work of relational engagement. This volume is the first publication of the center. Our hope is that it will inspire the building and deepening of relationships throughout the Jewish community as a fitting echo of that first "coffee date" between Susie Buffett and Dorothy Kripke some sixty-five years ago.

Introduction

It's all about relationships. People will come to synagogues, Jewish Community Centers, Jewish Federations, and other Jewish organizations for programs, but they will stay for relationships. Programs are wonderful opportunities for community members to gather, to celebrate, to learn. There is nothing "wrong" with programs; every organization has them. But, if the program designers have given no thought to how the experience will offer participants a deeper connection to each other, with the community and with Judaism itself, then it will likely be another lovely evening, afternoon, or morning ... with little or no lasting impact....

It's not about programs.

It's not about marketing.

It's not about branding, labels, logos, clever titles, website or smartphone apps.

It's not even about institutions.

It's about relationships.

—*Relational Judaism*, pages 2–3

The Relational Judaism Handbook is designed for Jewish institutional leadership—both professional and lay—to create a Relational Engagement Campaign, a comprehensive strategy for building and deepening relationships throughout your organization.

We begin with an overview of the tiers of engagement that will form the basis of the campaign: "offer participants a deeper connection to each other, with the community, and with Judaism itself." Read in reverse order, we see the three tiers of relational engagement as *Judaism, community,* and *each other.*

Why Judaism first? Because this is our ultimate mission: to strengthen each individual's relationship with Judaism—it's religion, values, culture, and peoplehood. Goal: *connecting with the Jewish experience.*

Second, community. Each of you in leadership, whether professional or lay, is an ambassador of your organization. Your role in welcoming, serving, and connecting every person to your community is indispensable. Our cards on the table: Engagement cannot be the sole responsibility of professional staff. It is up to each and every person in leadership to accept the responsibility of building relationships with our members and guests and to guide them to find their place in the community. Goal: *connecting with leadership.*

Third, a deeper connection to each other. A simple fact: it's much easier to quit an organization than to quit a friend. When you are connected to a group of friends who will be there for you in good times and bad, you have a deeper relationship with the community of which you are a part. Thus a major goal of a Relational Engagement Campaign is to connect our people to each other, primarily in small groups. Goal: *connecting with friends.*

Together, the three tiers of relational engagement represent a road map for the work of building a sacred community of relationships. Consider this well-known text from Psalm 133:1:

הִנֵּה מַה־טּוֹב וּמַה־נָּעִים שֶׁבֶת אַחִים גַּם־יָחַד

Hinei ma tov u'ma na'im shevet achim gam yachad.

Hey, how good and how pleasing it is when we all dwell together!

The key word is *yachad,* "together." "Together" is the clarion call of Relational Judaism. When we are "together" in a community of sacred relationships, it is indeed good and pleasing. Curiously, though, there is a Hebrew word in the text that on the surface looks to be unnecessary: *gam,* "also." The sentence could easily have been written *Hinei ma tov u'ma na'im shevet achim yachad* and it would have had the same meaning. So why the word *gam*? It looks to be extraneous.

But we are taught that there is no extraneous word in the Torah. Every word has a meaning. What, then, is the meaning of this apparently extra word *gam*? The Zohar, the foundational text of Jewish mysticism, offers an explanation:

> What is the meaning of *shevet achim gam yachad*? The word
> *gam* (in the expression *gam yachad*, "together") signifies the
> inclusion of the Shekhinah with them. (Zohar 3:59b)

In other words, when we sit as one, when we are not separated from each other, each in our own atomistic bubble, when we truly come together face-to-face, each of us a *tzelem Elohim*, a human being fashioned in the image of God, it is in this relationship, in this "between," where the Shekhinah—God's presence—can be found. The word *gam*, "also," means that when we are present with each other, God is also present.

If that is not sufficient to instruct us as to the power of relationship, the Zohar continues:

> Furthermore, the Holy One, blessed be God, listens to their
> words and it is *na'im*—pleasing to God, for God takes joy in
> them. (Zohar 3:59b)

Thus the presence of the word *gam* not only indicates the presence of God in our sacred communities of relationships, but it also embellishes the meaning of the word *na'im* in the psalm. When we are together, it is not only pleasing to us, but it is also pleasing to God!

This is the undeniable power of sacred community when it works well. When we find our place in it, being part of a community is *good* because it helps us find *meaning*, an answer to the age-old question of human existence: What does it all add up to? It helps us find *purpose*. We ask ourselves, "What am I supposed to do with my God-given spiritual gifts and talents?" And being part of a community is pleasing because it gives us a sense of *belonging*—to a group of friends who will be there with us and for us in good times and bad—and *blessing*—a place to celebrate, and count, and share the many sacred moments in our lives.

We believe it is this value offer of a face-to-face community of relationships that is good and pleasing precisely because it provides a path to a meaningful, purposeful, connected, and blessed life.

Transformative Change

What could you imagine for your community if more people made relationships—with Judaism, between leadership and the community, and amongst peers—the central focus of their work? We believe that any amount of work a synagogue or organization does toward this end can make a difference. Simply changing the way people are greeted at the front door can mean the difference between a negative and positive first impression. By asking people to wear name tags, for example, we may find that both new and existing community members feel more comfortable attending our events because there is no longer awkwardness about asking (again?) for someone's name.

But the real reason we, and any of us, get into this work is to aim high, shoot for the stars, and attempt to create *transformative* change. We Jews have always had a messianic bent, and so we are comfortable saying that, one day, we imagine Relational Judaism as one of the gateways into a deeply committed and engaged Jewish future. We have seen time and again the ways in which an organization can benefit from commitment to moving from programmatic to relational. The organization discovers more leadership in its ranks, becomes more creative in the ways it seeks to engage its members, increases its fundraising capacity, and finds its clergy and leadership to be more satisfied with their work. Most importantly, this commitment to Relational Judaism reveals a Judaism that is relevant to our time and place, fulfilling the words of Rav Kook to "make the old new, and make the new sacred."

This is why investing in your Relational Engagement Campaign is so important. Creating transformational change takes patience; the results of cultural change may well play out over the course of a decade or more. It will take dedication of time and resources that could easily be spent elsewhere. It will require laser-beam focus on the major questions of our time, including "What do my members and guests need to live lives of meaning?" and "What of our tradition is being called forward to address these needs?" It will at times require sacrifice as you prioritize this campaign over other worthy programs or initiatives. Yet by embracing the low-hanging fruit of relational engagement—much of which requires no significant money (it costs nothing to create a welcoming ambience)—you will likely see immediate impact in your organization, even as you pursue the path of transformative change. It is helpful to remember that the path you are on is perfectly crafted to take you to your destination. So what kind of destination do you want to reach? If transformational change is a part of that answer, this is the path for you.

How to Use This Book

This handbook can be used as a guide for a series of meetings to consider the three tiers of relational engagement and what you will do as a result of your deliberations. It sets out the importance of relational engagement and offers exercises and experiences that will help your team understand the dynamics of engagement. "Torah Study" gives you the opportunity to root your work within a spiritual framework. "Takeaways" and "Spotlights on Best Practice" feature strategies that have proved effective in organizations. Several case studies document how other organizations have created their engagement campaigns. The handbook also provides space for you to commit in writing to your "Next Steps" going forward.

Each meeting of your leadership team should model relational engagement by including one or more of these components:

1. *Check-in.* A short go-around-the-table (tables with a maximum of six people, if you have a large group) session for each person to share something personal or to pose a question related to the purpose of the meeting. For example, if your team is considering a welcoming strategy, you might ask, "What's one place where you have felt truly welcomed?" (Don't be shocked if you hear about hotels; they are in the hospitality business!) Strictly limit each response to *three sentences* or less. If you cannot think of a question related to the purpose of the meeting, you can try one of these all-purpose questions:

   a. What is one thing no one knows about you?

   b. What is something wonderful that has happened lately?

c. What is your favorite Jewish holiday and why?

d. What is something you are proud of?

e. Where is your favorite place to visit?

f. What is one thing from your day you're bringing with you into the meeting, or one thing you would like to leave behind, so that you can be fully present?

You will be surprised at how little people know about each other. These few minutes of check-in can help build a culture of connection that will permeate the organization.

2. *A relational moment.* Instead of a "go-around," ask each team member to spend five minutes, one-to-one, with someone among the group they don't know or don't know well. Suggest people share a story about something relevant to the purpose of the meeting, the current moment in the Jewish calendar, or how they became involved with the organization.

3. *Hevruta study.* Spend five minutes studying a Torah text in pairs. You could use the relevant texts we have provided in each part of the handbook—or choose your own. Whichever text you use, always have a good translation and discussion questions that help participants relate the text to their own experience.

A few additional tips:

• Schedule these team meetings well in advance to ensure maximum participation.

• Announce at the first meeting that you will be honoring everyone's time by beginning and ending on time—and stick to it! People are much more willing to come if they know they can count on concluding on time.

• For each meeting, provide an agenda that explicitly states the purpose of the meeting and what you hope to achieve by the end.

- Once decisions have been made about steps you will take, create a culture of accountability by following up to ensure the work is done.

- Be as transparent as possible about your efforts. Publicize the work of the team to the community, celebrate victories, and build on your successes.

A Word about Words

Whenever we use the term *members*, we refer to those people who *you* identify as members of the organization. Often these are the people you include on your membership lists who have contributed funds or paid dues or fees. By *guests* we mean prospective members or actual guests attending a one-shot program or family event. Of course, your objective may be to convert guests into members, which is typically a deeper level of engagement. *Leadership* or *leaders* refers to your organizational leaders—board members, committee chairs, and professional staff: CEOs, CFOs, development professionals, clergy, educators, engagement directors, program directors, office managers, even your custodial and security folks—anyone who is a paid employee of the organization. *Community* has two meanings, depending on the context: It can refer to the organization—for example, the community of the synagogue or the community of the JCC. *Sacred community* or *spiritual community* refers to a synagogue or independent minyan. Otherwise, *community* refers to the broader Jewish community that encompasses all the organizations of our people.

Let's begin!

Part One

Connecting with the Jewish Experience

Torah Study

When we are still in the womb, Rabbi Bunim says in a famous midrash (Talmud, *Niddah* 30b), an angel sits by our side and whispers in our ear all of the secrets of living. She whispers the tales of our ancestors, the wisdom of our hearts, the longings of our future generations. She whispers to us the keys we need to create a life of meaning and purpose, of joy and equanimity. But then just as we are born into the world, the angel touches us above our mouths and under our noses, creating that little indention (the philtrum), which causes us to *forget* that wisdom that we already know to be true. Except not all of it. Some of it remains in our hearts and comes out as we encounter truth and love in our lives.

That is the point of our Jewish tradition with all of its commandments, holidays, stories, and visions for the world; we are always relearning what it means to find meaning and purpose in our lives.

It's important to keep our eyes on the ball or, better, the goal line. Many Jewish organizations spend a lot of resources—physical, psychic, and financial—on strategic planning and visioning exercises that often fail to focus on the true objectives of our work as a community. The ultimate mission/purpose/goal of a Relational Engagement Campaign is to deepen individual salience of "being Jewish" and to strengthen commitment to the Jewish communal enterprise. We have marveled at Rabbi Steve Leder, senior rabbi of Wilshire Boulevard Temple in Los Angeles, who raised $165 million to reimagine the synagogue with a campaign centered on just three words: "We Make Jews."

So what is the content of "making Jews"? We believe Rabbi Leder is right on target. "Making Jews" is about connecting each person with the Jewish experience through active engagement with the life of the community. We foster engagement by cultivating relationships; we have identified Nine Levels of Relationship that represent a comprehensive set of objectives designed to deepen the connection with Judaism for every individual in your organization. We also foster engagement through readiness; it's important that we have the resources and communal commitment to carry us through the inevitable challenges of transformative change. This is why it is critical to take the time to assess where we are and whether we are ready to embark on a Relational Engagement Campaign.

Setting the Foundation: The Nine Levels of Relationship

The Hebrew word *bayn* means "between." This is the word that signifies engagement and connection. When we are in relationship, we stand in the "between."

In *Relational Judaism*, I (RW) describe the *"bayns* of our existence" as Nine Levels of Relationship. Simply put, a Jewish institution should aspire to build these Nine Levels of Relationship with every single person we encounter, young and old. This is what our programs, our in-reach and outreach, our teaching seeks to do.

Let's review the nine levels briefly from the perspective of the individual with a series of questions about your organization. As you review these levels, think about how your institution works to create and deepen these relationships.

The first four are personal:

1. *Bayn adam l'atzmo*: Between you and yourself.

    How does your programming enhance the personal identity of your people? Will you have the audacity to say, "Engage with us and your life will be different, deeper, more meaningful and purposeful"?

2. *Bayn adam l'mishpachah*: Between you and your family.

    How does your work strengthen the "family"? We define *family* as one or more people living under the same roof.

3. *Bayn adam l'haveiro*: Between you and your friend(s).

How will you connect each person to a group of friends in your community?

4. *Bayn adam l'Yahadut*: Between you and Jewish living and learning.
   How are you teaching enduring Jewish values and practice?

The next four are communal:

5. *Bayn adam l'kehillah*: Between you and your community, both sacred and secular.
   How do you connect people to a sacred or spiritual community and to the communal institutions such as Federation, JCC, Hadassah, and the many organizations in the Jewish community?

6. *Bayn adam l'am*: Between you and Jewish peoplehood, wherever Jews are.
   How do we create a sense of belonging to the Jewish people all over the world? Why is it that the first thing Jews visiting in Rome want to do—Jews who will not step into their local synagogue or JCC—is visit a synagogue or eat in a Jewish deli in the Jewish ghetto? Or they see someone wearing a "Magen David" necklace and think, "Oh, *landsman*, a Jewish sister or brother!" That is a palpable sense of connection to the Jewish people.

7. *Bayn adam l'Yisrael*: Between you and the State of Israel.
   Love it, argue with it—just be in relationship with the Jewish homeland. How are you creating and sustaining that connection?

8. *Bayn adam l'olam*: Between you and the whole world.
   How do you inspire people to see Judaism as a world religion with the imperative to repair the brokenness in the world (*tikkun olam*)?

This last level of relationship is perhaps the most challenging, yet it can ignite the other eight:

9. *Bayn adam l'Makom*: Between you and God.
   Believe or disbelieve, either way, how do you encourage a willingness to wrestle with the Divine?

The word *makom* literally means "place." It is one of one hundred names for God in Jewish tradition. This notion of God is that we can find sparks of divinity everywhere, especially within each of us human beings who, as Torah teaches, has been fashioned *b'tzelem Elohim*, "in the image of God." In Relational Judaism, *makom* also represents a key challenge and opportunity for leaders: How does everything we do to engage our people in the Jewish experience on all Nine Levels of Relationship help guide them to find their *makom*, their place in the community? When people find their place, they feel connected and engaged in a community that offers them a path to meaning, purpose, belonging, and blessing. How we can do this work of relational engagement is the goal of this handbook.

Takeaways

Review how your current programming and engagement efforts address individual identity, family, friendships, Jewish living, and learning. Explore how it fosters connection with community, the Jewish people, Israel, the world, and God. The goal of deepening our engagement work is to strengthen each of these relationships in a lifelong commitment to Judaism, Jewish living, the Jewish community, and the Jewish people.

Our Next Steps

_____

_____

_____

The *Emet* of Engagement:
Why It's Worth the Effort

From the coauthors: Our friend and teacher Rabbi Asher Knight offers this visionary explanation of the transformational potential of engagement, which sets the stage for the work you are about to do.

The Landscape

The Hebrew word for *truth* is *emet*. *Emet* is spelled with three Hebrew letters: *aleph*, *mem*, and *tav*. *Aleph* is the first letter of the aleph-bet. *Mem* is the middle letter. *Tav* is the last letter. Hidden in the word *emet—truth—* is the notion that we reveal truth by exploring complexity—the beginning, middle, and end. The difficulty of *emet* is that several truths often exist at once.

Our modern congregations are facing complexity in trying to engage members. Staff and clergy want to create exciting and affective programming that brings people together to share in the rhythms of Jewish time and life. Leaders want to financially sustain their staffs, who are housed in buildings that are increasingly more difficult and expensive to maintain. Members want to make Judaism relevant in their homes. People are seeking intimate and unique opportunities to learn and laugh, to rest and rejuvenate, to act for justice, and to engage as proud Jews in our multicultural, multi-ethnic, and multireligious world.

Even with these desires, Jews are being challenged by our modern society. We feel enslaved to an American culture that emphasizes ambition, busyness, and superficial digital interactions. We are being pulled by powerful forces of careers, immersive technology, and long commutes. We are often trying to do *more* with *less* resources.

The landscape before us is complicated. As shapers of our collective future, we need to be cognizant that the *emet*—the truth—of our modern society is affecting the very desires we have for our community and spiritual selves. *Emet* is affecting our Jewish journeys and our sense of belonging. For Judaism to continue living, we must be willing to ask: What kind of living tradition will our generation build for the future? How will we confront, head-on, the very real issues we are experiencing? How will we build it in partnership and relationship with one another?

What Is Engagement?

Engagement is about creating relationships and deep connections that inspire personal growth and cultivate meaning so we can transform ourselves, our communities, and our world. Engagement is about developing stakeholders, members who own their own Jewish lives and feel intimately connected to other Jews. For the purposes of this handbook, engagement is about small groups of people who are:

> *Learning together* through the pursuit of Jewish wisdom.
>
> *Praying together* and developing personal spiritual practices and inspiring worship that uplifts the soul and connects to God.
>
> *Acting together* through ongoing significant acts of lovingkindness and world repair.
>
> *Playing together* in fun social settings where people can relax, laugh, and be themselves.
>
> *Caring for each other* by valuing and supporting one another in times of joy and sorrow.
>
> *Accountable to each other* through shared leadership that serves the individuals' and community's best interests.

Our lives are at the center of it all. Engagement is about the holistic Jewish soul, opening the door to sacred encounter, where the relationships developed in small groups help us grow in our Jewish learning, spiritual practices, and deeds. Engagement is about changing people's understanding of themselves, of their roles and responsibilities to their

Jewish community, the broader world, and our responsibilities in it. While engaged Jews will certainly attend affective and fun programming or communal worship service, what makes for engagement isn't programs but rather a committed group of people living Jewish lives together.

The Difference Between Programmatic and Engagement Models

In truth, many synagogues choose to approach the idea of engagement through a programmatic and consequently a consumerist model. While there is nothing wrong with providing a great program for a community, we should be clear that engagement does not simply equate to more people attending more programming. To understand why not, we have to understand the difference between a programmatic versus engagement approach and their end results.

Programmatic/Consumerist Approach	Engagement Approach
• Start with determining a program, event, or service that you want people to attend: Shabbat service, speaker presentation, adult education program, social justice event, etc. • Professional staff, experts, or involved small group of lay leaders define, develop, and plan the program. • Market and advertise to people to get them to "come to us." You try to produce events and worship that are attractive. • You hope that the programs are well attended. • Reflect and evaluate so that you can program more effectively. • You understand the synagogue to be the dispenser of Jewish religious goods and services.	• Start with listening. Get to know your constituencies, what motivates them and their lives. • Invest in and develop leaders who work together to own, define, and develop a vision of Judaism that is relevant to their lives. • Rely on leaders to build personal relationships and invite others to consider their holistic Jewish lives. • Create and support small groups of enlivened stakeholders. • Build organic and imaginative community of communities that is owned and supported by those who have worked for their creation. • Small groups are focused on dynamic Jewish learning and living, the development of Jewish spiritual practices, acts of lovingkindness, and meaning making. • Personal transformation leads to communal transformation.
End Result: A program where a few people develop attractive programming that hopefully meets the needs of the "consumer," that is, the member. Congregants choose whether the programming as advertised is something they will or will not attend. People attend to have their needs met through quality programs and to be Jewishly educated (or have their kids educated) by professionals and experts.	**End Result:** Relationships are formed through an organized process; social fabric is woven; members become stakeholders. Identify and train new leaders who support small groups of congregants who are working together to live Jewish lives that have personal relevance and meaning.

We need to be careful to not approach engagement as another program. Rather, engagement is about helping people discover the best that is within themselves; connecting and building impactful relationships so that they can transform their souls in holistic and relational ways. When we do this, we can connect to the very best within ourselves and the wisdom of our Jewish tradition, and we elevate each other toward the godliness embedded in each of our souls and in the universe.

Engagement Is about Authentic Living

Knowing that we need connection in our lives does not always lead us toward developing community. Even when we have the best intentions, we sometimes need support and a hand reaching out to us, inviting us to come along, prodding us to leave the comforts of home and to put ourselves out there. Authentic and genuine living is about growing and becoming who we are, at every stage of life, in relationship with one another. But this isn't something that Jewish professional and lay leaders can simply do for people through programming. We need to help people consider how Judaism isn't something that we consume but rather something that we grow, produce, and cultivate in our lives. Engagement can't be a buzzword, a membership plug, or a request to come to temple programming. A solid community is more than paying dues and asking what the temple can deliver to its members. Engagement is about building a vibrant, inclusive community where we feel strongly connected to our congregation because we are actually connected to each other. Engagement is about fostering relationships that motivate all of us to live meaningful and impactful Jewish lives. By doing so, we can extend the perimeter of our Jewish lives well beyond the confines of the synagogue building. Engagement is about the ultimately rewarding task of creating connection, meaning, happiness, and safety.

In a world that can overwhelm and mystify us, we are hungry for authentic, genuine, real-life connections. Within the darkness of our world, it is in smaller circles of relationship that we will kindle the light for our lives. It is not in isolation but rather in community that we experience real safety, that we can foster creativity. It is in community where we will yet imagine the possibility of a tomorrow built upon the human and spiritual foundations that will sustain our homes, our lives, our relationships, and help us pass our faith to future generations.

Takeaways

The modern suburban synagogues and Jewish institutions as we know them today were created in middle of the twentieth century by a generation of Jews who sought to address the needs of their communities. In so many ways, they flourished. But we live today in a radically different world, and our synagogues and institutions must adapt and change to address this new world. But as Jewish leaders, we do not have to face the unknown future alone. In fact, best practice suggests that we should do so in partnership and relationship with the people we serve.

Engagement is about creating relationships and deep connections that inspire personal growth and cultivate meaning so we can transform ourselves, our communities, and our world. To do so, we need to be clear about the difference between programmatic and engagement approaches.

Our Next Steps

What does *engagement* mean to our team?

_____

_____

_____

What work do we do that falls into the programmatic approach? The engagement approach?

_____

_____

_____

Are You Ready?

The Nine Levels of Relationship are central to how we understand ourselves and our Jewish tradition. But each level of relationship needs tending; without paying attention to its seeding and rooting, its growth and development, we can never expect to reap the fullest benefits of these relationships for ourselves or our communities. So we must invest. Still, it is important to know when the best time for planting might be. Before jumping in, here are some important questions you may want to ask.

What Else Is Going On Right Now That Might Need to Take Priority?

For those undertaking other significant transitions, such as major budget questions or new senior leadership, this may not be the right time for you to begin. The relative stability of the organization is important for this work because of the need for widespread participation and support. Does your leadership have sufficient "bandwidth" to make an organization-wide campaign a focus? If your community has other major priorities at this time, you may want to wait until some of them are settled before embarking on this initiative.

Does Our Senior Leadership Share Our Vision?

Complete agreement of the senior leadership, such as clergy and top executives, is a huge factor in the success or failure of a Relational Engagement Campaign. If you are not in one of these roles, you will need to start with a series of conversations in which you dream together about the impact this effort could have on your community. You may also want to ask one another to think about the effect of *not* working toward such a campaign. If you are in one of these senior leadership roles, you will need to determine who you need on your team to garner the enthusiasm of others who may be slower to adopt the idea. For example, at The Temple in Atlanta, Georgia, the senior rabbi, executive director, and board president were fully committed from the beginning. They pitched it to board members, clergy, staff, and big donors in board meetings, one-to-one meetings, staff retreats, clergy retreats, sermons to the congregation, and all the various modes of publicity, so that everyone co-owned the idea; they felt they were on the ground floor of something exciting. This process took the better part of a year.

Another successful strategy is to ask each stakeholder to remember from their own experience or to sample a small-scale, newly crafted Relational Judaism experience. Once they experience a few conversations and interactions that focus on engagement with Judaism, their community, and one another, they begin to see the potential firsthand for a Relational Engagement Campaign. For example, one clergy team has been gathering every three or four months to simply participate with one another in a fun outing or activity that relates to a creative expression of their synagogue's vision and values. To lift up the value "We are our history, our future," they took a walking food tour of a historic neighborhood in their city. The activity gave them time to talk informally, bond further as a team, and generate enthusiasm for the participation of others in the synagogue in relational engagement. Now all these clergy are ambassadors for the initiative.

Are We Addressing a Need Articulated by Our Members?

The answer to this question may only be deeply understood by conducting a listening campaign, described in detail below. But through initial conversations with staff, board members, and trusted lay leaders, you may have already discovered that your members are craving something different. A distinguishing feature of a relational engagement culture is a bottom-up style of leadership that allows the articulated needs of the community to drive the change. As leaders of the change, our job is to help the community more clearly articulate what they feel they need and create a framework to help them provide it for one another.

Are We Clear on the *Why* of a Relational Engagement Campaign for Our Community?

After you have determined that building a more engaged community is a priority, and you have leadership that understands and agrees on the necessity of a Relational Engagement Campaign, and it is a need articulated by the membership, you will need to get clear on the reasons for your campaign. What are your major goals? How will you know you are moving in the right direction? The more specific and concise you are, the better. A good measure is your answer to this question: Can you pitch it in an elevator? Imagine you are inviting someone into a new initiative that is a part of your campaign. You might say to potential participants: "We are creating _____ because it's important for our community to be more dedicated and self-directed Jewish learners." Or "We are creating _____ because we believe we are a stronger community when people know each other well and invest in one another's well-being." Or "Join _____ so that you can feel what it means to be connected to our community. We believe that no one should feel alone here." Whatever your motivation might be, it will be important to clearly define the reasons you are investing time and energy—and other people's time and energy—into this campaign.

Who Should Be on Our Team for This Campaign?

Ideally, *everyone*. One of the main messages of this effort will be that engagement does not require huge funds for new buildings, but it will require a reorientation of how leadership and community members spend their time getting to know, serving, and engaging members and guests.

Takeaways

To know whether or not your organization is ready to begin a Relational Engagement Campaign, it will be helpful to answer the following questions together:

What else is going on right now?

Does our senior leadership share our vision?

Are we addressing needs articulated by our members?

Are we clear on the why?

Our Next Steps

Determine who else needs to be brought on board at this early stage. Begin to articulate why your congregation or organization might want to create an all-encompassing strategy for deepening relationships. It does not have to be perfect at this stage. But to practice coalescing a vision, ask each person on your team to write down their top three reasons and then compare them with one another. Can you begin to create a coherent *why*?

What would look different if the members of our organization were more deeply connected?

_____

_____

_____

Part Two

Connecting with the Relational Community

In the description of the building of the *mishkan*—the Tabernacle—in the desert, God instructs the Israelites to build an ark for the Ten Commandment tablets (Exodus 25–27). On either side of the top of the ark, they are to place two *k'ruvim* (cherubim), creatures with humanlike, animallike, and birdlike features, with their wings spreading out over the cover of the ark. Most importantly: *they shall face each other* (Exodus 25:18–20).

Yet in 2 Chronicles 3:13, we learn that when King Solomon built the First Temple, "the wingspread of these cherubim was thus twenty cubits across, and they were standing up facing the [Temple]." This discrepancy leads to a debate in the Talmud:

> How should the *k'ruvim* stand? Rabbi Yochanan taught that the two *k'ruvim* faced one another, while Rabbi Elazar taught that they faced the Temple. This (difference in text) does not pose a problem, as their faces miraculously changed direction in reflection of the Jewish people's relationship to God. Here, when it states that the *k'ruvim* faced each other, it was when the Jewish people do the will of God. There, the verse that describes that the *k'ruvim* faced the Sanctuary and not toward each other was when the Jewish people do not do the will of God.
>
> (Baba Batra 99a)

17

The Talmud is teaching a critical lesson about the relationship between God and the Jewish people: When the Israelites behaved properly and the relationship was good, the *k'ruvim* faced each other. But when there were difficulties in the relationship, the *k'ruvim* looked away from one another.

Is it not the same with our relationships with fellow human beings? When we are good to each other, when we see eye to eye, we face one another with ease. When things go poorly and the relationship frays, we tend to turn away; we can barely look at one another.

In a community of strong relationships, we do not turn away from anyone. We believe that we don't always need to see eye to eye to walk hand in hand, especially when we all work to build a relational community. We encourage face-to-face meetings, meetings in which we may actually find godliness "in the between." When we are face-to-face, we are the *k'ruvim*, charged with guarding the Torah and its teachings, our spiritual road map to a meaningful and purposeful life.

Moreover, with a play on the Hebrew words, we are also the *keiruvim*, those who practice *keiruv*, the act of bringing others closer to Judaism. *Keiruv* does not only mean reaching out to those who are not Jewish; it can also mean reaching in, bringing anyone—our peripheral members, our children, anyone committed to raising a Jewish family—closer to Jewish practice and ideas and to the community itself. The best way to bring anyone closer to Judaism is through personal encounter.

So spread your wings, *keiruvim*, and prepare to meet your people!

Welcoming You

Here is the key question about the people we seek to engage in any program or worship experience we offer:

> Has anything happened during the time they were at the program to deepen their relationship to the community, to the sponsoring institution, and most importantly, to each other?...
> A rabbi confides in me, "A woman who was a member of my synagogue for twenty years resigned. I was shocked because she showed up to all of our programs. So, I called her to ask why she was leaving. You know what she said? 'I came to everything, and I never met anybody.'" (*Relational Judaism*, p. 17)

Since *Relational Judaism* was published, this is the single most frequently quoted passage in the book. With his permission, I can now reveal the rabbi who told me the story is Rabbi David Stern, senior rabbi of Temple Emanu-El in Dallas, Texas. As a result, he has led his professional colleagues and lay leadership in a major Relational Engagement Campaign that has transformed his congregation.

The first step in building relationships is to welcome other human beings. Instead of thinking of your organization as a building, an institution, or a calendar of programs, consider instead how your community would be different if at its heart were strategies and opportunities to empower people to meet each other, *panim el panim* (face-to-face). This is especially important for leaders of our organizations who hope to engage newcomers and guests. A warm welcome is the very first step in building a relationship. Without it, there is little to no chance for further engagement.

When you think of a program, prayer service, board meeting, or committee meeting, what are the component parts you spend most of your time planning? The subject matter, the content, the physical setting, the refreshments, the marketing? All these are important aspects of any gathering, yet the one thing that matters most is the most overlooked: How will we facilitate face-to-face interactions among the people we seek to engage? Will they leave the experience having met someone—either lay or professional—with whom they may want to continue to build a relationship?

Pastor Rick Warren, the founder of the twenty-five-thousand-member Saddleback Church, teaches that the first thing people wonder when they show up at a church is not "Where is the restroom?" It is "Is there anyone else here who looks like me? In my demographic? With kids the same ages as mine? Someone interesting? Someone interested in me and my story? People I would want to be with again?" That is why when you visit Saddleback Church in Lake Forest, California, the first people you encounter—the greeters—are volunteers drawn from across the demographic they seek to recruit into membership: young professionals, middle-age parents with kids, singles, seniors. They wear name tags and T-shirts that are welcoming: "I Can Help!" They are stationed at key locations on the one-hundred-acre campus: the parking lot, the entrance of the campus, the front door of the worship center, the "Welcome Booth" in the gathering plaza. Even more importantly, Pastor Warren has consistently taught his congregants that they are *all* representatives of Saddleback, all ambassadors of their faith, and all doing God's work by welcoming the stranger. This, of course, he learned from our Torah in the example of Abraham and Sarah, who rushed to welcome three strangers into their tent.

Torah Study

Let's study the beginning of the Torah section Vayeira. Pair up with one friend, preferably someone you don't know well or at all, sit face-to-face, knee-to-knee. Spend a minute or two welcoming each other: share your name and something about yourself—where you went to college, what you like to do, how you got involved in the organization. Try to make a connection on a personal level. Then place the text *in between* you. Read the text and questions aloud and answer this question: "How does this text teach us to personally encounter a stranger?" Make a list of the takeaways you can use in creating your welcoming ambience.

Genesis 18:1–8 Vayeira

וַיֵּרָא אֵלָיו יְהֹוָה בְּאֵלֹנֵי מַמְרֵא וְהוּא יֹשֵׁב פֶּתַח־הָאֹהֶל כְּחֹם הַיּוֹם:

Vayeira eilav Adonai b'eilonei Mamrei v'hu yosheiv petach-ha'ohel k'chom hayom.

The Lord appeared to him by the terebinths [oak trees] of Mamre; he was sitting at the entrance of the tent as the day grew hot.

וַיִּשָּׂא עֵינָיו וַיַּרְא וְהִנֵּה שְׁלֹשָׁה אֲנָשִׁים נִצָּבִים עָלָיו וַיַּרְא וַיָּרָץ לִקְרָאתָם מִפֶּתַח הָאֹהֶל וַיִּשְׁתַּחוּ אָרְצָה:

Va-yi'sa einav vayar v'hinei sh'loshah anashim nitzavim alav vayar va-yaratz likratam mi-petach ha'ohel vayishtachu artzah.

Looking up, he saw three men standing near him. As soon as he saw them, he ran from the entrance of the tent to greet them and, bowing to the ground,

וַיֹּאמַר אֲדֹנָי אִם־נָא מָצָאתִי חֵן בְּעֵינֶיךָ אַל־נָא תַעֲבֹר מֵעַל עַבְדֶּךָ:

Vayomar adonai im-na matzati chein b'einecha al-na ta'avor mei'al avdecha.

he said, "My lords, if it please you, do not go on past your servant.

יֻקַּח־נָא מְעַט־מַיִם וְרַחֲצוּ רַגְלֵיכֶם וְהִשָּׁעֲנוּ תַּחַת הָעֵץ:

Yukach-na m'at-mayim v'rachatzu ragleikhem v'hisha'anu tachat ha'eitz.

Let a little water be brought; bathe your feet and recline under the tree.

וְאֶקְחָה פַת־לֶחֶם וְסַעֲדוּ לִבְּכֶם אַחַר תַּעֲבֹרוּ כִּי־עַל־כֵּן עֲבַרְתֶּם עַל־עַבְדְּכֶם וַיֹּאמְרוּ כֵּן תַּעֲשֶׂה כַּאֲשֶׁר דִּבַּרְתָּ:

V'ekchah faht-lechem v'sa'adu lib'khem achar ta'avoru ki-al-kein avartem al-avd'khem vayomru kein ta'aseh ka'asher dibarta.

And let me fetch a morsel of bread that you may refresh yourselves; then go on—seeing that you have come your servant's way." They replied, "Do as you have said."

וַיְמַהֵר אַבְרָהָם הָאֹהֱלָה אֶל־שָׂרָה וַיֹּאמֶר מַהֲרִי שְׁלֹשׁ סְאִים קֶמַח סֹלֶת לוּשִׁי וַעֲשִׂי עֻגוֹת:

Va-y'maheir Avraham ha'ohelah el-Sarah vayomer mahari sh'losh s'im kemach solet lushi va'asi ugot.

Abraham hastened into the tent to Sarah, and said, "Quick, three *seahs* of choice flour! Knead and make cakes!"

וְאֶל־הַבָּקָר רָץ אַבְרָהָם וַיִּקַּח בֶּן־בָּקָר רַךְ וָטוֹב וַיִּתֵּן אֶל־הַנַּעַר וַיְמַהֵר לַעֲשׂוֹת אֹתוֹ:

V'el-habakar ratz Avraham vayikach ben-bakar rakh vatov vayitein el-ha-na'ar va-y'maheir la'asot oto.

Then Abraham ran to the herd, took a calf, tender and choice, and gave it to a servant-boy, who hastened to prepare it.

וַיִּקַּח חֶמְאָה וְחָלָב וּבֶן־הַבָּקָר אֲשֶׁר עָשָׂה וַיִּתֵּן לִפְנֵיהֶם וְהוּא־עֹמֵד עֲלֵיהֶם תַּחַת הָעֵץ וַיֹּאכֵלוּ:

Vayikach chem'ah v'chalav u-ven-habakar asher asah va-yitein lifneihem v'hu omeid aleihem tachat ha'eitz va-yokheilu.

He took curds and milk and the calf that had been prepared and set these before them; and he waited on them under the tree as they ate.

Takeaways

After your team has studied the text, collect your takeaways from the story that illustrate the power of hospitality and how you might improve your welcoming ambience.

_____

_____

_____

_____

_____

_____

Here are some takeaways we've heard:

Looking up. Sitting at the entrance of his tent, Abraham lifts up his eyes (*va-yi'sa einav*) in anticipation. Relational communities are on the "look out" and the "look up" for the strangers in their midst, the first-timers, the guests of the Bar/Bat Mitzvah, the spiritual seekers, the preschool parents, the newcomers to the community.

Make the first move. Abraham doesn't wait for the strangers to announce themselves.

Run to greet. Look again carefully at the words describing the action; the verbs in the Torah tell you the whole story. They all indicate running: "he ran [*va-yaratz*]," "Abraham hastened [*va-y'maheir*]," "Quick! [*mahari*]," "Abraham ran [*ratz Avraham*] to the herd," "the servant-boy hastened [*va-y'maheir*] to prepare it." As I (RW) wrote in my book *The Spirituality of Welcoming*, this is a text in a hurry!

Ouch! What is Abraham's physical condition at the beginning of this story? In the sentence before this *parasha* (section) begins, we learn that Abraham circumcised himself ... at the age of ninety-nine! Yet off he runs to greet the strangers. Are there ever any good excuses for not welcoming a stranger if this one was not employed? No!

Welcome first, ask questions later. Abraham has no idea who the strangers are. Neither do you know who walks into your building: Jewish or not, rich or poor, single or married, gay or straight. And it should not matter in a community that believes every human being is "made in the image of God."

Hospitality is the most important value. What is Abraham doing at the beginning of this tale? Look at the first words: "The Lord appeared to him [Abraham]...." The commentators have a field day with this. Rashi deduces that God is practicing the mitzvah of *bikkur holim*, visiting the sick, which Abraham clearly must have been after his surgery. Others suggest Abraham was either study-ing, which is the way we hear God's voice, or praying, which is the way we talk to God. In any case, Abraham is in a relational moment with God, three strangers appear, and what does Abraham do? It is as if he says, "Excuse me, God, gotta run to greet these guys!" He breaks off his engagement with God! From this the Talmud deduces the following conclusion: "*Hachnasat orchim*, welcom-ing strangers, is a greater mitzvah than welcoming the Shekhinah, God's presence" (Shabbat 127a).

Under-promise, over-deliver. Abraham offers the strangers a "mor-sel of bread" but produces a feast. In the quality service world, this is called "exceeding expectations." How can you exceed the expectations of your members and guests?

Serve them ... your best food! Abraham selects one of his best animals—"tender and choice"—to prepare for the strangers. (Don't be surprised about the milk mixed with meat. The laws of kashrut as we know them come from the rabbinic period.) How is the coffee served in your place? Seriously, is it really, really good? When people walk in carrying a Starbucks cup, your coffee is not good enough if you want them to come in from the parking lot and hang out.

Rally the troops. Abraham realizes he alone cannot provide for his guests. He recruits his wife, Sarah, and his servant-boy to help out. This is the most important lesson for organizations hoping to create a relational community: it takes *everyone*—not just greet-ers—to create a truly warm and welcoming ambience as the first step in building relationships.

As we visit in various communities, the understanding that "every-one is a greeter" is not only the most important maxim but also the most challenging. It is so common for the leadership, the volunteers, and the "regulars"—those who frequent their orga-nizations most often—to feel at home, to immediately gravitate to welcoming each other—the friends they already know—rather than reaching out to guests. Often this leads to the formation of cliques, a few people who tend to sit together, eat together, and kibbitz together, forming a nearly impenetrable barrier to newcomers wanting "in." A clique is different from a small group, an issue we will address below. A clique is a closed group, whereas a small group is open to new people.

Spotlight on Best Practice

Rose and Murray Geller (may he rest in peace) had been longtime members of Valley Beth Shalom, a Conservative synagogue in Encino, California. Like many "regulars" in synagogues, they had their "regular" seats in the sanctuary: sixth row center, on the aisle. One Shabbat morning they came to shul a little late and found two strangers sitting in "their seats." Instead of saying, "You're sitting in our seats," the Gellers said exactly the appropriate first thing to say: "*Shabbat shalom!* We haven't seen you here before. Are you new? Welcome!" They knew these were visitors and so they offered a warm greeting. But, of course, they still hoped to sit in their "established place" (in Hebrew, *makom kavu'a*) in the sanctuary. So they then asked the second appropriate thing to say: "May we sit with you?" The visitors were thrilled ... and *moved over two seats!*

The story gets better. During the first Torah procession, the Gellers began to chat with the visitors, learning their names—Joy and Chuck Feldman. They were not visiting for the Bat Mitzvah that morning as the Gellers suspected; they were from Toronto and had heard about Valley Beth Shalom and wanted to experience it. During the second Torah procession, the Gellers invited the Feldmans to sit with them at the kiddush luncheon. Over enchiladas (some shuls have cholent, a stew; Valley Beth Shalom serves enchiladas), the Gellers and the Feldmans continued to bond, promising to stay in touch. Fast-forward to 2016. I (RW) gave a talk in Toronto to a large crowd of synagogue leaders and told the story of the Gellers welcoming strangers to their congregation. Suddenly two people started waving wildly: "It's us, it's us!" they yelled. Sure enough, it was the Feldmans, who proceeded to confirm the story. "We've been friends with the Gellers for more than fifteen years. We've been to each other's simchas, comforted each other in times of loss. We love them!" A wonderful friendship born of the simple gesture of welcoming the stranger.

Murray and Rose Geller were not professional staff at Valley Beth Shalom. They were not board directors. They were people who understood their responsibility to welcome the stranger. As we shall soon discuss, there is a tremendous hospitality and customer service industry that depends on the warm welcome of strangers. At first glance, one would think that the professional staff in hotels, restaurants, and tourist sites are the key people who are trained to be hospitable. They most certainly are important to creating a culture of welcome in a community. But perhaps even more important are the regular citizens.

Spotlight on Best Practice

In Philadelphia, community leaders understand how important it is to encourage every citizen to be a welcoming ambassador for visitors. They created "PHL Welcomes U," a "free educational program empowering Philadelphians on the front lines of service and interaction in public-facing roles with the tools they need to create meaningful, positive experiences for visitors to our great city." In six short online videos, participants are taught the art of greeting, how to create experiences that exceed expectations, and essential interpersonal skills such as listening for needs. While the series of six modules are targeted mainly to workers in the hospitality industry, all Philadelphians are welcome to enroll. One participant wrote in his testimonial: "Thank you for the opportunity to be part of the program. It is a great way to show love for the city you live in and be able to promote it to visitors" (phlwelcomesu.com).

Case Study

Rabbi Mike Uram, executive director, Hillel at the University of Pennsylvania; author, *Next Generation Judaism*

I learned something important about legacy organizations my first High Holy Day season working at Penn Hillel. At first glance, it was an impressive operation. We offered several large services filled with three thousand students and community members. It was only when I walked outside the auditorium around campus that I realized something: while we were busy running services for thousands of students, other campus Jewish groups were building relationships with students, offering learner services, and hosting intimate holiday meals. It's not that Hillel didn't want to be doing this relational work; it was that we were already too busy just running services.

This is a common problem for Penn Hillel and many other legacy organizations, and it's one that makes it difficult to change and innovate. We had so many community and programmatic responsibilities that we didn't have enough time, money, and creative energy left to reach new students. At the time, Penn Hillel was still among the best Hillels in the world, and yet we were only reaching about 50 percent of the Jewish students on campus. While we were constantly trying to attract new students, it seemed that every time we tried to create a new program, it just ended up attracting the same students who were already deeply engaged.

We were left with a few nagging questions:

1. How could we reach the other 50 percent of students?

2. How could we break the cycle of being so busy that we never have time to reach new students?

3. How could we reinvent Hillel so it didn't have the same social, educational, religious, and geographic barriers to involvement?

4. How could we engage a generation of Jews who came of age with the Internet and who expected their Jewish experiences

to be equally as fast and customized as everything else in their lives?

While we are constantly asking ourselves these kinds of questions, today Penn Hillel has grown dramatically in our ability to respond to many adaptive challenges. A key to our success was the decision to develop and simultaneously run two different operating systems for Jewish life. One is called Hillel, and the events usually take place in the building and are designed to empower students to create a dizzying array of expressions of Jewish life that include everything that an excellent synagogue, Federation, or JCC might provide. The operating system for Jewish life under the Hillel banner has all of the same strengths and trappings of how other legacy Jewish organization function.

The second operating system is the Jewish Renaissance Project (JRP). We created it to be a Jewish startup that functions in a totally different way than Hillel does. JRP operates outside of the building, bringing Jewish life to students wherever they live, work, and play. It is geared for students who, for a whole host of reasons, aren't interested in "coming to Hillel." It is essential to point out that we don't think of these students as uninvolved. Rather, their Jewish experiences, interests, and needs require a different type of engagement than the students who are motivated to come to Hillel.

Today JRP has nearly double the number of Jewish students Hillel reaches, helping us to engage over 90 percent of Jews on campus.

What Led to the Creation of the Jewish Renaissance Project?

Much like other well-established Jewish organizations, Penn Hillel had become a victim of its own success. With the nearly three hundred events per month, five hundred student participants per week, and over a thousand different students engaged each year, Penn Hillel's institutional resources were stretched to the limit with its core programmatic offerings alone. Even though the staff and student leadership were deeply committed to reaching every Jew on campus, Hillel didn't have the capacity to reach new students. More than that, it was so focused on programs, attendance, and getting large numbers of people into the building that the relational approach was often overlooked.

Running Two Operating Systems at Once

For years, our approach to engagement was to plan new programs that would attract new people. It never worked. We used the same staff, same student leaders, and same processes to create something new. Inevitably the program intended for newcomers attracted a majority of "regulars" and ended up looking and feeling similar to regular Hillel. When new students would show up, they often ended up feeling like outsiders, and it confirmed their preexisting sense that Hillel wasn't for them.

After much experimentation, we found a workable strategy for overcoming these challenges:

> *Role of multiple brands.* Hillel needed a separate brand to reach new populations. Corporate marketers figured this out decades ago, but in the Jewish professional sector, we were still trying to connect every Jew on campus to the same organization. We spent a lot of time thinking about the way Gap, Old Navy, and Banana Republic were three brands that helped one company reach new people who wanted different styles of clothing and different prices. Why couldn't Jewish organizations do the same?

> *Rule of bifurcation.* Before we could add something new to our work, we had to divide staff between those who worked in the building with regulars and those who would work outside of the building with engagement students. (We use this term to describe Jews who feel just as Jewish as other Jews, but have shorter resumes of experience with formal Jewish institutions, who may have fewer Jewish friends, and who may not feel the need to show up in Jewish spaces in order to ignite their Judaism.) There was no way for the same overworked staff to also try to engage large groups of new students. We moved the offices of three staff members out of the Hillel building and onto campus where students lived and congregated. These new JRP staff

members were relieved of their responsibilities to attend, advise, or run the standard Hillel programs. Instead, they were charged with meeting hundreds of Jews who were not already connected to organized Jewish life.

Rule of epidemics. Key to our theory of change is that real innovation doesn't happen in incremental steps; rather, we need to make a quantum leap forward to do something new. One of Hillel's great limitations is that it has to be all things to all people all the time. That made it nearly impossible to excel in any area or to focus on the needs of one particular population. By starting from scratch, JRP could be intentionally designed to be sleeker, nimbler, and more relationally focused in its approach.

Rule of curated spaces. One of the biggest problems we had in connecting new people to existing Hillel programs was that no matter how welcoming we tried to be, the new people still needed to leave their "regular" lives and social networks to enter the Hillel space. Finding your way into an already existing "club" is never easy, especially considering students' wide variety of Jewish backgrounds. We found that the most successful approach to reach new students wasn't to try to get them into Hillel but rather into intentionally curated new spaces where we could carefully control the experience and the environment. We could make sure all the people were new, were coming from similar backgrounds, and would have something in common. By changing our methodology, we could change the entire newcomer experience even if the event was essentially the same. For example, while engagement students were hesitant and intimidated to come to Hillel for a discussion about Israel, hosted by an existing Israel group, they were excited to be part of new group of people just like them that was being convened for that exact purpose. Simply by curating a new Jewish space outside of institutional confines, we were able to minimize many of the social dynamics and barriers to involvement that plague most large programmatic offerings. Curating these kinds of new spaces can help any organization increase the numbers and diversity of people they reach.

Rule of microcommunities. Both current research and our own experience have shown that engagement Jews are resistant to just showing up to be part of large, general Jewish programming. They fear that it will be bland or agenda laden or, worse, that they will be exposed as Jewishly inauthentic. This doesn't mean that they are uninterested in getting more engaged in Jewish life. Rather, engagement Jews tend to be more interested in Jewish experiences that are relationally driven and intimate, customized, and rich with Jewish content. When engagement Jews choose to engage with Jewish life, they access it through a relationship, not an institution, and they want it to be deep, distinctive, and special.

What JRP Really Looks Today

While the methodology has continued to evolve, JRP and Hillel still look as described above. Penn Hillel still runs two different operating systems under two different brands, with two different staffs.

The only major difference from the original JRP model is that it has grown dramatically in both numbers and depth. Today, JRP comprises eleven different initiatives. We have three staff members working outside of the Hillel building, including a rabbinic educator. Most JRP initiatives include student interns who participate in weekly small-group sessions that are heavily focused on Jewish exploration and leadership development. Student interns are paid $400 per year to engage sixty friends and host one event per month. Each internship is customized for different types of students, living in different places, with different interests: freshmen in the Quad, sophomores in the Greek system, juniors and seniors living off campus. Taken together, JRP staff and student interns generate impressive numbers:

- 1,400 new students engaged each year (unduplicated)

- 10,709 in total participation (duplicated)

- 3,865 different events and one-to-one interactions

Ten years into this experiment, Penn Hillel now engages twice as many students as we used to. More important than the increase in overall numbers is that Penn Hillel is reaching a more diverse group of Jews and is having a greater impact on their Jewish lives.

Another positive outcome of JRP is that it became a fundraising boom for Penn Hillel. Today we raise over $500,000 a year for JRP in addition to our annual fundraising that supports our core programs. Many donors who were reluctant to support Hillel are now excited to support JRP because it's different and the idea of engaging students outside of the building resonates with their own Jewish experience. Some of the donors who get engaged through JRP also end up supporting Hillel more broadly. I point this out not to brag, but to make an important point: success breeds success. The only way for an organization that feels stuck to move forward is to take risks and do something transformative for people.

The Art of Name Tags

In *The Spirituality of Welcoming*, I reported on churches that regularly invite their congregants and guests to wear name tags during services and events in the community. Some congregations and most other organizations took up the idea and provided name tags, not just for the leadership and staff but also for all members and guests. Frankly, others would not do so, either for ritual reasons (not writing on Shabbat, for example) or because members simply did not like the idea. It really depends on your community whether name tags for all is the right way to go. There is no doubt that name tags for board leadership and staff is a good idea, especially if you are serious about engaging newcomers and guests. Moreover, when building relational moments into your programming to facilitate people meeting each other, name tags are indispensable.

One of the most pervasive—incorrect—assumptions in Jewish organizations, especially synagogues, is that everyone knows everyone else's name. This could not be further from the truth, even with teenagers in your community who you might think, "Surely, the kids know each other's names!" Think again, as this story from Rabbi Asher Knight illustrates.

In 2011, I took our confirmation students to a ropes course to participate in group building exercises. All the students had been enrolled in the religious school since at least the seventh grade. Most of them had joined the Confirmation Facebook page. The facilitator asked me if he needed to begin with name games. "Not with this class," I said. They were already connected. Fifteen minutes later the facilitator called for a quick break. He came over to me and said, "Rabbi, they don't know each other's names." I didn't believe him.

I asked the students to form two lines, with one line facing the other. Then I asked each student to name the person across from them. Only twelve of the forty-three students could name the student standing right across from them. Baffled, I asked the students to tell me which high schools they attended. The class attended fourteen different high schools. They lived in twenty different zip codes.

This isn't a critique of the congregation or leadership or the religious school. This is about understanding the competing truths and realities of our members' lives. We are struggling with an alone-together modernity, compounded by the fact that we live in an area with huge urban and suburban sprawl. Our children's lack of relationship—the fact that they don't know each other's names—is symptomatic of the much larger systemic reality within our lives. We would be foolish to think these dynamics aren't affecting our congregations' and our people's future.

Name tags are always an important way to help build connections. If your decision is to use name tags, there is an art to creating name tags that are truly helpful in connecting strangers.

1. The most important and visible feature of the name tag should be your FIRST NAME in bold print, easy to read from a distance. The family name can be underneath the first name in smaller letters.

2. The name tag itself should be placed just under your right-hand collarbone. Not on the left. Not on a lanyard with the name tag dangling in front of your *pipik* (belly button). Why? Because when

you go to shake hands with someone, you extend your right hand. Your new friend extends her or his right hand, and her or his eye naturally goes to the right, not to the left, and not to the *pipik*.

3. There are several ways to affix the name tag. Paper name tags often have adhesives, while more permanent name tags have a pin that must be secured through clothing. And, yes, there are lanyards that avoid both by dangling like a long necklace, with the name tag resting either on your chest or, you guessed it, your *pipik*. There are those who do not want to "ruin" their clothing with adhesive or pinpricks, which is why lanyards are used. Yet the most effective placement of name tags is just below the right collarbone.

4. Who wears a name tag? Here, you have choices:

   a. *Staff.* Most organizations ask staff members to wear name tags when at work.

   b. *Board.* Some boards ask their directors to wear name tags.

   c. *Members.* Some synagogues have creatively devised ways to enable all members to have name tags.

d. *Every participant.* Blank name tags are provided at the entrance of an event, and people are asked to create their own. Alternatively, participants are asked to answer a prompt, which can be general in nature or related to the season or event. For example, after a name tag asks for the name, it might read:

I'm celebrating …

I'm grateful for …

I'm visiting here from …

I'm praying for …

Ask me about my week because …

Another idea: some organizations add the cities of birth to employee name tags. So mine (RW) might look like this:

RON
Woltson
Omaha, Nebraska

Adding information such as cities of birth can be an effective way to stimulate story sharing during a relational moment in a program.

Welcoming is such an important first step in creating a relational community because of the *value* it represents to your organization:

Hospitality is a significant *Jewish value*, emphasized throughout Jewish sacred texts.

A warm, personal, face-to-face welcome into a relational community is a significant *value offer* to those looking for relationships beyond social media.

A welcoming ambience can be a *quantifiable value* to a Jewish organization in improved recruitment, engagement, and retention of members.

Takeaways

How is the welcoming ambience in your organization? Don't ask each other; ask guests and newcomers.

Establish a team of volunteer greeters. Teach them the art of effective greeting. Deploy them at key moments. Remind them that they are doing sacred work.

Develop a strategy for facilitating relationship building, beginning with personal encounters.

Make a decision about name tags. Who will wear them? What will they look like? How will people retrieve them when entering the building? How might you use prompts on name tags to help people share their stories?

Think of your institution as a gracious, hospitable home. How would you welcome, feed, and engage your guests?

Our Next Steps

_____

_____

_____

_____

Getting to Know You

After a warm welcome, the next step in building relationships is to begin the process of getting to know the other.

Relational Moments

Nearly every program or worship experience has three common outcomes:

A *cognitive* component: what you want people to *learn*

An *affective* component: what you want people to *feel*

A *relational* component: how you want people to *meet, engage, interact with one another*

An easy way to remember these outcomes is by the acronym CAR: cognitive, affective, relational. Using CAR, you can get your community headed in the direction you'd like to go!

We program planners are pretty good at the cognitive and affective, but we're not so good at the relational. One way to build the relational component in your programming and experiences is to always include a *relational moment*. In the church world, this moment is called "pass the peace." The leader asks participants to turn to those around them and offer a greeting. Typically this takes about thirty seconds. The gesture immediately changes the ambience in the room from cold to warm. This is a good first step, but the chances are slim that people learn enough about the other that they are interested or willing in building a relationship together.

Let's go beyond "pass the peace" and consider how to carve out some time in all our gatherings to encourage personal encounters in relational moments. Here are some examples that mirror our suggestions for your own leadership team meetings:

Torah study. Imagine engaging in *hevruta* Torah study during a prayer service. Some congregations do this on a regular basis in lieu of or as part of a sermon. Others offer Torah study before services, usually on Shabbat morning. The key for clergy and educators is to allow for people to engage the text and each other in addition to any direct teaching they may offer.

Checking in. Check-in is an opportunity for everyone to share a few words about what is happening in their personal lives. If you prefer a more directive instruction, you might ask, "Tell us one thing about you that we don't know—for example, a hidden talent or an experience you had as a child." Put a time limit on the sharing: "Please tell us in one sentence what's happening." Or if you can devote more time and you have a smaller group, use a one-minute sand timer. In a larger group, form groups of four to share among each other. This personal disclosure often results in people learning interesting things that can lead to further connection between folks.

Meeting a stranger. Any lecture or workshop I (RW) offer includes a five-minute relational moment: "I invite you to meet someone in the group you do not know or do not know well. Pair up, just two of you in face-to-face encounter. First, introduce yourself to each other and see if you have a connection: someone you both know, where you went to school, how you like to spend your time. This should take one minute. Then share your answer to one of these three questions: (1) "What keeps you up at night?" (This is what you are worried about. "My prostate" is not an acceptable answer.) (2) "What gets you up in the morning?" (This is what you are passionate about.) (3) "Where y'at?" (In New Orleans, this is what strangers will ask you, meaning "Where are you at? What's your story?") Suggest the new friends exchange contact information: business cards, email addresses, phone numbers, "See you on Facebook," or "Let's connect after Shabbat." Before letting the group go, finish your instructions by creating some signal to bring the group back together after five minutes: "If you can hear the sound of my voice, clap once," flip a light switch, begin to sing a well-known song. Debrief the experience by asking if anyone made a connection that surprised them. Emphasize the power of relational moments to build a relational community.

At a community-wide workshop on Relational Judaism in Nyack, New York, I introduced a five-minute relational moment to the 150 leaders from different synagogues and organizations in the town. Within one minute, I heard screaming and laughing from two women who had just met each other. They were hugging and crying. I walked over and asked, "What's going on here?" They said, "Ron, you told us to meet someone we didn't know ... we were in fourth grade together ... and we haven't seen each other in forty years!" If I had not invited the group to experience this relational moment, these two women would have left that evening having not reconnected, never realizing that their journeys brought them to that program as presidents of two different synagogues in Nyack. Surely they reignited their relationship that night, a thrilling example of the power of personal encounters within our programs.

One-to-Ones

A powerful strategy for personal encounters is the "one-to-one" (1:1) meeting popularized by community organizers. Sometimes done over a cup of coffee, these conversations between two people enable leaders of organizations to learn much more about the person they are hoping to engage than the typical survey or demographic form handed out to new members or prospects.

The purpose of the one-to-one encounter is *not* for you to talk but rather for you to *listen*. The goal is not to promote your organization but rather to hear the invitees share their stories, interests, and talents so that you can begin to suggest ways for the person to find their place in the community. The best outcome of a one-to-one is when the invitee explores potential points of connection with the leadership and mission of your institution and, perhaps, even takes a further step toward engagement.

Community organizing groups such as JOIN for Justice offer intensive workshops on how to conduct one-to-one meetings. You might consider inviting a local trainer to meet with your leadership group to conduct a how-to session. Some organizations do this in preparation for a "listening campaign," a major effort to host dozens or even hundreds of one-to-one conversations, all designed to surface issues, concerns, and gaps in serving the people of their communities. We will present a strategy for conducting a listening campaign below in the section on small groups.

Spotlight on Best Practice

Rabbi Gordon Tucker and the leadership of Temple Israel Center in White Plains, New York, conducted a listening campaign that involved several hundred one-to-one conversations. One of the issues that surfaced was the fact that many of the elderly members of the congregation had stopped coming to services. What they learned amazed them and led to significant change in the way the community served the elderly.

The seniors were unable to come to Friday night services and dinners in the synagogue building because they could not drive at night. I (RW) visited a major synagogue that offered seniors taxi vouchers to solve this problem. Rabbi Tucker's group came up with a much better, more relational solution: they organized a group of volunteer drivers willing to pick up the seniors, bring them to shul, and take them home. Why was this better? During the rides to and from the synagogue, the seniors had someone to talk with, someone who was caring for them, someone with whom they could build a relationship. The seniors loved it, and the volunteer drivers loved the experience even more.

The second problem the seniors faced was even more daunting. In the one-to-one conversations, many of them complained of being "trampled" by the famished Jews attacking the buffet tables at the kiddush luncheon after services on Saturday morning! Some even admitted they stopped coming to services because of this. Rabbi Tucker's group considered several ways to solve this problem and decided not only to reserve tables for the seniors but also to provide waiters who brought the food to them.

Spotlight on Best Practice

We heard of a congregation where the rabbi during Friday night services asked if anyone was celebrating a special occasion. A woman stood up and said, "I just had a hip replacement." The rabbi congratulated her and then spontaneously asked, "Does anyone else have a new body part?" The people laughed heartily and then a man stood up and said, "Yes, I have a new knee!" At the Oneg Shabbat afterward, people approached the bionic members to wish them well.

As with the effort to create a more welcoming ambience, *everyone* in a leadership role in the community has a role to play in implementing a comprehensive Relational Engagement Campaign (the third time we have emphasized this point).

Many organizations enlist a core team to conduct one-to-one meetings with members. Much as you would do in a fundraising campaign, the team should include leaders who are comfortable meeting with strangers over coffee and are both good listeners and gregarious conversationalists. Remember, the goal of these one-to-one encounters is *not* to sell the organization, nor is it to ask for anything. The goal is to listen carefully to the person's story, surface their talents and passions, and then make some preliminary suggestions about how the person can find their place in the community.

What are some "connecting" nodes for those seeking a place in a community?

> *With whom can I connect?* Where will I find my friends? Rick Warren teaches if a member knows five to seven people in a congregation, they will feel a sense of belonging. Some likely places to find friends include others in the same age and stage of life: preschool parents, seniors, empty nesters, parents of the same-age kids, newcomers to the community, neighbors, carpool networks, members of the health club, people working out, and so forth. We will suggest additional strategies in the chapter on small groups.

> *With whom might I worship?* Synagogues with a daily minyan know that the regular "minyannaires" often become lifelong friends. Many

congregations now offer a variety of worship experiences, even on the same Shabbat evening and morning. Which minyan best meets your spiritual needs? You will likely find a group who shares your preference for worship style.

With whom will I study? Congregations and JCCs offer adult education classes, Torah study groups (often on Shabbat morning), *hevruta* learning, national programs such as Melton Mini-School, men's groups, women's groups, and more. Like the "minyannaires," people who study together often become good friends.

With whom shall I repair the world? Those who gather together for *tikkun olam* projects discover the shared value of social justice work.

With whom would it be fun to play? There are softball teams, mahjong groups, and all sorts of other recreational activities that bring people together. JCCs sponsor "Maccabiah" teams and leagues where friendships are created.

With whom will I serve? Yes, standing committees responsible for the business of the organization and short-term groups dedicated to achieving a specific task provide volunteer leadership opportunities that often result in bonding experiences. Or kvetching experiences—but that's the subject of another book.

Clergy/Staff Encounters

One of the greatest compliments a rabbi and cantor can hear is "she is *my* rabbi" or "he is *my* cantor." One of the greatest compliments a CEO or director of a JCC or Federation is "she is my friend" or "he is my leader." Even more than "this is my synagogue or my JCC or my Federation or my chapter of Hadassah," when a leader is referred to with the adjective *my*, it indicates that a relationship has been established. This powerful connection often becomes a crucial component for relational engagement between a member and the community.

Creating this bond is squarely on the shoulders of the leaders, and it is a formidable challenge. With the normal administrative, pastoral, and teaching tasks assigned to them, professional staff are very, very busy people. It can be difficult to find time for the sort of relationship building advocated here. Thus the first thing for the leadership to understand is that if you want your clergy or staff to spend a number of hours each week in personal encounter with your members, something on their very full plates will have to give.

Our Next Steps

What meetings can we take off the plate of the clergy or staff to enable them to spend time meeting with members and prospective members?

_____

_____

_____

Spotlight on Best Practice

In *Relational Judaism*, I (RW) reported on Rabbi David-Seth Kirshner, rabbi of Temple Emanu-El in Closter, New Jersey, who insisted the congregation create a budget item for catered and waitered Shabbat meals in his home once a month. I visited Rabbi Kirshner's congregation as a scholar-in-residence in October 2015 to see for myself the impact of this practice and to observe his now famous Friday night dinners.

The first thing I learned is that what began as once-a-month events have grown into *nearly weekly* Shabbat dinners in the lovely home of Rabbi and Dori Kirshner. They begin hosting people—four to six couples and single guests every Shabbat—from Rosh Hashanah through the end of May, taking off the summer months. In addition, there is an annual new families barbeque, leadership dinners, and youth events. Four times a year they host a Shabbat dinner for wedding couples for whom the rabbi officiates. Rabbi Kirshner estimates nearly two thousand individuals have been hosted in their home over the nine years he and Dori have served the congregation.

There is a waitperson who sets up the dinner, makes some small dishes (Rabbi Kirshner has become a real foodie during this process and does much of the cooking), serves, and cleans up. Dori is a full-time professional during the week, and during the meal she is a superb and engaging full-time host. All costs for the food and help are covered by the temple.

The evening begins with the rabbi gathering everyone around the "adult" table in the dining room, including the inevitable gaggle of kids who tag along and make quick friends with the Kirshner children. The traditional Shabbat table ritual is performed in a relaxed and joyous manner—nothing at all stiff about being at the rabbi's table. Once the blessings are completed, the kids either stay at the table or are excused to eat dinner at their own tables in an adjacent room and then go play in the basement, which is well stocked with Shabbat-style games. There is an assortment of excellent kosher wines, freshly baked challot, and an incredibly delicious avalanche of entrees and side dishes presented on the kitchen island.

On the evening Susie and I were guests, there were three other couples—two couples were members of the congregation and one couple had been invited by one of the member couples to come along as a recruitment effort. The couples were seated across the table from each other so each person has two new people on either side to converse with.

In addition to hosting the wonderful meal, the rabbi and Dori are excellent conversationalists, encouraging everyone at the table to tell a story or two about themselves. At one point our hosts introduced their dog, Brisket, who, amazingly, can tell the difference between kosher and *treif*. There was no pressure whatsoever placed on the nonmember couple, only heartfelt testimonials from the member couples about the congregation.

When the other guests departed, I learned more details from Rabbi Kirshner about his strategy. Most importantly, he has taught his congregation to expect being invited to his Shabbat table only once. Only if you are bringing along a prospective member are you invited a second time. This idea is right out of the Shlomo Bardin playbook. Bardin created the Brandeis College Institute in Simi Valley, a four-week intensive exploration of Judaism for college students, who could only attend once. This allows Rabbi Kirshner to avoid the trap many clergy fall into by inviting only a close circle of friends and leadership into their homes. Rabbi Kirshner has explained to his congregation that their investment pays off best when he is able to invite a wide swath of congregational membership and prospective members to their home.

The bottom line is impressive indeed. In the very competitive environment of New Jersey—with a synagogue on nearly every corner, it seems—and in a time when most synagogues are very happy to hold their membership numbers steady, Temple Emanu-El has seen an increase of 250 membership units over the nine years of Rabbi Kirshner's tenure. Clearly the Shabbat dinners have more than paid for themselves. More importantly, the rabbi has built relationships with hundreds of members and helped recruit hundreds more to engage with Jewish life through the congregation.

Rabbi Kirshner shared another wonderful consequence of his engagement work:

> This is a team effort. I have an amazing partner and cooperative kids. When people ask how we grew the shul, the answer is "one by one." Breakfasts and dinners and snacks and coffees and one-to-one meetings: these things all make people feel closer.
>
> We recently offered a new inclusivity initiative at the shul. Most accepted this with open arms; some did not. Two people who opposed what we were doing, I invited for coffee. They were menschy about their disagreements, but they were not swayed. Yet we left cordially. Three weeks later, we held our High Holy Day appeal. Each of the two people increased gifts—one from $1,000 to $1,800 and the other from $250 to $3,600! A major leap, proving my theory that "rabbi time" and one-to-one time spent connecting and listening matters more than agreeing on all items. If our colleagues were less governed by fear and more governed by connecting one-to-one, our movement would be in a better place.

Certainly there are other rabbis who, like Rabbi Kirshner, demonstrate an easy-going style on the pulpit, offer powerful sermons with great substance and humor, have fluency with popular culture as well as sacred texts, invite people to join hands at the end of the service for the priestly benediction, "work the room" at the Oneg, and regularly schedule missions to Israel. But very few have been willing to open their homes in such a generous manner, with the full support of a congregation that is enjoying the fruits of their investment.

Spotlight on Best Practice

I (RW) recall the days when clergy stood at the back of the sanctuary to greet worshippers after services in a "receiving line." At Valley Beth Shalom, Rabbi Harold Schulweis, may he rest in peace, would ask the congregation to remain in place while he escorted the Bar/Bat Mitzvah families to the back of the sanctuary, where they were positioned to accept the congratulations and appreciation for the service. With large crowds, this could take a half hour. If people did not want to wait in line, they could find him in the lobby or the social hall during lunch. He was accessible and his congregants and guests deeply appreciated it. Perhaps it is time to bring back the "receiving line."

Phone Calls

The next best thing to personal face-to-face encounter is a phone call. Many synagogues now call members at least once a year to connect, often just before major holidays such as Rosh Hashanah, Passover, or Hanukkah. Some call on birthdays or special anniversaries.

I (RW) met with the board of trustees of a large organization. What was their biggest complaint? "No one calls! We get weekly emails, we get bills, we get requests for donations, but we can go years without receiving a single phone call from anyone."

Conversely, a single phone call from a CEO, an executive director, a rabbi, an educator—just to check in—can make a huge impression on the recipient. Carefully time your calls—not before breakfast, at dinner time, late at night, on Shabbat or Jewish holidays. There should be no hint that the call is about the "business" of the organization; you are simply calling to demonstrate you care about them.

And, please, no robocalls!

Spotlight on Best Practice

In *Relational Judaism*, I (RW) wrote of Rabbi Dan Moskovitz, who, when assuming the pulpit of Temple Sholom in Vancouver, Canada, realized he knew nothing about the people named on the weekly yahrzeit list of fifty to sixty names read in the fifty-year-old synagogue every Shabbat. In a remarkable move, Rabbi Moskovitz decided to call a family member remembering each person on the list, with a simple request: "Please tell me a story about your loved one." Most members receiving these calls were shocked. One member said to the rabbi, "This simple act immediately impressed everyone in the congregation."

When I shared this engagement strategy in a presentation to members of the Jewish Communal Professionals of Southern California, a former student of mine, Brian Greene, executive director of the Westside Jewish Community Center in Los Angeles, rushed up to me after the talk to relate the following story:

> You may remember, I'm from Vancouver. My mother, Marilynn Greene, had a very close and meaningful relationship with her rabbi at Temple Sholom. When he retired, a new rabbi had come to the temple, she had not met him, and she told me she was feeling a bit distant from the temple now that her rabbi was not there. She was probably about eighty years old at the time, living alone in a senior living center. One day she got a phone call out of the blue from the new rabbi. He introduced himself as Rabbi Dan and shared that he noticed it was the yahrzeit day

for her father. He asked questions about her father, who had died when she was a teenager. They had a really nice conversation about him, and then Rabbi Dan asked how she was doing. My mother called me afterward and said, "Nobody has asked me about my father in fifty years. I've been telling all my friends about the great new rabbi the temple hired!"

Rabbi Dan reports it took him two to three hours to make the calls, beginning on Thursday and ending before Shabbat. "It took awhile to do, but it was often the most sacred thing I did all week," this busy rabbi says. The payoff: his temple membership has climbed by 140 units and the religious school population has tripled in the four years he has been at the synagogue.

House Meetings

Taking another page from the community organizing handbook, many synagogues have found that gathering small groups of members in homes—"house meetings"—is an effective way to engage people. For some communities, this is a more successful strategy than one-to-ones.

At IKAR in Los Angeles, members did not find the one-to-one strategy fit their people. Instead, they adopted house meetings as their main mode of listening to their members. Rabbi Sharon Brous says, "With one-to-ones that don't go well, you can be looking at your watch. When you get ten people—a minyan—in a room, there are fireworks!"

Spotlight on Best Practice

Rabbi Angela Warnick Buchdahl, senior rabbi, Central Synagogue, New York City

Many years before I arrived at Central, Rabbi Peter Rubinstein initiated an audacious project—to invite every adult in the congregation to a small-group conversation (twenty to forty people) in a member's home in a series of cocktail parties. The precipitating event was Central's fire in 1998. The congregation was much smaller then, around twelve hundred families, and the fire was a crisis moment. Rabbi Rubinstein wanted to personally connect with the community in order to help rebuild and renew the congregation. Since then, approximately every four to six years, Central embarks on another round of these intimate conversations. As the congregation has grown, the number of gatherings has as well.

We did a series of cocktail parties, approximately forty of them in 2006 when I arrived as the new senior cantor, and it was a way for me to meet the congregation. We did another round in 2010 as an outgrowth of our community organizing campaign. In this round we called them "house meetings," and we discussed issues of Jewish continuity as part of our "Pass It On" initiative. The most recent round was completed in 2015. Clergy and senior leadership alternated attending events, and I attended all of them.

We had a small lay committee who helped run the initiative and found hosts for the house meetings. We planned two gatherings in an evening: the first one from 6:00 to 7:30, serving cocktails. The second from 8:00 to 9:30, serving desserts. People mingled, ate, and talked for the first half hour. Then we gathered everyone to do a round of an icebreaker question with name introductions, then an interactive d'var torah, and then we led the group in a thirty- to forty-minute conversation about the issue at hand. A member of the board took notes at every gathering, and findings were compiled to help inform the strategic direction of the congregation.

These congregational meetings had so many important benefits: members met new members and began new relationships; clergy and senior leadership had a chance to know many more congregants on a personal level; hosts felt a sense of ownership and pride to have Central in their home. In each iteration, we were able to truly take the pulse of the congregation on an important issue or topic. It has helped fulfill our goal to have the soul and warmth of a haimish (warm) shul in a large synagogue.

Listening

"When new members join a synagogue or JCC, what do they get?" When asking this question during workshops, someone inevitably yells, "A bill!" Sadly, this is too often the case. (We love executive directors, but if we are to move from a transactional to relational paradigm, it's the rabbi who should be the first point of contact—even for the business side of the relationship.) Rather than a warm letter from the rabbi, the new member packet typically consists of information about various groups in the organization; a list of volunteer positions on committees, which few sign up for in fear of being made chair of the committee immediately and involvement being a life sentence—you'll never get off the committee; and a demographic survey to complete and return, which no one reads. Even if the form asks for talents or hobbies, a demographic survey is not a great way to really come to know another human being.

Why is personal disclosure important? Because when you share your story with someone, you feel closer to them. You have revealed something intimate about your life. Conversely, the listener feels closer to the teller—you relate to them. Often you are touched emotionally. Personal encounters are still the best way to hear someone's story, but what are some other ways to encourage members to engage in personal disclosure?

If done publicly, telling stories can become a powerful way to build a relational community. In the twentieth century, testimonials were often heard in churches but rarely in synagogues and JCCs. In fact, in most synagogues it was unusual to hear anyone's voice other than the rabbi sermonizing, the cantor singing, and the president of the congregation greeting and making announcements.

Yet consider the power of testimony. Yelp, Amazon, and Goodreads are websites that encourage people to write reviews that are essentially testimonials about the experience of products or service providers. Watch almost any daytime television program and what you hear are testimonials and stories. Fundraisers know that perhaps the most effective way to motivate a financial contribution is to have those touched by the philanthropy share testimony and appreciation for the work of the organization.

At The Temple, we (LM) have group leaders testify to their personal experiences during an annual Shabbat service that celebrates our Relational Engagement Campaign. The attendees of that service are always moved by these testimonials, and many seek out or create small groups at the next opportunity. At Central Synagogue, we (NA) have small-group members speak at Yom Kippur services as a way to recruit new members into groups forming immediately after the holidays. At IKAR, an independent spiritual community in Los Angeles, members were asked to submit one-paragraph stories about "a simple expression of love, empathy, or shared humanity ... someone's gesture, gift, acknowledgment that really made a difference." The 109-page booklet of inspiring stories, *Every Little Thing*, was self-published and distributed at Rosh Hashanah services. Some synagogues and JCCs post stories of their members on their websites, social media sites, and in columns in their newsletters.

Spotlight on Best Practice

I (RW) am sitting in Congregation Rodef Sholom in Marin County, California, on a Friday night. The service has been lovely and there is a large crowd. Just before the Mourner's Kaddish, the rabbi introduces a member of the congregation "who will share a story about her mother whose yahrzeit is this week." Walking to the bimah from the congregation, a woman in her forties approaches the lectern. She is a bit nervous; public speaking is not her profession. Yet as she begins to speak, it is clear this will be a deeply heartfelt tribute to her beloved mother. The stories are funny, poignant, and moving. People in the congregation are sobbing; they identify with this woman and her testimony. The whole talk takes less than five minutes. She is welcomed back to her seat by her family and synagogue members sitting nearby, embracing her with hugs and kisses. (See our website, www.relationaljudaismhandbook.com, for Hagar Ben-Eliezer's amazing *azkara*.)

Rabbi Stacy Friedman, Rabbi Elana Rosen-Brown, and Moji Javid, director of community engagement, report the *azkara* (a remembrance) is offered three times a month at Friday night Shabbat services in lieu of the previous practice of reciting a responsive reading. Every month, a lay volunteer—an "*azkara* captain"—coordinates the choosing of the person to offer the *azkara* and coaches her or him on how to properly prepare and deliver the two- to three-minute remembrance. (I have always loved Rodef Sholom. The synagogue asks congregants to deliver freshly baked challot from their "Mitzvah Kitchen," which meets every Thursday night, to homebound members after Friday night services. This congregation placed the *mezuzot* in the synagogue building far down on the door mantles so those in wheelchairs, walkers, and young people can reach them.)

Moji admits that sometimes the *azkara* giver will run a bit long, but never more than five minutes. In the three years the congregation has been offering these stories of loved ones, there have been no complaints—quite the opposite. Members are genuinely moved by many of these presentations. Moreover, both the *azkara* givers and the captains are honored to be asked, feel more connected to the congregation, and consider the act of remembering their loved ones a deeply spiritual experience.

In *Relational Judaism*, I (RW) wrote of the practice at IKAR of inviting congregants to submit short stories about the loved ones they are remembering for a self-published *Yizkor* booklet distributed at the memorial service on Yom Kippur, much like the *Every Little Thing* book mentioned above. This transforms the typical simple listing of names into an extraordinarily engaging and moving book of memory.

Rabbis use other strategies to engage congregants personally during the worship service. It is common for those standing to offer a *mi sheberakh* for the ill to call out the names of those they are praying for. Many rabbis ask those observing a yahrzeit to identify the relationship they have to the deceased by asking, "Who are you remembering?" The congregant answers, "My mother, Bernice Paperny Wolfson." This notion of personalizing the yahrzeit list, the *Yizkor* book, and the Mourner's Kaddish is a wonderful way to encourage storytelling that deepens connection.

As a community, we come together to pray for the sick and mourn for the dead, but many communities also use worship services to celebrate milestones. Some are more obvious: birthdays, *aufruf*, Bar/Bat Mitzvah. Some congregations ask members to share more. One congregation asked people to identify their own reasons for celebration. One child said he passed his deep-water swim test.

Spotlight on Best Practice

Recall from *Relational Judaism* the best practice of Valley Beth Shalom, which gathers small groups of new members to meet with clergy and top lay leaders in a "new member induction" ceremony. After bagels and coffee in the lobby, a circle of chairs is placed on the pulpit of the sanctuary, and everyone takes turns telling the story of "how I got to Valley Beth Shalom," their spiritual journey story. The synagogue leaders do not "hard sell" the programs of the congregation. Instead they invite the new members to explore the many opportunities to connect with the congregation and other congregants. At the end of the hour, the rabbi takes the Torah scrolls out of the ark and hands them one by one to each person, marking the act of joining a spiritual moment. The *shehecheyanu* is recited. Many people are brought to tears.

Spotlight on Best Practice

Rabbi Susan Leider, Congregation Kol Shofar, Tiburon, California

When someone becomes a synagogue member or renews their membership, they usually pay their dues and show up when they want to. But what if they could opt into a membership model to help them find their place in the community? Could this option be offered alongside traditional synagogue membership?

Our board and community studied *Relational Judaism*, and we engage in community organizing that emphasizes the importance of one-to-one meetings and building relationships. Our midsized Conservative congregation has grown from 440 units to 519, but we are still well below our peak. In many demographics, there are opportunities for connecting socially and sharing experiences together apart from ritual and prayer. We are known by many to be haimish, warm and welcoming.

But in many ways, we have a long way to go. I recently received an email from a relatively new member who shared that he was not renewing his membership, as he found it to be one of the coldest and most unwelcoming synagogues for new people. He wrote, "Often after attending services, I just stood there. No one ever made an attempt to welcome me to sit with them at kiddush lunch." Others echo this, saying, "I walk into kiddush and I still don't know where to sit. People here have known each other for ages."

Together with our board, we began to imagine what an initiative to integrate new members based on Rick Warren's "ministry" model of membership might look like in a synagogue. The result we call *Makom*—Finding Our Place. We seek to address the importance of fostering deep relationships and shared experiences, truly listening to and understanding each other, putting skills and talents to work for the whole, making meaning in people's lives, and helping new members find one's *makom*, their place in the congregation. We believe that the outcome will lead us to discover new leadership, increase our financial viability, and connect our members more deeply to the congregation.

Makom is an optional membership track offered to members as an enhancement to traditional synagogue membership. *Makom* members still complete an application and pay dues, but they also commit to participating in a series of intergenerational cohort group meetings over the course of a year, with a mutually agreed upon outcome of committing to service to the community in a specific role. Through these cohort meetings, existing leadership and *Makom* members explore together what significant synagogue involvement could look like for each individual.

Meeting Number 1—Your Jewish Journey. Here we focus exclusively on listening to each other's Jewish journeys. How did you end up at Kol Shofar? If you were born Jewish, what has your path been like? If you came to Judaism later in life or you aren't Jewish, tell us about your journey. This is the first step in deepening relationships with the community, discovering common threads that unite us.

Meeting Number 2—Get to Know Kol Shofar. What makes Kol Shofar tick? How do things happen in this particular community? Learn how to navigate the community. How do we care for each other? What demographic groups are part of the synagogue?

Meeting Number 3—Where do I Fit In? In this meeting, we deepen our understanding of congregant talents, gifts, interests, and skills. Where do they see themselves volunteering and getting involved in service?

The first cohort of twenty-three members is under way, and the feedback has been extraordinarily positive. (See our website, relationaljudaismhandbook.com, for a full description of the program, invitation to participate letter, FAQs, and other documents.)

Takeaways

In your leadership team, plan to implement the following action items:

Greeters. Create a dedicated and well-trained corps of volunteer greeters. See *The Spirituality of Welcoming,* pages 45–82, for suggestions and material for training purposes.

Our Next Steps

_____ _____

_____

_____

Name tags. Decide on who will wear name tags (if anyone, but you know how we feel). Design the name tag. Create a way to store the name tags in an accessible place in the building. Be sure your top leadership wear the tags to demonstrate the importance of the practice. If your observance allows or during weekday programs, offer all participants a name tag template to write on and wear. Use the name tags at some point in your event; if they are not useful, people will stop wearing them.

Our Next Steps

_____

_____

_____

Take five. Ask your leadership team to devote five minutes at every program, worship service, Oneg Shabbat, and meeting to greet and meet people they don't know. Do not say, "Welcome to our congregation"—they may have been members for years! Instead say, "Wonderful to see you!"

Our Next Steps

_____

_____

_____

Never ignore. Encourage your professional staff to never walk by someone in the hall without recognizing their presence with a simple greeting. Model the practice of welcoming strangers; it is the first step in creating a relational ambience in your organization.

Our Next Steps

_____

_____

_____

Food and drink. Assess the quality of the food and drink you offer at the synagogue. If people complain about the Shabbat dinner offerings or the "terrible coffee," then you have work to do. Think of the cuisine you would serve at your own home; you, like Abraham and Sarah, would offer the best. Likewise, if your Shabbat dinners are expensive and inedible, people might come once, but that's it. Be transparent and brutally honest, even if you fear stepping on the toes of caterers or volunteers. Consider a "pop-up" coffee and bagel café during high traffic times in the building. In addition to the great food and drink, be sure there is free and password-free Wi-Fi, comfortable seating and air flow, and Jewish books and periodicals available for browsing or even borrowing.

Our Next Steps

Relational moments. Discuss with your clergy how to offer short relational moments within programming and worship services. Use a variety of types of relational moments to keep things fresh.

Our Next Steps

Phone calls. When will you call your members? Who will make the calls?

Our Next Steps

Clergy/staff visits. How will you empower your clergy and staff to spend time meeting your members and potential members? What's in your budget to make this happen? How can you provide relief from other duties to allow time for personal encounters?

Our Next Steps

_____

_____

_____

Tasks. Who will agree to do which task for your welcoming efforts?

Our Next Steps

_____

_____

_____

Serving You

The next step in crafting a Relational Engagement Campaign is to think carefully about the "quality service" that permeates your efforts. Our members and guests interact with a wide variety of companies, institutions, businesses, and, yes, Jewish organizations. Their experience with these groups is often defined by the quality of the service they provide. Great "customer service" experience engenders loyalty, while poor service inevitably leads to the end of any relationship whatsoever with providers.

Granted, businesses are different from nonprofits. Their motive for providing excellent service is primarily profit. They understand that their relationship with customers is transactional at its core. The goal of a Jewish organization is to create a deeper relational relationship. Yet there is much to learn from the business world's "quality service" literature that can help improve the relationship between our institutions and their members and guests.

Everyone Is a Greeter: Disney

A great relationship story: When I (RW) joined with Rabbi Lawrence Hoffman to create Synagogue 2000/3000 in 1995, I learned that the Walt Disney Company had just opened "Disney University," the internal training division, to outsiders by offering a series of seminars on their strategies for providing their guests a superior experience. I wanted to attend "The Disney Secrets of Quality Experience" seminar, but I couldn't get in. Enrollment was closed, yet I was eager to attend. I told Larry about it and he called Stanley Gold, who at that time was the chair of the Board of Governors of Hebrew Union College and a member of Disney's board of directors and counsel to Roy Disney. One phone call later I was on my way to Disney World in Orlando to attend the seminar.

As I approached the ballroom in the Dolphin Hotel, I immediately felt elated that I had made the right choice. Who do you think was standing at the entrance of the ballroom to greet every one of the seventy-five participants? Not Mickey Mouse. Not Walt Disney (he's dead). Not Michael Eisner, CEO of Disney at the time. The two people greeting everyone were the two trainers from Disney University, our instructors for the next four days. (Ever since my very first teaching experience, I have been greeting my students at the front door of the classroom ... and I continue to do so at scholar-in-residence presentations and lectures. For me, it's a way to connect personally with all the people who are about to become my "students." Witnessing the same phenomenon at Disney was validating indeed.)

The first segment of the seminar was titled "Traditions." We learned the history of the Walt Disney Company and how Walt had innovated animation and transformed dingy carnivals into the sparkling Disney parks designed to immerse guests in a living experience of the classic movies. This story was related through testimonials, videos, and "insider" information that made us feel as if we were privy to "backstage" knowledge. They promised that over the next four days, we would learn the secrets of Disney's extraordinarily successful strategies of hospitality, service, and crafting memorable experiences. By lunchtime, we felt privileged to be welcomed into the Disney family.

The top three insights I learned were:

1. *Everyone is a greeter.* How many Disney employees, or "cast members," do you meet before you get on the first ride? The answer is seven. There are cast members (1) at the entrance of the parking structure, (2) directing you to a tram, (3) on the tram welcoming you to the park, (4) at the security checkpoint, (5) selling you passes at the ticket booth, (6) taking your ticket, (7) renting you a stroller. You are barely inside the front gate and you have met all these representatives of the Disney company, the frontline providers of the Disney quality service experience. Their genuine smiles, use of eye contact, and helpful information and guidance can make a great start to your day.

2. *Everyone in leadership is an ambassador for the organization.* Greeters are great but not nearly enough to create an ambience of welcome throughout the experience.

3. *Everyone is an educator.* The first visit to a Disney park can be overwhelming. The Disney people understand this. They know lots of people feel disoriented, even with the directional signs and maps. A well-staffed "Guest Services" desk is positioned near the entrance of the park where guests can ask questions, yet Disney people know that many people will never walk into it; they are too embarrassed to admit they are "lost." Who gets the most questions from guests at Disney parks? The sweepers, the cast members who are seemingly everywhere keeping the park pristine. So Disney ensures that the sweepers know as much about the park as the Guest Services agents.

We also have guests and even members who will be too embarrassed to ask a Jewish question to a rabbi, so they may ask a receptionist or other office staff. They may ask other congregants. Recall Saddleback Church's strategy of dozens of lay leaders strategically located throughout the campus dressed in T-shirts that read "I CAN HELP!"

Visitors to Disney parks have very high expectations that their experience will be outstanding. Yet there can be challenges: long lines, fussy and tired children to drag along, exhaustion from walking distances. Disney knows all this and does everything it can to ameliorate the situation: the famous winding Disney waiting line that fools you into thinking you are closer to the entrance than you really are, the "pre-show" during your wait in line to keep you entertained. Moreover, every Disney employee is instructed to "take five," meaning spend five minutes during the shift to do something "extraordinary" and "unexpected" for a guest.

Takeaways

How can your organization exceed expectations of your members and guests? Are there parking spaces for first-time visitors? Are there welcome gestures when new members join?

Are there surprise gifts for Bar/Bat Mitzvah families? Are there annual phone calls to wish members happy birthday, anniversary, Passover, or new year?

Personalized Attention: Nordstrom

The Nordstrom department stores are known for their "legendary" service. Examples abound of clerks paying *personal attention* to each and every customer interaction. The story is often told of a delivery company leaving a $200 pair of shoes in the rain at the doorstep of a customer. When the customer called Nordstrom to complain, instead of being directed to contact the delivery company, which was legally responsible for the ruined shoes, the Nordstrom employee who sold the shoes to the customer said, "I'm incredibly sorry that happened. Will you be home in the next forty-five minutes?" The employee then brought over a new pair of shoes.

Takeaways

Know your people. Apologize when things go wrong—even if you are not at fault. Solve the problem as soon as possible.

The Power of a Personal Note: Chase Bank

On my birthday a few years ago, I received 456 "happy birthday" messages on Facebook and four—count 'em, four—handwritten birthday cards. One was hand-delivered (with chocolate cake and presents in bed, a Wolfson family tradition) by my wife, Susie. The second and third cards came in the snail mail: one from our daughter, Havi, and her family and the other from our son, Michael. The fourth card also came via the postal service. It was from Valerie, my Chase Bank teller. On Chase Bank stationary, the handwritten card read:

> Dear Mr. Wolfson,
> Happy Birthday! I hope you have a wonderful day.

When you were in the branch last week, you mentioned you were seeing your grandchildren to celebrate. How was your visit? Next time they are in Los Angeles, please bring them by the branch so we might meet them.

Enjoy!

Valerie, your Chase Bank teller

I was so impressed I made a beeline to the bank—on my birthday!—to thank Valerie for the card and to ask her a question: "Were you instructed to write this?"

"Not really," Valerie admitted. "But we have been encouraged to interact more with our clients. I noticed your birthday was coming up, and I had a little extra time to write something."

It then became clear to me. Marina, the bank manager, now patrolled the lobby, welcoming customers instead of working back in her cubicle. Another teller was stationed near the ATM machines, ready to help people navigating the technology. You cannot get more transactional than a bank! Yet they clearly had decided to ratchet up their client engagement strategies, to encourage tellers to address clients by name and to build relationships, all in an effort to transform a transactional experience into a relational one.

Takeaways

In this Facebook era, there is nothing more impactful than a handwritten card and a personal phone call. This is especially true when the communication is not about money. When does your community connect in a personal way, beyond social media postings and bulletins?

Anticipating Needs: Marriott Hotels

I am visiting a congregation in an East Coast city, staying in a Marriott hotel. I am energized by the presentations and conversations with the synagogue leadership over Shabbat. Tomorrow morning I will be leading a workshop on Relational Judaism, and an idea comes to me in my sleep.

I wake up. It's three o'clock in the morning. I turn to the nightstand and, whaddaya know, there is a pad of paper and pen! How did Mr. Marriott know I would be looking for exactly that at three in the morning?

The answer: Mr. Marriott anticipated my needs. Just as he put an ironing board in every hotel room. Just as most public institutions have put baby-changing tables in every restroom, including the men's.

When we anticipate the needs of our members and guests, we can be proactive about providing answers and solutions to questions and needs they have, even before they realize they have them. How do we anticipate the needs of Bar/Bat Mitzvah families who are as anxious about the party as they are about the ceremony itself? How do we anticipate the needs of the family members who will be chanting blessings over the Torah in an unfamiliar language? How do we anticipate the needs of the JCC members—umbrellas at the front door?

Takeaways

Put yourself in the shoes of your members and guests: new members, preschool families, pre–Bar/Bat Mitzvah families, health club members, parents with special needs children, empty nesters, seniors, adult children caring for aging parents, guests on Shabbat morning. What are their needs, both physical and spiritual, at key times of their engagement with community? Compile a list and consider how you are meeting these needs.

Answering Questions: Apple Genius Bar

If I get stuck trying to figure out the technology on my iPhone, iPad, or Mac computer, I can make an appointment to visit the "Genius Bar" in my nearby Apple Store. Imagine creating a pop-up "Jewish Genius Bar" at key times during the calendar year, especially in the weeks before Passover. Historically, rabbis gave sermons only twice a year: on Yom Kippur and on the Shabbat immediately prior to the Passover holiday. In the latter, the rabbi often reviewed specific instructions and suggestions for how to make the seder an engaging and meaningful experience.

Takeaways

Create opportunities for members of all ages to see the community as a resource center for celebrating Jewish life, not only at the institution but also, more importantly, at home.

Spotlight on Best Practice

At Congregation B'nai Jehoshua Beth Elohim in Deerfield, Illinois, Rabbi Karyn Kedar deconstructed the library at their facility. Instead of stacks of books in a room deep in the building that nobody uses, she built bookshelves into their large—and beautiful—lobby, inviting people to check out the books on an honors system. That is the kind of accessible resource center for Jewish life that every Jewish institution can offer. This synagogue lobby looks more like a reading room in a modern public library, with sitting areas for adults, a play area for children, and a pop-up café at high traffic times. The columns are inscribed with key values of the congregation: "Wisdom, "Courage," "Faith." Extraordinary!

Take Me There: Barnes and Noble

Twenty years ago, when you asked a clerk at Barnes and Noble if they had a certain book, the clerk would look it up on the computer and direct you to "the third floor, aisle thirteen." Today when you ask if the store has a specific title, the clerk looks it up on the computer, takes you to "the third floor, aisle thirteen," finds the book on the shelf, and hands it to you—a totally different level of service.

When strangers or guests of the Bar/Bat Mitzvah enter a synagogue service and cannot find the page number in the siddur, there are three things you could do: (1) ignore them, (2) tell them the page number, or (3) hand them your siddur turned to the correct page—you can find the page again easily in another copy of the siddur. In some Orthodox synagogues, a hand-cranked device (like a low-tech "Take-a-Number" display in the bakery) keeps the congregation alerted to the current page.

Another example of people being "lost": navigating the labyrinth of hallways to find a location within a building. Many JCC and synagogue buildings are notorious for poor or nonexistent signage. One solution is better directional signage. Another is to station volunteers at key entry points and intersections within the building to assist guests. In *The Spirituality of Welcoming*, I (RW) suggest leaders take a walking tour of the building in order to see it through the eyes of guests.

Takeaways

Encourage staff and members to be on the lookout for guests and members looking "lost" and help them along to their destination. "Lost" can also mean not knowing how to follow along in worship services in a synagogue or during a particular ritual in a JCC preschool. Always provide transliterations of Hebrew, give precise instructions, and translate commonly used Jewish lingo (even expressions such as *mazel tov*—"Congratulations!") for those who are new to Jewish terms. The goal is to make folks as comfortable as possible in navigating the experience.

Knowing Your People: Louis Market

My (RW) grandfather, Louis Paperny, built the first modern supermarket in Nebraska. In the front of the store he created a "courtesy counter," a place where his customers could cash checks, return soda pop bottles, and meet Louie (everyone called him Louie). There they could find him, at the very entrance of the market, greeting his customers by name, offering credit to those who needed more time to pay bills, chatting about kids and grandkids. There is where Louie established relationships with his loyal clientele, people who traded with him for generations.

Many synagogues have no such "courtesy counter" in the lobby of the building (JCCs are better at this). There is no check-in space or concierge desk, as in a hotel. No reception desk, as in offices. No place to welcome visitors and help them connect with the people or events they have come to encounter. We can do better.

Spotlight on Best Practice

At Valley Beth Shalom in Encino, California, the lobby of the congregation is a very long hallway that members often refer to as "the bowling alley." Realizing the cold and unwelcoming first impression this gave to visitors and members, the synagogue leadership decided to completely transform a difficult space. First, they added a "welcome desk" just inside the front doors, staffed by an office worker who functions as a greeter and direction giver for those unfamiliar with the building. Two sitting areas were created with comfortable chairs and couches. A free coffee machine was set up nearby. One long wall became an art gallery. The gift shop, which had diminishing sales due to online shopping, was closed and the space renovated as a youth lounge.

Bins to collect items for the food pantry were placed in prominent spots. Banners of welcome and announcements of various activities and programs were hung from the rafters. A video displays a loop of advertisements for events and photos of the clergy. A tasteful and understated display of donors was installed along another wall. The central pillars of the synagogue—*Torah, Avodah, Gemilut Hasadim,* and *Chevrah*—are illustrated along another wall with dynamic photos of congregants engaged in study, prayer, acts of social justice, and community building. The overall message is one of welcome and invitation to engagement.

Spotlight on Best Practice

Imagine what might happen if your leadership was connected to every member of your organization. You would be able to recognize their names, visualize their faces, know something personal about their stories, tick off their kids' and grandkids' names, know their talents and passions. Someone on your team would recall their points of engagement with the community—how they have volunteered (if at all), when they tend to show up. All of this information would be gathered into a database and decisions would be made about attempts to deepen their connection to the organization and to others.

At Cold Springs Middle School near Reno, Nevada, this ongoing assessment is standard practice. It's "a foundation of our middle school," according to principal Roberta Duvall. Several times a year, all the teachers gather in the library where posters filled with the names of every child in the 980-student school line the walls. Next to each name are rows of columns labeled "Name/Face," "Something Personal," "Personal/Family Story," "Hobbies." The teachers make notes in the columns, cross-referencing information with each other about each student. Principal Duvall reinforces the importance of the effort: "Every student needs to belong and connect to at least one teacher or one adult in this building every day."

Why does the school do this? To increase attendance and to drastically improve graduation rates. And it is working. Teachers are ramping up their three "signature classroom practices" for social and emotional learning: welcome rituals and routines, more engaging teaching methods, and end-of-class reflections. They welcome students individually at the door, hold "feel-good family circles" to promote a sense of belonging, and encourage students to write compliments, anonymously, about their peers to help each person feel known and appreciated in the group (https://www.edutopia.org/article/power-being-seen).

These best principles of relational engagement can be readily applied to your organization. Take the time to review your membership lists to ensure no one remains anonymous. Identify their interests, talents, and passions and find ways to encourage their use in the community. Find ways to compliment, appreciate, and recognize people in testimonials and reports. Be sure no one comes to a program or worship experience and sits alone. Connect people to your leadership and to each other—and watch your level of engagement rise and your membership recruitment and retention improve.

Takeaways

Look at your walkway from the parking lot into the main entrance of the building. Inside the lobby, establish a greeting area with a concierge desk staffed by a welcoming personality, comfortable seating, free and password-free Wi-Fi, excellent coffee, and Jewish periodicals or even books to borrow. Be sure there are photos of your members doing great things. Ask yourself, "Can I find the coat room, the office, the restroom, the health club, the library, the pre-school, the rabbi's study—without asking directions?" If the answer is no, improve the signage.

Outstanding Service: Ritz-Carlton Hotels

The job description of a Ritz-Carlton Hotel employee is as simple as it gets: "Ladies and gentlemen serving ladies and gentlemen." How does the company teach their staff how to be "ladies and gentlemen" and how to serve? Here are the twelve principles—the "gold standard"—that every employee knows:

1. I build strong relationships and create Ritz-Carlton guests for life.

2. I am always responsive to the expressed and unexpressed wishes and needs of our guests.

3. I am empowered to create unique, memorable, and personal experiences for our guests.

4. I understand my role in achieving the key success factors, embracing community footprints, and creating the Ritz-Carlton mystique.

5. I continuously seek opportunities to innovate and improve the Ritz-Carlton experience.

6. I own and immediately resolve guest problems.

7. I create a work environment of teamwork and lateral service so that the needs of our guests and each other are met.

8. I have the opportunity to continuously learn and grow.

9. I am involved in planning the work that affects me.

10. I am proud of my professional appearance, language, and behavior.

11. I protect the privacy and security of our guests, my fellow employees, and the company's confidential information and assets.

12. I am responsible for uncompromising levels of cleanliness and creating a safe and accident-free environment.

Takeaways

Imagine such a list for your professional staff and volunteer leadership:

1. I build strong relationships and create members for life.

2. I am always responsive to the expressed and unexpressed wishes and needs of our members and guests.

3. I am empowered to create unique, memorable, and personal experiences for our members and guests.

4. I understand my role in welcoming and engaging our members and guests.

5. I continuously seek opportunities to innovate and improve the synagogue or JCC experience.

6. I own and immediately resolve members' and guests' problems.

7. I create a work environment of teamwork and lateral service so that the needs of our members and each other are met. No silos! (See explanation below.)

8. I have the opportunity to continuously learn and grow, both Jewishly and in my chosen profession.

9. I am involved in planning the work that affects me.

10. I am proud of my professional appearance, language, and behavior.

11. I protect the privacy and security of our members and guests, my fellow employees, and the organization's confidential information and assets.

12. I am responsible for uncompromising levels of hospitality and creating a spiritually safe and blame-free culture of honor.

A special note about "silos." In the Midwest, many farms have individual silos for corn, wheat, and soybeans. The three silos stand alone, much like the departments in our institutions. The youth group people have no clue what's going on in senior services. The health club staff have little contact with the cultural arts people. Teachers have little knowledge of synagogue programming. The social justice folks barely know the "minyannaires." In a great relational community there is, at minimum, good understanding of every area of the institution and, at best, cross-collaboration and integration of services and programming.

The Power of Testimonials: University of Michigan

When our (R and SW) daughter, Havi, visited the colleges she was interested in attending, she considered the most powerful presentation to be the experience at the University of Michigan in Ann Arbor. A student was assigned to her as a personal guide throughout the visit. She took Havi on the tour of campus, sat with her at meals, and answered all her questions. Most importantly, the student offered a personal testimonial about her positive experiences at the school. Havi emerged from the visit sold on attending the university.

Takeaways

Testimonials are powerful messages to both members and guests. In most synagogues, the only testimonial is the annual talk by the president on the High Holy Days. Certainly synagogue presidents offer announcements at the end of worship services, but announcements are not testimonials. Some synagogues have invited members to give short testimonials during announcements or on the High Holy Days. JCCs often feature testimonials in their communications, both online and printed. The focus of these testimonials is to tell the story of how engagement with some aspects of the community has impacted their lives.

Pride in Ownership: Green Bay Packers

When a Green Bay Packers wide receiver catches a touchdown pass in Lambeau Field, he does something remarkable to celebrate. He jumps into the stands, fans "*pahtch* his *tuches*," and the crowd goes wild. It's called the "Lambeau Leap." There is more to the leap than meets the eye. The Green Bay Packers is not owned by a billionaire or a conglomerate like every other professional sports team in North America; it is owned by the citizens of Green Bay, Wisconsin. In many homes throughout the city, people proudly display their framed shares on the walls of their living rooms. So when the wide receiver celebrates with the Lambeau Leap, there is a pride of ownership that is qualitatively different from that of any other city in the country. When Green Bay citizens wear Packers jerseys and "cheeseheads" and refer to them as "our team," it has a totally different meaning than in any other city.

Takeaways

There is no greater compliment for a Jewish institution than when members proudly proclaim it is "my shul" or "my J." Just as when applied to professional staff, these words *my* and *our* indicate a level of relationship that comes from a sense of belonging that transcends transactional. How do you get there? Only through a concentrated effort to engage each individual in the community. A deep connection can lead to pride of ownership that sustains engagement and continuous support of the institution.

A Setting Designed to Connect:
The Tonight Show

Speaking of jumping into the stands, *The Tonight Show* learned the power of direct connection when Jay Leno took over from Johnny Carson. Carson used to deliver his nightly monologue in front of a blue curtain set off to one side of the studio, somewhat distant from the studio audience. When Leno began his run as host of the show, he too presented his monologue in the same space—and he was bombing! It took the producers a month or so before they realized why Leno was not connecting with the studio audience: they were too far away from him. Leno developed his skills in comedy clubs where the stage is directly in front of the people, very close to the comedian.

(This reminds me [RW] of the very funny *Curb Your Enthusiasm* episode when Larry David has no tickets for entering a synagogue on the High Holy Days. He asks his friend Jeff what he can do. Jeff points to a shady character lurking near the entrance to the building: "He's a scalper … of High Holy Day tickets." Amazed, Larry David approaches him surreptitiously and whispers, "You got tickets?" The scalper responds, "Yep. Great seats." David asks, "How much?" The scalper says, "One thousand dollars." Larry is nonplussed and complains, "A thousand dollars!" The scalper explains, "Yeah, but you'll be sitting so close, the cantor will be spitting on you!")

Once the producers realized what was happening to Jay Leno, they junked Johnny Carson's set and built Jay a "thrust stage" that jutted into the studio audience. Once he had access to the people, Leno came bounding out to begin the show by shaking hands with the crowd that rushed the thrust stage. He was greeting people on national television every weekday night. Leno's successor, Jimmy Fallon, rushes into the crowd at the end of the show to give high fives. Even Stephen Colbert has taken to slapping hands with those in the front row of the Ed Sullivan Theatre at the beginning of his TV program, *The Late Show with Stephen Colbert*.

Takeaways

Many synagogues built in the 1950s and 1960s or earlier feature very high pulpits that place the clergy at far distances from the congregants. Today, many prefer a more intimate setting, both for more engaging participatory worship and to reflect a hoped-for intimacy with the Divine. Moreover, some twenty-two years ago when we began the Synagogue 2000 project, most Reform temples did not bring the Torah scroll out into the congregation. Rather, they would take the scroll out of the ark and pass it along from "generation to generation"—grandparents to parents to Bar/Bat Mitzvah children—before placing it on the reading table. This began to change when rabbis realized the value of bringing the Torah scroll—and themselves!—out into the congregation. Not only did this offer the worshippers access to touch and/or kiss the Torah as a sign of respect, but the rabbis could greet congregants as the Torah parade wound its way through the sanctuary—a relational moment.

As Conservative and Orthodox synagogues know well, this act also provides an opportunity for people to greet and kibbitz with each other—a relational moment for the community.

Our Next Steps

What are some things we can do to improve the quality service of our community?

_____

_____

_____

Part Three

Connecting with Each Other

The goal of a Relational Engagement Campaign is for every member of the organization to know and care about other people in the community. The best way to achieve this goal is to create a full range of small groups through which members can connect with each other.

We (LM and NA) are writing from our experience developing small groups within synagogues, particularly our own: The Temple in Atlanta, Georgia, and Central Synagogue in New York. We believe the principles of small-group engagement you find below can be extrapolated and used in any organization. In the "Spotlights on Best Practice" and case studies, we present successful small-groups initiatives from the Jewish Community Center and Hillel worlds, as well as from congregations of diverse sizes. Whatever your organization, as you work through this part of the handbook, think about the principles and apply them to your setting in a way that will lead to our ultimate goal: connecting people to each other.

Small Groups as Minyans of Meaning

Torah teaches us, "God said, 'Let them build me a sanctuary and I will dwell among them'" (Exodus 25:8). Commentators later ask, shouldn't God have said, "And I will dwell in *it*," in other words, in the sanctuary? The answer is that God doesn't need a building; people do. The same is true of social structures, the ways we organize ourselves in relationship to one another. We need to build social structures that allow God to dwell among us. When we come together to care for one another, we act as a sanctuary, a place where goodness, holiness, and respite exist. Small groups are a wonderful way to create moments that allow God to dwell among us, that allow for holiness to become embodied.

The idea that small groups can foster relationships and allow us to lead more meaningful lives is not new. Our tradition recognizes that there are times when we need a minyan for support and that finding a group of ten (or so) fellow travelers is the first step in creating a vibrant Jewish community. Likewise, the *havurah* movement that originated in the late 1960s has allowed lay people to create intimate and self-sustaining spiritual communities over which they exercise ownership rather than acting as spiritual consumers. And, of course, our communities are full of groups of people who come together around shared passions and commitments: choirs, soup kitchen committees, classes, morning prayer groups, Israel trips, social justice work, and sisterhoods and men's clubs.

All these gatherings of like-minded people are important, but none are exactly what we mean when we speak about employing a "small-group" strategy for a Relational Engagement Campaign. Instead, we are referring to a particular approach to building and supporting lay-led groups of (usually eight to twelve) congregants who come together on a regular basis—weekly, biweekly, or monthly over the course of a programming year—in order to deepen their connections to one another, to the broader community, to Jewish tradition, and perhaps ultimately to God. Because fostering and deepening relationships is the *ikar*, the main principle, of small-group life, we want the number of people in the group to be large enough to keep things interesting but small enough so that members get to know each other intimately. Because growth and transformation are central to relationship building, each group member shares in the responsibility of owning the group and crafting its culture and specific agenda.

The modern mavens of this approach to congregational engagement are Christian megachurches such as Saddleback Church in Lake Forest, California, and Willow Creek Church in Chicago, Illinois. For these congregations, which have satellite campuses in many places in the United States and even around the world, the small group is the cornerstone to their efforts to build authentic communities in which each member is known and supported in their spiritual journey. These groups, which typically meet weekly, are where church members "do life together"—studying, praying, offering support, and socializing. If someone is sick, their small-group members support them. If someone is seeking to improve some aspect of their lives, their small-group members keep them accountable. (See "For Further Learning" for some great books about how church leaders teach about small groups.)

The Benefits of Small Groups

More recently, Jewish congregations have begun to experiment with this small-group model to create a greater sense of connection in our own communities. The response has been overwhelmingly positive. Clergy and lay leaders have reported many benefits to this approach:

> *Relationships.* Ultimately, whether groups are formed around interest, age, geography, or schedule, the goal is the same: to offer members the opportunity to deepen their relationships with other congregants and with the community as a whole.

Greater sense of belonging. Members have reported that after joining a group, they feel less anonymous. When they come to an event, they are more likely to know people and feel comfortable taking part.

Finding your makom—*your place.* When members forge relationships with others and feel a sense of belonging, they begin to find their place in the community. The organization can even become their *third place*—home is first, work is second. The synagogue, JCC, Hillel, or Federation becomes a place for members to use their talents and passions, to serve others, and to feel connected in a deeper way than merely transactional.

Opportunity to be part of a caring community. Small groups offer members authentic opportunities to care for each other. Instead of a one-off visit from someone on the "caring committee," members can rely on the deep relationships they've built with one another. When life happens, they can support one another as part of a genuine and ongoing relationship.

Growing new leaders. Small groups offer a new model of leadership. Our organizations are full of members who might not think of themselves as leaders but who are expert connectors, listeners, and conversation facilitators. Small groups lift up these leaders and allow the organizations to invest in their growth.

Organization-wide conversations. Through listening campaigns or curricula employed by many small groups simultaneously, organizations can encourage their members to engage in conversations on common themes through small groups. When leadership listens to their people, the people feel more connected and invested in the ideas the organization is exploring.

You Mean *Havurot*?

One of the first questions that Jews typically ask when they hear about these kinds of small groups is how (if at all) they differ from *havurot*, synagogue-based friendship groups that began in the 1960s. There are certainly similarities; both are small, intentional Jewish communities.

There are, however, a few key differences between the small groups we are talking about and the *havurot* that our members may have grown up with.

First, a *havurah* was planned to be a lifelong commitment; in the small-groups model, some groups may remain together for years, while others come together for a few weeks. As explained later in the chapter on forming small groups, one important attribute of small groups is that they have carefully delineated "on-ramps" and "off-ramps," with an expectation that a group may come together for just one season or program year, unless it chooses to continue.

Second, some synagogue *havurot* evolved to hold their own independent services and to become, in effect, self-sustaining mini shuls. In the small-groups model, it is clear from the outset that the small groups are subsets of a larger community, which continues to worship and learn together as a whole. Instead of picturing these groups as a constellation of separate communities, picture them as cells in a single organism. Ideally they augment the functioning of the larger community rather than divide it.

Third, *havurot* were often formed and sustained based on social chemistry; if the social chemistry was not good, the *havurah* often fell apart. Small groups are organized in a number of different ways, and part of the fun (and challenge) of these groups may be the interactions its members have with people who are very different from themselves.

Spotlight on Best Practice

Rabbi Angela Warnick Buchdahl, senior rabbi, Central Synagogue, New York City

When I thought about the people at Central who felt most deeply connected to our community, most transformed by their experience of being a member, they all shared one thing in common: they were all part of a small group within Central—a bereavement group, a book club, a wise aging cohort, a leadership development group. The organizing principle of these groups varied, but they were all sized from eight to fifteen people, they had sustained contact over time, and they not only learned together but shared something of themselves in the process. Several years ago, Central had approximately twenty of these smaller groups that had formed organically over time. Most of our small groups were led by people on the professional staff, and they met at the synagogue. While twenty groups was a respectable number, we were still only reaching a fraction of our membership. We knew that if we wanted to help all of our members feel this deep sense of community, we would need to find a way to preserve the best of the experience while adjusting the model to take it to scale.

We did some research on the small-groups experience from the *havurah* movement as well as megachurches today and developed the model of "CORE Groups" that would be facilitated by trained members, meet in each other's homes, and have a curriculum provided by Central. Taking these groups off site and making them lay-led enables us to grow the initiative infinitely, so that we could eventually meet our aspiration of having everyone in our congregation a member of a CORE Group within Central. As New Yorkers, living in one of the biggest cities in the world, we know that this city feels like home because it is actually made up of a series of little neighborhoods—our little corners of the world where we greet others by name and are known. In a large synagogue, we too want each person to find their "neighborhood" within it—the small cell within the larger organism of the community where we know each other's stories, celebrate our tradition together, and care for each other in times of need. Our CORE Groups are a key strategy for making Central a deep, meaningful, and transformative experience for every one of our members.

Torah Study: *Shema/V'ahavta* for Small Groups

You've said it a bazillion times, but we invite you to read Deuteronomy 6:4–9 again as if for the first time:

שְׁמַע יִשְׂרָאֵל יְהוָה אֱלֹהֵינוּ יְהוָה אֶחָד
בָּרוּךְ שֵׁם כְּבוֹד מַלְכוּתוֹ לְעוֹלָם וָעֶד

Shema Yisrael, Adonai Eloheinu, Adonai Echad.
Barukh shem kavod malkhuto l'olam va-ed.

Listen, O Israel, Adonai is our God, Adonai is One.
Blessed is God's glorious name forever and ever.

וְאָהַבְתָּ אֵת יְהוָה אֱלֹהֶיךָ בְּכָל־לְבָבְךָ וּבְכָל־נַפְשְׁךָ וּבְכָל־מְאֹדֶךָ
וְהָיוּ הַדְּבָרִים הָאֵלֶּה אֲשֶׁר אָנֹכִי מְצַוְּךָ הַיּוֹם עַל־לְבָבֶךָ
וְשִׁנַּנְתָּם לְבָנֶיךָ וְדִבַּרְתָּ בָּם בְּשִׁבְתְּךָ בְּבֵיתֶךָ וּבְלֶכְתְּךָ בַדֶּרֶךְ וּבְשָׁכְבְּךָ וּבְקוּמֶךָ
וּקְשַׁרְתָּם לְאוֹת עַל־יָדֶךָ וְהָיוּ לְטֹטָפֹת בֵּין עֵינֶיךָ וּכְתַבְתָּם עַל־מְזֻזוֹת בֵּיתֶךָ וּבִשְׁעָרֶיךָ

V'ahavta eit Adonai Elohekha b'khol l'vav'kha uv'khol naf'sh'kha uv'khol
m'odekha. V'hayu had'varim ha'eileh asher anokhi m'tzav'kha hayom al
l'vavekha. V'shinan'tam l'vanekha v'dibar'ta bam, b'shiv't'kha b'veitekha
uv'lekh't'kha vaderekh uv'shakh'b'kha uv'kumekha. Uk'shar'tam l'ot al yadekha
v'hayu l'totafot bein einekha. Ukh'tav'tam al m'zuzot beitekha uvish'arekha.

You shall love Adonai your God with all your heart and with all your soul and
with all your might. Take to heart these instructions with which I charge you
this day. Impress them upon your children. Recite them when you stay at
home and when you are away, when you lie down and when you get up. Bind
them as a sign on your hand and let them serve as a symbol on your fore-
head, inscribe them on the doorposts of your house and on your gates.

לְמַעַן תִּזְכְּרוּ וַעֲשִׂיתֶם אֶת־כָּל־מִצְוֹתָי וִהְיִיתֶם קְדֹשִׁים לֵאלֹהֵיכֶם: אֲנִי יְהוָה אֱלֹהֵיכֶם
אֲשֶׁר הוֹצֵאתִי אֶתְכֶם מֵאֶרֶץ מִצְרַיִם לִהְיוֹת לָכֶם לֵאלֹהִים אֲנִי יְהוָה אֱלֹהֵיכֶם

L'ma'an tiz'k'ru va'asitem et kol mitz'votai vih'yitem k'doshim lei'loheikhem.
Ani Adonai Eloheikhem asher hotzei'ti et'khem mei'eretz Mitz'rayim lih'yot
lakhem leilohim. Ani Adonai Eloheikhem!

Thus you (read: y'all) shall be reminded to observe all My commandments
and to be holy to your God. I, Adonai, am your God, who brought you out of
the land of Egypt to be your God: I, Adonai, am your God.

Break into *hevruta*, read the text aloud, and consider the question: How does this text suggest we relate to God and therefore to each other? How is the *Shema/V'ahavta* related to small groups?

While we make it no secret that we've learned a lot about the nuts and bolts of small groups from our Christian brothers and sisters, the truth is that small groups and the purpose behind them are central to and grounded in our own tradition. We do not have to look far to find an entire treatise for small groups—the *Shema/V'ahavta*! From an experiential perspective, the stories that people share from their small groups come to fully describe this small-groups theology.

It begins with *Shema Yisrael*—Listen and understand, Israel. *Adonai Echad*—God is One, and everyone around us is linked to each other, to all humanity, and God is in all of it. Every encounter is an opportunity to know God better. Knowing each other, in a sense, is coming to understand and know God—and also to love God.

How do we love God? Not only with our heads, not primarily with our intellects, but instead with our hearts. We may seek to understand God with our minds also, and certainly Jewish tradition has emphasized this type of knowing at different points in our history. But the *V'ahavta* teaches us about relating to God. Since we are all connected as one human family, we connect with our hearts first—we take time for real relationship, for listening to one another, for really seeing one another. This is the foundation of small-group experience, to deeply know that the other people in our group experience the breadth of life with all the joys and sufferings of the heart, just as we do.

Then—still not with our minds but with our souls—a level deeper: we are asked to love each other for the simple fact that we are made *b'tzelem Elohim*, made in the image of God. Externally we look different, but our souls are all made from the same God stuff.

Then—*still* not our minds but our *m'odekha*, our effort and actions—we love God by doing the things that show love: showing up for one another, bringing soup, caring for the sick, burying the dead, celebrating simchas together—the things that come to pass when one is a part of a small group.

We learned from Rabbi Jonathan Slater about the types of love we see mentioned in Torah as proof. Here and there, we do find *love* used to describe the feeling between a couple or between a parent and child. But most often we see *love* used in one of three ways:

1. To describe how we should treat those in our known community (love your neighbor as yourself).

2. To describe how we should care for those whom we don't know (love the stranger in your midst).

3. To describe how we should relate to God (love Adonai your God).

In these ways, love is less an emotive state and more a series of actions. Perhaps this list is purposeful in its order: we love one another and act on one another's behalf; only then can we imagine what it might mean to love the stranger, someone less familiar to us. Then, as we see the way this love shapes our world, we may begin to understand how God loves us and how we might love God. One can argue that we can only know how to love God by considering how we act toward ourselves, our friends and relations, and the strangers in our midst. The *Shema* teaches that at the center of Jewish thought and law is love, as expressed in the relationships that create meaning in our lives. When we engage in small groups, we expand our circle of concern beyond our families, relations, and usual friends to act on behalf of those who are different from us, whom we might not have otherwise ever known. Small-group encounters help us to love new people and in different ways, such that we express our love for God, as the *Shema* describes, through our acts of love toward one another. In this way we bring holiness into our midst.

Only after using our hearts, souls, and effort do we engage the intellect in our love for God: *v'hayu had'varim ha'eileh asher anokhi m'tzav'kha hayom al l'vavekha.* We take *into our hearts* the instructions of how to construct, celebrate, and protect a sacred community; we learn them as they were commanded in the Torah. These commandments are often considered the center of Jewish thought and law—indeed, it wouldn't be Judaism without them—but learning them through the lens of love and relationship is sometimes missing. *V'shinan'tam l'vanekha*, and we should "teach them to our children," through our most precious relationships, with heart, passion, and compassion, so that they love each other and therefore love God too.

Where should these things happen? *B'veitekha* and *vaderekh*—in our homes and out in the world. You'll notice that never does it say that Jewish life, learning, and experiencing must happen solely within the walls of an institution such as a synagogue, JCC, or *beit midrash* (school). A Jewish institution can serve as a great hub of Jewish learning, living, and experiencing, but it is only *one* place among all the places where that is possible. Torah expected that we would do this learning *in our homes* and *out in the world*—in cafes, back corners of restaurants, and someone else's house.

Then, as we move from the first to the last paragraph of the *V'ahavta*, we shift from the singular to the plural, from *kha*, "you" singular, to *khem*, "you" plural—or as we say down South, "all y'all." With that shift we learn that we can do none of this alone: we cannot love alone; we cannot live Jewish life alone; we cannot ensure the continuation of Jewish life if we pretend we are an island, as individuals, as families, even as communities. We must come together in small groups so that people can come to really know each other and take bold steps outside our comfort zones. In this way, when we truly see each other, when we love each other, when we seek to build authentic relationships with one another, when we invest in one another, when we trust one another with our vulnerability, we will become more holy to one another, freeing each other from any stagnancy in Jewish life and moving toward, ever closer, the Source of life and love.

Case Study

Rabbi Esther Lederman, director of congregational innovation, Union for Reform Judaism

In 2007 I was privileged to serve as a rabbinic intern at Central Synagogue in Manhattan, where I helped lead what has now become a common term in our congregations—a listening campaign. I worked with a dedicated group of leaders who set out to have one-to-one conversations with members from all walks of life in the congregation. The purpose: to get to know these people and learn what fired them up and what got them down, what kept them up at night and what got them up in the morning. We heard some incredible stories.

Here was one that has stayed with me to this day, told by an older single woman whose family was no longer local. Describing her experiences of coming to services on Friday night, she said, "I come alone, I sit alone, and I leave alone." Many of us were saddened by this story. I do realize there may be some of you who think this description sounds heavenly, as I do now that I am a harried working mother of two. But she was lonely and didn't want to be. And she was not alone in sharing this sentiment.

The early decades of the twenty-first century will be remembered for introducing us to the likes of Facebook, Instagram, and Twitter—virtual tools that connect us to one another. Yet, in spite of these vehicles, we live in a world that is increasingly isolating. Even the most connected among us surprisingly lack the handful of relationships that both ground us and challenge us to ask the important questions of life. Author and MIT professor Sherry Turkle, in her book *Alone Together*, shares an anecdote of how technology is affecting relationships: "A thirteen-year-old tells me she 'hates the phone and never listens to voicemail.' Texting offers just the right amount of access, just the right amount of control. She is a modern Goldilocks: for her, texting puts people not too close, not too far, but at just the right distance. The world is now full of modern Goldilockses, people who take comfort in being in touch with a lot of people whom they also keep at bay."

In the Jewish world in general, and in the congregational world in particular, we are not immune from the challenges of isolation and loneliness. In congregations across our nation, some version of these stories are playing out, in places both large and small. Clergy and lay leaders are experiencing a moment of sacred discontent, a feeling and belief that congregational life cannot continue as is. We have spent decades worrying about programs and not enough about people. The time has come for us to laser focus on relationships by building small communities within our congregations.

I am proud to say that the Union for Reform Judaism, the organization for which I work as the director of congregational innovation, has been a catalyst in congregations engaging in this challenging and transforming work. After three years of working with congregations across our movement who are experimenting with creating small groups, we are reaching a tipping point in transforming our congregations to be more relational, engaging, and relevant to the lives of its members.

As Rabbis Kerry Olitzky and Rachel Sabath-Halachmi write in *Striving Toward Virtues*, "The Torah clearly teaches what our own life experiences affirm: We were not created alone, or to be alone. We are part of a larger community of human beings, whose presence in the world adds texture to our lives, individually and collectively. Because we know that we are not alone, we must always be aware of others as we attempt to understand the world and what it means to be alive. As a result, how we see ourselves is often dependent on how we see others and how others see us. Only in the process of recognizing the 'other' can we begin to understand what being human truly means."

In many ways, this is the ideal of what small groups can create and achieve. The stories we have gleaned from participants tell us how it has helped them to become a more engaged Jew and a more intentional human being. These groups fight against the loneliness and isolation that our modern society has wrought. These groups help us see the Divine in each other.

Imagine hundreds of people gathering regularly in small groups, around dinner tables, in homes, on bike trails, in cafes, and yes, in synagogues, to relate and connect, to laugh and rejuvenate, and to deepen their sense of belonging to themselves, to one another, to the congregation, and to the Jewish people.

Hundreds of people in small groups. But it's no longer in our imagination. It's already happening—from New York to Palo Alto, in Atlanta, and Boston, and Dallas. Small groups are helping us reimagine congregational life.

Joining a small group is not a "show up when you can" endeavor. It's a commitment to come to every monthly meeting, to prioritize the meeting on the calendar, and then, while there, to put away the cell phone and fully participate. As one leader explained, "We are trying to move synagogue membership from a business transaction to an emotional investment." These groups are the high point of emotional investment for the participants.

From congregations across the country, I hear stories that exemplify how small groups can transform congregational life. When community garden members at Temple Emanu-El in Dallas participated in an early pilot of a small group, a longtime congregant had this reaction: "I thought I knew these people. I had been gardening next to them for years. It turns out I knew nothing about them. Today I feel much closer to them; we have supported each other through periods of mourning with meals made from the garden's produce, shared hilarious moments of camaraderie, and developed meaningful spiritual practices."

And back where I began this journey, at Central Synagogue, a member of the small group for people in their twenties and thirties, whose members typically are in a transient stage of life, spoke volumes about the work of small groups when she said, "I'm going to miss New York City and the great things about this place. But the hardest thing is leaving my small group."

The first time in Torah that God declares something *lo tov*, "not good," is in the early moments of creation when God recognizes the utter aloneness of Adam: *lo tov heyot ha'adam levado*, "it is not good for a human being to be alone" (Genesis 2:18). That fundamental truth still lives with us today. Small groups of people, really meeting each other where they are, learning each others' stories, developing deep bonds, are our answer to God's despair that humans should not live alone.

We believe that communities of small groups in our congregations are the future of our synagogues. As Rabbi Ben Spratt wrote in a sermon introducing the concept to his community: "For the heart of Judaism, the house of God, rests in the power of people gathering, where each person counts." Not surprisingly, their small-groups initiative is called Minyan. This is about each person counting and each person mattering. Or to quote one of the authors of this book, Rabbi Nicole Auerbach: "Let this be a year where we recognize that God doesn't show up one day a year in the holy of holies; God shows up when we show up for one another." People in our congregation want to show up for each other. They want to see and be seen. They just need to experience the possibility.

Our Next Steps

We can see our team using the *V'ahavta* text study above in the following settings:

_____

_____

_____

_____

_____

What You Need to Know to Get Your Small-Groups Initiative Started

As mentioned previously, a Relational Engagement Campaign should begin where the people are. Relational engagement, as a general rule, is conducted from the bottom up as opposed to the top down. Once your leadership decides that it wants to begin to create small groups, it is important to understand the everyday needs of your community so that you can point the small groups in the right direction. You will only know where to take your community once you have asked them. Plus, you will inevitably pick up new, enthusiastic leadership along the way.

One question you will want to address as you begin is how these small groups will eventually become a part of your organization's permanent landscape.

As you begin, you may want to clarify what your ultimate vision is for the role groups will play in your community. Do you envision becoming a community *with* small groups or a community *of* small groups? There is no one right answer to this question. But as you explore this idea with your board and leadership, you will want to be clear about the scope of the institutional change you are seeking.

Case Study

Rabbi Asher Knight, senior rabbi, Temple Beth El, Charlotte, North Carolina; former associate rabbi, Temple Emanu-El, Dallas, Texas

Small groups are focused on *personal* and *communal* transformation. On a personal level, we want our members to feel changed, different, less lonely, unburdened because they are able to share with others. We want members to have a strong feeling of belonging and connectedness, that they are not living life alone. We want our members to feel transformed in their Jewish lives through an increased connection to their spiritual selves, the development of spiritual practices, and living with Shabbat and the seasons and cycles of Jewish time. Through small groups, members will experience Judaism as having increasing relevance to their daily lives. We want our members to say:

- My small group has become a center of my life.

- My small group is a place where I can be myself, and it is nonjudgmental.

- I look forward to my small group, and it's worth my making time for it.

- My small group is like an extended family, with connectedness to others, responsibility for others, and accountability to others.

After a few years of small-groups experience, we want our members to be able to reflect on the ways that their small-groups experience has transformed their relationship with their synagogue. We want them to be able to say:

- This small-groups experience has helped me create better clarity about the meaning of life through Jewish learning and meaningful conversations

- Everything about being Jewish is clearer: the importance and possibility of connectedness, accountability, and responsibility to and for others.

- The increased exposure to Jewish texts and learning has helped me improve my comfort level with Judaism.

- Because of my small-groups experience, I have attended Shabbat services, holiday worship, a program, or a learning experience that I may not have previously attended.

- As a result of being in a small group, I feel I have increased clarity about living a Jewish life.

Visualizing the Small-Groups Model at Temple/Synagogue

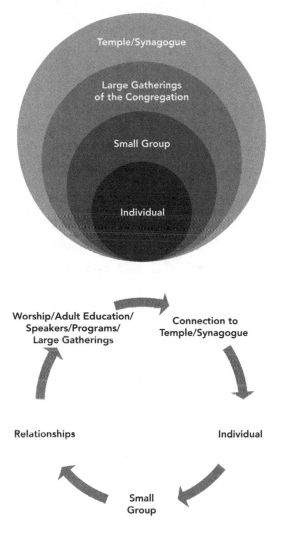

The key is to engage our members to become stakeholders and to develop a living Judaism that speaks to their daily interests, needs, concerns, and aspirations. Proper membership engagement will help steer the congregation's leaders toward weaving a strong social fabric and a meaningful and living Judaism.

Is a Small-Groups Culture Right for Us?

Just as with any other engagement initiative, the first and most important step is to determine whether the timing is right. (In part 1, see "Are You Ready?") Before you start recruiting group leaders, you'll want to ask: "Are there other goals that take priority right now?" "Is the senior leadership committed to making this a success?" "Is this meeting a need felt by our members (as opposed to meeting our own need to try something new)?" Most importantly, "Are we clear on the *why* of small groups in our community?" You will likely have asked these questions before beginning a comprehensive Relational Engagement Campaign. Ask them again with a focus on your small-groups initiative, which will likely require a more substantial investment of staff and resources.

Planning Your Small-Groups Listening Campaign

After you've determined that now is indeed the right time to begin, you'll want to organize a listening campaign. This listening campaign is similar to the one we've suggested you employ at the beginning of the Relational Engagement Campaign, except this one results in the creation of small groups. This first strategic step accomplishes many different goals. First, you'll understand the desires and needs of your community more deeply as they relate to the types of small groups to develop. Second, since a major strategy of a listening campaign is gathering ten people or so for a "house party" conducted by a peer, people already begin to experience what it might be like to join a small group that is hosted by a lay leader in someone's home. Third, people will begin the process of knowing one another better, which is likely central to your overarching goal. Even if you stopped with just this step, you'll have already had a win. Fourth, you will generate your first round of leaders, because those who are enthusiastic about their experiences in listening campaign house parties will trust you enough to take the second step into small groups with you!

Recruit Listening Campaign Leaders

To begin your listening campaign, gather together some of your tried-and-true lay leaders. You can add new people to your team as well, but it is great to start with some people whose circle of friends extends into the community. Also, you will want an inclusive group that represents the diversity of your community in as many ways as possible. As you individually invite each person, describe your vision of what you hope this effort will accomplish. Ask each person to share their vision with you. If possible, incorporate their ideas into your vision so that it is truly shared. Then schedule a meeting to begin their training so they understand the goals and expectations for your groups and so they are equipped to deal with basic issues of group dynamics. For more on training, see "The Importance of Lay Leadership."

Develop Questions

At the same time, you'll need to determine the questions you'd like to ask your community during the small-groups listening campaign. Three questions are usually plenty for an hour of good conversation for a group of ten people. For example, at The Temple we decided it was important to have our congregation reflect on the impact of community. So we asked, "When was there a time when community served you well? When was there a time when community let you down?" That the questions weren't specific to a synagogue community meant they could draw on many different experiences; the questions allowed them to consider the kind of community that synagogues could be. Our second question was borne out of a curiosity about the kinds of things people would like to do with one another. So we asked, "What would you do if you had a group of ten people who would join you?" From this we knew we'd be able to create an initial list of group offerings. The third question was borne out of an instinct that our synagogue might be able to increase its relevance because of the ways it could add meaning to people's lives during their major life transitions. We didn't know exactly how it would translate into small groups, but we knew that if it was important to our people, we had to address it. So we asked, "At what crossroads do you find yourself at this point in your life?"

When we finally embarked on the training, we focused on the questions we were going to ask, the reasoning behind them, the general stance we should take during the conversation—that of careful listener and open, nonjudgmental acceptance. We then practiced an actual run-through of the conversation to give our leaders some time and space to find their own answers, as they would act as role models in terms of depth in their answers. We went over the mechanics of how the process would work: Each person would invite their circle of ten friends to their homes, and with a designated note taker, they'd host their friends and lead the conversation. To make sure we got to as many people as possible, some of our leaders volunteered to lead extra conversations over Shabbat dinner at The Temple, after a Temple-organized seniors event, during preschool with young parents, and at similar events.

After running the campaign for four months, we had held face-to-face meetings with more than 250 people and collected reams of data. We capped the listening campaign with a feedback session, where we revealed the results of the campaign and officially launched the small-groups initiative. At the end of the session, attendees were asked to fill out a premade card with a list of all the small-group ideas and a blank to fill out if they wanted to be in our first cohort of small-groups leaders. From this group, we recruited our first round of leaders and participants.

Other Considerations as You Begin: Budget and Staff Resources

A common question when embarking on creating a small-groups culture is one of budget. Some larger organizations choose to hire full-time staff members to work exclusively on building a Relational Engagement Campaign. Other organizations reconfigure existing positions to reflect a shift in thinking, priorities, and programming—"program director" becomes "engagement director" or "engagement manager," for example, or the membership director or program director adds small-groups work to their to-do lists. Still others hire one person in a combined position—programmer, membership coordinator, and engagement director, for example. There is no one best way to achieve a more fully engaged membership from a staffing perspective. Once you have the will to make it a priority, each organization will have to examine its staffing structure and budget capacity to see what is possible.

The initial setup for small groups is time intensive; it could take approximately fifteen hours a week during the first few months or so. Setting up the system can be relatively staff intensive too. The listening campaign needs a lot of staff time to track down, collect, and upload the notes from each house party. Significant time is required to meet with many prospective group leaders and guide them toward a successful group idea. It takes time to find the right curriculum, if needed, and generate the publicity. But once the groups are up and going, they tend to be self-perpetuating, as they rely on the group leaders and group members to do the organizing and convening. Most of the time, the staff person only deals with groups in development stages, in order to train the leaders in problem solving.

In fact, sometimes when the professional staff have been tempted to intervene in a small-group issue, we've learned that the best approach is to help coaches and group leaders solve the problems together. In one example, a leader needed help with group dynamics. One of the group members was using sharp language to address his group leader and threatening to leave the group because of an instance in which he felt slighted. But with a little coaching from the clergy, the group leader was able to readdress the person himself, and together they worked out their miscommunication.

Once things are set up and running smoothly, actual programming expenses are quite minimal because so many of the events happen outside of the synagogue. When you consider how much small groups can strengthen your community, with such little regular upkeep and few work hours spent versus the hours that your congregants are getting meaningful time together, the efforts pay off in dividends. Creating a welcoming and engaged community means a paradigm shift in the way we invest in our relationship building, not in our buildings themselves.

Spotlight on Best Practice

Rabbi Peter Berg, senior rabbi, The Temple, Atlanta, Georgia

Having a full-time director of engagement is a game changer for us at The Temple. A few years ago, we made a conscious decision to move away from a programmatic-driven model to an engagement-driven model. Of course, we still have wonderful programs, but the emphasis is now on how our members and guests engage with each other and our community. Our best investment this decade has been combining the positions of membership director, program director, and more, into one position that focuses on congregational engagement.

Why did we put all our eggs in the director of engagement basket? It is through this position that we can best fulfill our mission and vision at The Temple: *inspiring lives, transforming our world.* It is human nature to ask ourselves big questions, the ones that life doesn't answer so easily. In one way or another, we are all on a journey to find meaning for our lives, and helping people in this search, at every age and stage, is the ultimate purpose of our temple in general and our engagement department in specific. Rabbi Medwin makes sure that we live by our mission and vision; it's what distinguishes us from being a club, a civic organization, or a Jewish community center. We are a generation of seekers, in search of sacred truths that give meaning to our lives. How did we get here? What happens after we die? Is there a deeper purpose to our lives? How can we alleviate war and poverty and save our planet? What must be done in the face of racism and anti-Semitism? Having a full-time engagement director allows our members to wrestle with these questions every day so that we can create a sacred community and find meaning in our lives.

Takeaways

From your listening campaign, you will learn more about your community and their needs, passions, gifts, and desire to know one another better. This will help you design a structure that allows your members' needs to be met in collaborative partnership with them.

It's important to plan for who will be the engine for this initiative from your staff and lay leadership. In the process, you'll want to access the kinds of resources, both monetary and staff time, you are willing to dedicate to the process.

As important as deciding what you will do is understanding what might be the main obstacles to your work and figuring out how to address them.

Our Next Steps

_____

_____

_____

Organizing Principles
for Small Groups

The goal of small groups is to bring people together. But *which* people? The answer to this question depends on the needs of your community and your members. There are four primary organizing principles you might use to form your groups:

1. Geography: your neighborhood

2. Demography: your age and stage in life

3. Availability: when you can meet

4. Affinity: your interests and needs

You can use any one of these to organize your groups, depending on the needs of your community. For example, if you are a rural or suburban congregation or JCC whose members are spread out across many miles or zip codes, you may consider creating groups based on geography, to allow people to connect with their neighbors and avoid lots of transit time. If you are a JCC or congregation looking to connect people based on their similar stage of life (empty nesters or young parents, for example), groups based on demography might make sense. If you want to harness the interests and passions of your members to create a multiplicity of different types of groups, affinity might be the appropriate lens. If you are looking to encourage diversity in your groups and engage your entire community on a single topic or focus, you might wish to simply group people based on when they are available to meet.

You can even use more than one of these lenses at a time. For example, you may organize a group of preschool parents who share similar demography (age and stage) that meets in the same geographic area (the same neighborhood). You may target young professionals in their twenties and thirties (demography) who gather to play sports (affinity).

To begin with, however, it is easiest to separate the question of *who* you will attract into the groups from the question of *what* the groups will do once they form.

Let's look at how these organizing principles can be used to form meaningful relationships.

Geography

Fewer and fewer of us live in small, mostly Jewish enclaves. Many of us commute to participate in Jewish communal life. At The Temple, for example, our four thousand individuals live in seventy-eight different zip codes across Atlanta and beyond. Offering small groups that meet in neighborhoods removes the barrier of distance to participating in Jewish life and offers the benefit of our members getting to know their neighbors.

Organizing small groups around geography brings people together where they live. In The Temple's experience, members are thrilled with a chance to meet one another, to "do Jewish" without having to venture far from home, and to find meaning in their connection. They find that they share a desire for Jewish community, continuity, and learning, regardless of how strongly connected they are to their tradition.

At The Temple, one group of suburban mothers with teens had been meeting for a year. During each session, one person was assigned to bring a topic of conversation. After a few sessions they noticed that their conversations often moved toward their personal connections to Jewish tradition. Someone suggested they organize an outing to a community mikvah. The group leader described the impact the experience had on her life and the lives of those in her group:

> One incredible story from today…. We have all been email-
> ing about the mikvah tour and discussion with the rabbi
> there yesterday. One of the members, a friend of mine for
> years, is in an interfaith marriage, is not raising her child

Jewish, but has always stayed strong in her faith. On a side note, she really does not love to cook—it's just not her thing. Today, though, she emailed and said how yesterday's experience [learning about the mikvah with her small group] really strengthened her connection to Judaism and she is cooking Shabbat dinner for her family! This is so huge for her; just seeing the mikvah and talking about the spiritual connection to our bodies in this ancient ritual struck a chord with her. It brought tears to my eyes, and I thought that this is really the goal: all of us strengthening our Judaism through each other's experiences and wisdom and standing beside each other as we grow. That is what our group—and our synagogue—is all about.

It is clear that the women in this group are finding more than just casual relationships with a few neighbors. These women are finding deep and meaningful experiences that are transforming their lives, their families' lives, and the experience of their larger community. They are discovering their own sense of spirituality, which we believe is a major component of the revitalization of Jewish life.

They inspired us to create Chai (Life) Neighborhood groups, a way for people in the same neighborhoods to meet one another and discover their many commonalities. Sometimes the group leaders prefer to mix geography with demography so that they can meet people in the same stage of life in their neighborhoods—young families go to their neighborhood playgrounds together, elementary school–aged children who also go to the same school do Temple community-action projects together, empty nesters log on to an online curriculum to guide their conversations, and seniors of the same neighborhood frequent local restaurants and cultural events. Some of these groups rely on curricula provided by the synagogue to increase their Jewish literacy and deepen their Jewish understanding. Like so many things about small groups, each group's schedule and topic are dependent on the stated interests and needs of its members.

Spotlight on Best Practice

I (RW) am visiting Temple Israel of Long Beach, California, as a scholar-in-residence when, at a meeting of the congregational leadership, someone asks me a great question: "How do we find unaffiliated Jewish people in our neighborhoods? We know they're there, but we don't know how to reach them." I told the group that I had just joined Next Door (nextdoor.com), a social media platform that is quickly growing in popularity. Organized by local neighborhoods—mine is "Next Door Encino (Haskell-405)"—the app enables neighbors to post concerns, announce events, and request help or referrals. To be sure, there are also "sponsored posts" that are ads. I get a daily email that alerts me to things going on in the neighborhood; it's an online expanded "neighborhood watch."

So I said to the good people of Temple Israel, "If I were you, I would have your key leadership join these Next Door groups and announce a neighborhood potluck Shabbat dinner, or Saturday night Havdalah dessert and discussion, or a sukkah reception, or a Hanukkah party hosted in a member's home. I bet you dollars to donuts that a few Jews would come out of the woodwork in each neighborhood, and you can begin the process of engaging them. Move out of your building and into the geographic areas of your community."

Suddenly Susan and David Philips told this story: "You know, this year we didn't have room in our backyard for our sukkah, so we put it up in the front yard instead. To be honest, we had some reticence to do it, but we did."

I asked, "What happened?"

David said, "We met all kinds of people we didn't know!"

"What a great idea!" I shouted. "You're going in this book!"

David continued, "There was a twenty-five-year-old kid on a skateboard who went by and yelled, *Chag sameach!*"

I concluded, "Why is it only Chabad that puts up a sukkah in a public place or on the back of a pickup truck? Let's take a page out of their playbook and get out into the community."

Our Next Steps

What geographically oriented groups might we launch?

_____

_____

_____

_____

Demography

Small groups based on demography are organized around the age of participants and their stage in life. People who share age and stage are often facing similar challenges and enjoying similar experiences. For example, parents of preschool children are interested in meeting other parents navigating the waters of early childhood. Adults caring for elderly parents are eager for information and strategies. Families of Bar/Bat Mitzvah children are eager to share the excitement of planning for the big day.

Again, it is important to note that _who_ is in a group is a separate question from _what the group does_ together. For example, at Central Synagogue, we have several successful groups made up of members in their third chapter of life—that is, those age sixty-five and up—who come together to discuss issues of "wise aging," guided by materials from the Institute for Jewish Spirituality. These materials allow members to consider how to use tools of mindfulness and Jewish wisdom to find greater meaning in this stage of their lives. In the case of these groups, the organizing principle that brought them together—age—is directly related to the subject of their discussions.

In other cases, the _who_ and the _what_ might be quite different. Take, for example, two other groups at Central: one for fathers of young children, and another for members in their twenties and thirties. These groups have been meeting for years, and their members greatly appreciate the relationships they have built with others in their stage of life. But the meetings do not necessarily focus on the age or stage of life of the members. The fathers-of-young-children group comes together to discuss sermons from Friday night services, and the twenties-and-thirties group discusses a range of books and articles that connect them to both current events and Jewish tradition. Because they were organized around demography, the personal stories they share during their meetings will, of course, relate to their age and stage. And there is a level of trust and camaraderie that comes from having something in common. But it need not be the sole, or even primary, focus of the group.

Our Next Steps

What demographics might we want to bring together?

_____

_____

_____

_____

Availability

Sometimes, instead of creating a wide variety of groups, you may wish to engage a large portion of your community in conversation around a particular issue or topic. In this case, you may wish to assign people to groups simply based on the times they are available to meet. This often results in groups that are quite diverse. When Central Synagogue first experimented with this approach, some staff and congregants were concerned that there would be insufficient chemistry in groups that were formed without any commonality other than time preference. We heard, "But what if I don't have anything in common with the other people?" In practice, this turned out not to be an issue. In our experience, there is no difference in member satisfaction or depth of connection in groups formed this way versus groups that are formed with an eye toward demography or some other commonality. In fact, members of these groups see their diversity as a huge asset. As one leader said, "The best thing about my group is that these are people of all different ages and professions and life experiences, whom I never would have met had it not been for this group."

Our Next Steps

How might we organize groups based on time availability?

_____

_____

_____

_____

Affinity

Affinity groups form around shared interests or needs. Some groups help people connect to one another by sharing in common interests, such as hiking, concert going, mahjong, or cooking. Other groups gather to support people through specific moments in their lives, such as grief or becoming an empty nester. Still others bring together participants based on shared moral outrage and a passion to work for justice. Other groups focus on celebrating Shabbat and holidays together through the small-groups framework. Affinity groups are based on an assumption that there will always be at least a handful of people in the community who share similar interests or needs, the most basic of which is simply friendship and companionship—the most human desire not to be alone and invisible.

Establishing affinity groups based on shared interests is one of the simplest ways to begin small groups at your organization. While we all suffer from the "too busy" syndrome, we have found that people typically make time for the things that fill them with joy. If they can do those things in the company of community members, or if they can share with others a gift they have been cultivating, our members may discover a renewed interest and energy in their organization. The Temple's most successful groups focus on games (mahjong and bridge), food (Gourmet Cooking, What's for Dinner?... Reservations!, Eating Explorers, Ladies Lunch Bunch), the arts (Theatre, Reel to Real, Temple Heads, Midtown Small Gems), and health (Mom and Tot Yoga, Chai on Life Moms, Sunday Runday). In these groups, the passion of the leaders fuels the participation of the members. An amateur cook or part-time playwright can indeed be quite talented, and the group that forms around that person benefits from the expertise and learning, the exposure to other enthusiasts, and other local resources. Some of these groups are so successful that they have waiting lists!

One story that sticks out relates to The Temple's first mahjong group. The leader of the group made it clear from the first meeting that they were playing a game, but the real reason for their gathering was to invest in each other and get to know one another well. Toward that end, she started each game with a blessing and then encouraged the players to kibbitz while playing instead of maintaining intense concentration on the game. (These games can get very serious, we've learned!) Over time, a few things began to happen. First, each player learned to RSVP that she was attending and always had a very good reason if she could not attend. After all, as the leader explained, the group counted on a certain number of people to make the game possible. They were building a *commitment* to one another and a sense of *accountability* to their leader. Second, the group began to diversify their meetings, sometimes adding lunch before or an activity together afterward. This turned into dinners out together, attending services together, and even sharing Passover seder together. They spoke to one another about their deeper concerns and offered *support* and love to each other through their tough moments. One woman needed her mahjong group's excitement but also counsel when her son got engaged. Another woman landed in the hospital after an accident, and her mahjong friends were there for her in a heartbeat, with food for her and her husband. Lastly, new mahjong groups began to sprout from the original. The group members wanted to share their powerful experience by leading their own groups, and thus was born four new groups over the course of two years. Group members have become group leaders, and one group leader is now a Temple small-groups coach to other small groups totally unrelated to mahjong. They had embraced the principle of *shared leadership*, so much so that group members had the confidence and know-how to lead their own set of members. Currently you can play mahjong at The Temple almost any day of the week.

A skeptic might think, "Mahjong small groups are just a bunch of women playing a game. That will transform lives?" Yes, it can. While it might be tempting to understand shared interest groups as "engagement lite," we see our shared interest groups as having the potential to inspire lives and transform the synagogue.

Spotlight on Best Practice

Abram Kukawka, a Polish Holocaust survivor, was my (RW) father-in-law. When he retired at the age of sixty-five from an exhausting factory job, my wife, Susie, and I bought him a membership to the Omaha JCC health club. He knew nobody, certainly not the lawyers, doctors, and business owners who frequented the club. He spoke with a thick accent that embarrassed him, so much so that he always had his daughter make phone calls for the family. He had never exercised a day in his life. But in the locker room on the first day, Isadore Bogdanov—everyone called him "Boggy"—welcomed Abe to the health club, helped him get a locker, and introduced him to a bunch of the members. After their workouts, after their *shvitz* in the steam room, after their showers, Boggy invited Abe to have coffee with twelve guys who every day gathered around a table in the foyer above the indoor swimming pool. They called themselves the "Men of the Round Table." They chatted about their workouts, their businesses, their families, their lives. They told their stories and they heard each other's stories. They built relationships. They cared about each other and for each other. They were a small affinity group at the JCC.

Abe thrived at the club. He took every exercise class. He worked out on the machines. He ran 5K races and beat guys half his age. He soon became well known, schmoozing with the *machers*— the big shots—in the whirlpool. He came early to make the coffee. He collected money for Christmas and Hanukkah gifts for the staff. Over the years he earned the number one locker in the club. Everyone loved Abe; he was an inspiration, a legend.

Abe did well when he had his first open-heart surgery to repair a valve at the age of eighty-five, and the Men of the Round Table were there for him. Ten years later, the valve became infected, and the doctors told him there was nothing they could do. But Abe said he didn't want to die. So we took him to the Mayo Clinic, where a world-famous heart surgeon saw Abe was in such great shape that he agreed to do a second open-heart surgery. But first the infection had to be cleared up. Do you know what Abe, ninety-five years old, did in the three weeks before the surgery? He bought himself a new car—and insisted on a ten-year warranty! Just before the surgery, he told the surgeon the story and said, "So, doctor, I vant the same deal on this new heart valve!" He got five years. By then, Abe was living at the Rose Blumkin Jewish Home, attached to the JCC, and he went every day to his beloved health club to continue his workouts and meet with his friends. Shortly after his one hundredth birthday party, Abe walked into his favorite place on earth—the *shvitz*—and fell asleep, and that was that. Susie and I will forever be grateful to the JCC for giving Abe the opportunity to build those relationships.

Spotlight on Best Practice

Fred Ezekiel, former professor at Massachusetts Institute of Technology and a longtime member of Temple Emunah in Lexington, Massachusetts, wanted to strengthen relationships between members by creating the Theme Minyan program. Members gather after the evening minyan to discuss a preannounced subject of common interest suggested by members. The first event, "MIT Night," attracted over sixty people. Some fifty-five such events, suggested and led by facilitators, have occurred in just two years: "Brandeis Night," "Startup Night," "Prayers," "Health Care," "Software," "Surviving Hearts," "Jewish Apps," "Play Readings," "Tesla," "Israel Ride," "Golf," "Knitting/Crocheting," "Jewish Diversity," "Jewish Antiques Roadshow," "Jews with Guns," "Pink Together," "Healthy Eating and Living," and the "Davids Night," attended by twenty-one of the twenty-three "Davids" in the congregation, including the rabbi and cantor. One David showed up dressed as Goliath! "Miriams Night" followed soon thereafter. Theme Minyan is a sensational example of melding affinity groups with the worship experience.

These events have boosted minyan attendance and enabled attendees to get to know each other better. Fred and others established the Ladle Fund, based on a Judeo-Arabic proverb, "What you put in the pot comes out in the ladle," to provide food and lower the costs of events for innovative activities that enrich member interaction and deepen personal relationships.

Our Next Steps

What affinity groups can we imagine bringing people together? How might we identify common interests or passions?

_____

_____

_____

What Kind of Garden Is Right for You?

One of the biggest questions with which an organization will need to wrestle is the tension between growth and control. The benefits of a control model is that one can invest more in the success of each group in terms of its continuance, depth, variety of content, and the like. But this kind of control can also limit the pace of growth and the diversity of group experiences. The benefits of a growth model is that many more people get to be involved more quickly, and groups have the space to innovate and create in ways that can be surprising and helpful. But what gets lost is the capacity to ensure that each group leader finds success and that each group member is having a transformative experience. Both models have their strengths. Ultimately it may come down to the tolerance levels of those running the Relational Engagement Campaign: Are campaign leaders or organizations the type who prefer an English garden or a wildflower garden?

The Temple prefers the wildflower garden, allowing members to experiment to see what might stick. Anyone with passion, an idea, and two friends who will join can start a group. Central Synagogue takes the English garden approach, slowly increasing the number of groups, and experimenting with one aspect (content, method of forming groups, and so forth) at a time. Both approaches have been successful.

Our Next Steps

What kind of garden might work for our organization? How will this impact our other stakeholders?

_____

_____

Takeaways

The four main ways to organize small groups are around the following principles:

1. Geography: your neighborhood

2. Demography: your age and stage in life

3. Availability: when you can meet

4. Affinity: your interests and needs

In order to know which one to use, you can review your learning from the listening campaign and reflect on your understanding of your members' needs.

Our Next Steps

Which people do we want to engage first?

What are their needs? How does what we heard in the listening campaign influence the organizing principle we might choose?

_____

_____

_____

What Do Small Groups Do Together?

Once groups are formed—whether based on geography, demography, availability, or affinity—what exactly do they do when they get together? This will vary widely depending on the type of group.

Discussion and Learning Groups

Some groups gather for the sole purpose of discussing life's big questions through a Jewish lens. Though conversations may center on Jewish texts or ideas, these groups are not classes, and the leaders are not "teachers." Rather, the conversations center on the "Torah" that each member brings to the group based on their lived experience. The goal is not to master material but rather to connect deeply to one another.

An excellent example of this type of guided discussion can be found in a series of discussion guides designed by the organization Ask Big Questions, in collaboration with Central Synagogue in New York and Temple Emanu-el of Dallas. These guides invite members to explore such big questions as "What will my legacy be?" and "Where do I feel at home?" through engaging with Jewish and secular texts. (These resources are available from the Ask Big Questions website. See our "For Further Learning" section for a link.)

Unlike many synagogues that begin their small-groups engagement initiative with affinity groups, Central Synagogue spent the first four years of our work focused on creating and supporting discussion groups. Central's groups use a range of discussion guides (some written in-house and some from outside partners) including the following:

Sermon discussion groups. Synagogues that begin small groups often worry about where to find suitable content. But your clergy most likely create compelling, relevant content in line with your values every week in the form of sermons. At Central Synagogue, we pick eight to ten sermons a year and create discussion guides that both explore the underlying texts and allow members to relate the sermons' themes to their own lives. On our website we post links to the videos of the sermons (for those who don't see them live) along with facilitator guides and participant text studies. These sermon discussion guides have been very popular with our groups because they allow groups to connect more deeply with one another and with the message of our clergy.

Mussar groups. *Mussar* is a traditional Jewish discipline of ethical development focused on fostering spiritual attributes such as patience, humility, and honor. In a *mussar* group, members study one of these attributes and then spend the time between meetings noticing how it manifests in their lives. At the next meeting, they debrief on what they noticed and then learn about the next attribute. *Mussar* groups allow members to hold one another accountable for their goals and to foster deep connections. A slightly more accessible version of *mussar* can be found in the 92Y's "Ben Franklin Meets Pirkei Avot" curriculum. (See our "For Further Learning" section for a link to this curriculum.)

Wise Aging groups. These groups use materials developed by the Institute for Jewish Spirituality to consider the spiritual dimensions of aging.

High Holy Days / Omer groups. As discussed further below, these groups come together to experience a period of Jewish time together, using materials that allow them to reflect and prepare for the holidays.

Support Groups

If there is one thing that all communities have in common, it is that members are going through similar life stages during which they benefit from communal support. While our clergy and heads of organizations are present for their members during moments of crisis and joy alike, fellow community members play a special role in helping each other mark and move through these moments. It is a commonly held belief that each person is going through a difficult crisis alone; surely we say to ourselves, I am the only one who has had this particular experience. Yet nothing could be further from the truth. None of us are alone in our experiences; there is a way to avoid adding loneliness to our list of grievances. Small groups help people in need of support find one another and provide structure for their gatherings. Organizations who host small groups focused on support serve their members in very meaningful and timely ways. Such support groups serve the larger community as well, because when people bond through difficult moments in life, they learn how to care for one another better and are often more willing to contribute to the care of the entire community.

Spotlight on Best Practice

At The Temple, one of our most valuable lessons is from the bereavement group started by Drs. Robert and Barbara Greene, a retired couple in their late eighties who are an oncologist and psychologist, respectively. They tragically lost an adult child recently and moved to Atlanta from Boston to help support the family. When they arrived at The Temple, they knew no one in Atlanta, and they were in search of a synagogue they could call home. As they became more comfortable, they approached me (LM) about starting a group for people who are bereaved; it would be free of charge and available when anyone needed it at any time, no commitment necessary. This couple simply wanted to give of their time, every other week for two hours, because they found it helped them with their grief to help others in this way. They even scheduled their fifty-fifth wedding anniversary trip back to Boston around these meetings. Sometimes seven people show up, and other times they have just one. For them, it doesn't matter; they just want to make sure that no one has to endure their grief alone. Their connection to The Temple, the clergy, their group members, and their Judaism has deepened because they have found their "place" and a meaningful way to contribute.

We learned an important lesson from this group. It is important to note here that The Temple staff had tried establishing a bereavement support group the year before the Drs. Greene arrived. We knew it would be a mitzvah to be able to provide our congregants a group such as this, because we, like all of our communities, have members who struggle with loss. We worked hard to find the right counselor, to recruit our congregants to come, and to figure out the right time, place, and cost. But it just would not come together.

Then the Greenes came along, and because of their own needs and passion, they were the key to the bereavement group's creation. The lesson? Sometimes the leaders of an organization really want a group to form, we want people to attend a program we've designed, and we pray that our community loves what we offer. But leaders of an organization cannot want a program more than our members want it. When it comes from organizational leadership, it is hit or miss. We have no idea whether our community members really need that particular programmatic offering. But when it comes from the members, it is sure to succeed, because they are expressing their own needs and coming with the passion it takes to make it happen.

Social Justice Groups

Many of our Jewish organizations are concerned with ways we can benefit people in need in our communities and beyond. We consider the ways we might bring more justice into a world that is broken and suffering. Our communities look to us as they search for ways to contribute more goodness to their world and to teach their children the value of *tikkun olam*. When we look at the twentieth-century models of food drives and mitzvah days, we often see them failing to grab the energy and imagination of our community members. These programs are still important, but there are yet more ways to engage our members and their deep desires to repair the world.

Social justice is a high priority and an identifying aspect of many of our organizations' culture and history. Like other synagogues, we (LM) are experimenting with using small groups as a way to activate our community so that more people can act together to advance the cause about which they are most passionate. At The Temple, we created the Rothschild Social Justice Institute (RSJI), a collaboration between the clergy of The Temple and dedicated and energized lay leaders. The RSJI is made up of ten small groups, each following the best practices of small-groups life: a dedicated volunteer group leader, emphasis on getting to know one another, and care for each other beyond the scope of their work together. Each group leader is also a part of our RSJI council, a small group that meets regularly and encourages collaboration and coordination among other RJSI groups. The council guides the overall vision of our engagement with social justice and supports each group individually. Through these small groups we have seen a significant increase in the number of people engaged on an ongoing basis with social justice efforts and the number of leaders who are deeply invested in these efforts. As a result, we are able to contribute more to the Jewish community and the wider Atlanta community. Because of the small groups, we are able to address topics such as women's rights, building Jewish-Muslim relationships, stopping domestic minor sex trafficking, environmental justice, racial justice, hunger and poverty, refugee resettlement, equity in education, LGBTQ rights, and gun safety and sensible legislation.

The structure of The Temple's social justice groups varies slightly from totally lay-led small groups. For instance, a clergyperson is assigned to each group so they can bring their connections and resources to bear on the group's efforts. One lay leader's sole responsibility is to administer the council, assembling resources for all ten groups and keeping the effort moving toward a set of shared objectives. But unlike typical synagogue social action committees, the small-groups structure empowers these groups to be much more nimble and specific in their scope. Group leaders and members are encouraged to share ownership, just as they would in any other small group, and they drive the pace and direction of the group through their own passions and energy. This allows the groups to make plans and attend meetings without being slowed down by a rabbi's busy schedule and priorities. The small-groups model has certainly had a huge impact on the ways in which we work on social justice issues. In just the last year, the RSJI has organized sessions to help parents talk to their children about gun safety in their friends' homes, hosted a Syrian Supper Club to help local refugees kick-start their catering business, facilitated lobbying training in order to better equip our anti-domestic minor sex trafficking group members to support or oppose bills at the state capital, and so much more.

Spotlight on Best Practice

At Central Synagogue in New York, one of our board members was an active volunteer in our Head Start tutoring program. She mentioned, though, that while she volunteered with the same people every week, she didn't really know them. Moreover, they had never discussed what was Jewish about the work they were doing. Her comments were the impetus for our creating an eight-session social justice curriculum for small groups. (A group of volunteers from our "breakfast program," which serves meals to our neighbors every week, participated as well.) The curriculum covers questions such as "What are my obligations to Jews, as opposed to others?" "What are my obligations to my local community versus the global community?" and "What would a redeemed world look like?"

A clear measure of success is that all groups that have used this curriculum have decided to keep meeting past the initial eight sessions. Some are entering their third year, using a variety of other discussion materials. Aside from the important work they do together, they have developed deep relationships and a greater sense of community within the congregation.

Living in Jewish Time

The Jewish calendar offers remarkable opportunities to find meaning and connection. These seasonal opportunities are a great way to allow members to live in Jewish time together and to take advantage of the opportunities our tradition provides for reflection.

In particular, the month of Elul, which leads up to Rosh Hashanah, and the period of the Omer, which stretches from Passover to Shavuot in the spring, offer wonderful opportunities for short-term, intensive small-groups experiences. These can be a change of pace for existing groups or a reason for new groups to form.

At Central Synagogue, we invited our congregants to experience in small groups the arc of Jewish time between the beginning of the month of Elul through Simchat Torah. Each group met three times over this seven-week period. Participants were invited to a kick-off session that explored the meaning of this moment in the Jewish calendar and also to attend Selichot and Simchat Torah services together. Finally, to support this spiritual journey through Jewish time, each participant was given an Elul preparation guide, which offered one personal attribute (for example, arrogance, compassion, silence) for each of the twenty-nine days of Elul. Each daily entry included relevant texts and a few reflection questions. Members were invited to pick a *hevruta* (partner) and to correspond with them every day via email or Facebook, reflecting on the attribute of the day. In this way, members were able to engage in the practice of creating a *heshbon nefesh* (accounting of the soul) in advance of the High Holy Days. Those who participated reported enthusiastically that it allowed them to experience the holidays in a new way. Even better, most of the new groups that formed for this short term experience decided to continue to meet after the holidays were over, using other discussion materials.

Central Synagogue, Temple Isaiah in Lexington, Massachusetts, and The Temple in Atlanta experimented with similar projects during the spring Omer period, again with good success.

Aside from the benefit of connecting our members to the Jewish calendar, these short-term groups have another significant benefit: they are a low-risk, low-commitment on-ramp for members who may not be ready to make a yearlong commitment. (For an explanation of on-ramps and off-ramps, see "Forming Small Groups.")

Case Study

Rabbi Ken Chasen, Rabbi Lisa Berney, Rabbi Benjamin Ross, and **Cantor Linda Kates,** Leo Baeck Temple, Los Angeles

An essential question we are always asking is: How do we deepen our congregants' relationships with the Jewish tradition as a vehicle for making meaning in their lives? Of course, the flip side also applies: How will their lived experience help them (and us) make more meaning of the tradition? These questions catalyzed *Torah Citizenship*, a turn of phrase that we define as the intersection of being an engaged Jew and an engaged citizen.

The first endeavor of *Torah Citizenship* was in the spring of 2017. We used the Counting of the Omer, the period between Passover and Shavuot during which, in biblical times, a daily grain offering was brought in preparation for the late spring harvest. Just as the mystics transformed the Omer period into a time of personal reflection and refinement in preparation for the revelation of Torah, we thought it would be compelling to reflect on how our texts speak to our role or identity or responsibility as citizens. Our strategy, miming the mystics and modern interpreters, was to send a daily email with a text drawn from our ancient and modern texts around one of our selected seven weekly themes: caring for the poor, personal responsibility, communal responsibility, caring for the stranger, human dignity, the role of faith, and engagement. With each thought-provoking text, we sent a question or two for personal or interactive consideration.

Here is an example from the week on personal responsibility:

> "Woe to him who builds his palace by unrighteousness, his upper rooms by injustice, making his own people work for nothing, not paying them for their labor" (Jeremiah 22:13).
>
> *Question:* If you're being truly honest with yourself, how have you advanced your own safety, wealth, or well-being at the expense of others? What more can you do to contain this very human impulse?

The response was extremely positive. A SurveyMonkey online evaluation received fifty-one responses—fifty positive. Anecdotally, we heard many stories of congregants who began each day by pondering these texts and questions, several of whom formed their own *hevruta* pairings or groups to discuss their reflections. The response encouraged us to press ahead.

We in turn launched our first small-groups experiment around the mission of spiritual preparation throughout Elul, the final month of the Jewish year, in anticipation of the coming High Holy Days. We had three groups with thirty-five participants. They met three times in lay leader–facilitated groups and then had three shared communal experiences at the synagogue; they launched with a Shabbat service and continued with Selichot and Simchat Torah. We were blessed with dynamic material from Central Synagogue and Ask Big Questions. The overwhelmingly positive response from our leaders and participants is encouraging us to explore a new round of small groups. For us, two essential learnings were (1) the great value of interweaving the small-groups home meetings with synagogue events to deepen relationships and to deepen the meaning and practice of specific holidays, and (2) the importance of cultivating and empowering creative lay leaders who were able to use the material as a jumping-off point but not as fixed menu. The path forward is wide open.

Spotlight on Best Practice

At The Temple, affinity group leaders learn how to structure group meetings, which usually begin with a "relational question," a suggestion for a way to start a conversation meant to deepen the relationships among participants. This is one way to strengthen any group's connection to Jewish time. The director of engagement emails the groups this relational question, usually related to the calendar, and always asks group members to share a story from their experience on the theme. Some examples include:

Rosh Hashanah. As we begin to think about the New Year, what do you hope your Jewish community will gift you this year? What do you expect to gift back?

Simchat Torah. We start the Torah again this month and reread the creation story in Genesis. Even though it is forbidden in the Talmud for Jews to speculate about the time before creation, they do anyway, as they want to know the reasons that God decided to create the world. One understanding they propose is simple: God was lonely and the only cure was to be in relationship. We are made in God's image (or we made God in our image) so we know that this is a fundamental need for humans as well—to know we are not alone. Please discuss as a group: When do we need each other?

Hanukkah. As the darkest part of the year is upon us, what is something that brings light into your life?

Tu B'Shvat. In what ways do you connect to nature? How does it feed you?

Purim. Purim is about turning things in our lives on their heads. What are some places in your life that you take very seriously? What are other parts that you hold more lightly? What would it look like to switch them every now and again? What kinds of joy might you discover?

Through these relational questions, we accomplish a few things at once. We are encouraging storytelling, the best way to get a group of people to know one another and see each other's humanity. We are also adding a touch of Jewish learning, dropping in bits and pieces of Jewish history, holiday customs, ritual, and values that many would not sign up to learn in a more formal classroom structure. Finally, we are teaching them the habit of engagement, such that when they come to a committee meeting or formal learning opportunity, they are not surprised when it too begins with a relational moment. It is a part of cultivating a new engagement-focused culture. We collect all the relational questions on our website in a "Relational Question

Bank," which can be easily accessed by anyone and can be adapted by group leaders, committee chairs, and even clergy seeking to write their own questions (See our "For Further Learning" section for a link.)

Spirituality in Small Groups

The question of where spirituality is found in these small groups is an important one *and* one that is still developing. People are clearly hungry for spiritual discussions and insights rooted in tradition and applicable to today. Nothing illustrated this for me (LM) more than when, over winter break, each member of The Temple's core team read a book about Christian small-groups structures, best practices, and resources. We learned about ten different small-groups models from churches of various size and backgrounds across the country, and we adopted many tips and tricks to suit our own context. But the one thing that was so desired by our core team and yet so difficult to imagine was the Jewish correlate to "growing in Christ." A big part of the fulfillment people were getting from their Christian small groups was an expanded sense of connection with their God. It's possible for Jewish small groups to focus on fostering a deeper connection with God, but given the general discomfort with talking about "God" in many Jewish communities, it would require a creative approach to get participants interested and comfortable with committing to spiritual development. This may be the next frontier in small-groups thinking. Who is ready to take up the charge with us?

Case Study

Rabbi Jill Perlman, associate rabbi, Temple Isaiah, Lexington, Massachusetts

Isaiah Together began as an idea and a dream in the spring of 2014. While our community calendars and those of our chairs were relatively full at Temple Isaiah, we knew that those were not the measures by which we wanted to determine if we were living up to our potential as a center and hub for thriving Jewish life. We dreamed of a culture change where relationship would be at the center of who we are. A relational approach, we believed, would lead to deeper, more meaningful engagement both within the community and with Judaism. We engaged in a listening campaign to take the pulse of where we were on that front and to test out this new dream.

A key part of this test was through a new initiative that we call Isaiah Together. Isaiah Together is a small-groups model, comprising both long-term small groups (yearlong or more) as well as short-term intensive small-groups experiences (six to seven weeks). We believed that if we could gather people together in small groups in living rooms and other more intimate spaces that we would begin to scratch away at the feeling of anonymity that goes along with being part of a larger organization. We believed that if we partnered with our congregants and built curricula together based on their interests and passions, and empowered them as leaders of these small groups, that we would be a step closer to making relevant Judaism's great wisdom for our current day.

Isaiah Together is more than a model. It's an ethos that is beginning to permeate throughout the congregation. As we consider different programs, classes, and outreach, committee chairs and staff members are asking themselves: How can I make this event more relational? How are congregants engaging with other congregants in this program? How are we translating the "big" of synagogue life to the intimacy or the "small" that helps us connect? How does this event, class, or program align with the rest of what is happening at Temple Isaiah? How does it align with "together"?

Our small-groups model has been an exciting and effective way for us to "un-silo" parts of our congregation that have traditionally operated apart from one another. After running several series of spirituality-based short-term small groups, we recently moved into using our small-groups model to explore issues of justice, specifically racial justice. Our passionate, serious learners and our *tikkun olam* warriors, who are not always the same folks, get to not only be in the same room but also engage together in meaningful ways, using text against the backdrop of an unjust world. This is just the beginning of the transformation that can take place when we intentionally place relationship at the center of who we are.

Seeking Balance in Small Groups

If a group has come together around a shared love of gourmet cooking, chances are that much of their time together will be spent in the kitchen or sharing meals. Likewise, a group of empty nesters that comes together to discuss sermons will likely spend the majority of their time in conversation. Even in groups that have a clear focus, however, members should spend some time doing other things as well, such as attending services, volunteering together, learning, or simply socializing. This creates balance, and it maximizes the group's sense of connection. This idea of a "balanced" group was first developed at Saddleback Church, but it is no less important in Jewish community. (See Rabbi Asher Knight's case study on page 146 for a demonstration of how one congregation incorporated the idea of "balance" into its groups).

Case Study

Rabbi Elie Kaplan Spitz, Congregation B'nai Israel, Tustin, California

In 2015 I published *Increasing Wholeness: Jewish Wisdom and Guided Meditations to Strengthen and Calm Body, Heart, Mind and Spirit* (Jewish Lights Publishing). The book explores how the Jewish tradition develops aspects of our inner life, which aids in reaching out to others. Each chapter contains information on the topic as well as suggested practical exercises and guided meditations that are accessible on YouTube. After Ron read my book and saw the videos, he said, "You have produced the material for your small-groups launch. Do it!" And I did.

I began by meeting with a business-savvy congregant, to discuss how to best initiate small groups, and with my office operations specialist, who would help me produce the needed materials. My congregant advised titling the campaign "40 Days to Becoming Your Best." We decided to launch on Erev Kol Nidre because the theme fit and the congregation would be gathered together. I called a philanthropic couple, told them of the goal, and they agreed to purchase five hundred copies of my book so that each participant would receive their own copy, which would also serve as an incentive to join a group.

I prepared a booklet of weekly discussion questions for hosts, a small study guide for readers, and quotes to send out to participants by email each day. The five weekly sessions were as follows: (1) Body, (2) Heart, (3) Mind, (4) Spirit, and (5) Hand. Two months before the High Holy Days, we put up a couple of large banners and distributed fliers that described the topics and goal. I spoke at a board meeting and asked my leaders to sign up as hosts, and I passed around a sign-up sheet. Most did. I wrote about the project in the synagogue newsletter, and we added to our weekly announcements a paragraph description and a web link to sign up. At Selichot I spoke about the theme of "becoming your best." On Rosh Hashanah we handed out attractive bookmarks on which was printed a quote, "Apply your mind to discipline and your ears to wise sayings" (Proverbs 23:12), a couple of related questions, and the website address where those interested could sign up to be small-groups hosts. We had a table in our courtyard during Rosh Hashanah services staffed with volunteers to answer questions and recruit. We offered attractive cloth bags—similar to the ones we had used at Purim for *mishloach manot* (the traditional gifts of food)—now stuffed with two copies of my book, along with the booklets for a host. Going into Rosh Hashanah I already had thirty hosts out of a congregation of 450 families. People could receive the goody bag if they agreed to host, along with a button that read "I am a host." The numbers went up to seventy.

We asked hosts to email the office with the names and email addresses of all those in their groups, with the promise of both daily suitable quotes and a concluding Shabbat celebration for participants. I carried the cloth bags in my car and approached congregants and nonmember community leaders to consider hosting. By Kol Nidre, we had ninety-four hosts. Our groups averaged four to six participants; some were family groups where they would study the material with their children at home or via Skype, and some groups included non-Jewish neighbors. Each of my Rosh Hashanah sermons dealt with an aspect of the topic that would be covered in the material.

Close to a third of the people in the room on Kol Nidre had agreed to participate in small groups. I was genuinely delighted and surprised.

We set up a group Facebook page for people to report on how their group meetings were progressing. We did not get many posts. We learned that some of the groups had consolidated once they learned that their friends had also created groups. In the end, we had eighty-five groups that maintained the program. I found a donor to underwrite a Friday night meal of conclusion. During the six weeks of meetings, I met again with Steve Gladen, the pastor of small groups at Saddleback who had mentored me in preparing for our launch, and with Pastor Rick Warren. They were both so supportive and happy for the widespread participation. Pastor Rick said, "It is the topic that will motivate people to prioritize their time and the fellowship that will keep them coming." They encouraged me to consider how to keep the groups going with other study topics once the campaign concluded. At Saddleback they draw from the material of previous campaigns, plus some groups just meet weekly to discuss the sermon of the previous week.

At the culminating Friday night dinner, people sat at round tables with members of their group. We drew 150 adults for the gathering. I had them discuss with each other what they had taken from their participation, and then I employed an instruction that Pastor Steve Gladen had mentioned: "From what you have heard from each other this evening, please volunteer another member of your group to share." What was brilliant about this suggestion is that the people who tend to speak volunteered someone else. The people chosen already knew what they were going to say and felt honored that they were asked. The comments followed a consistent theme: "When my friends in the group and I get together we usually talk about restaurants, sports, or our families. In this setting we spoke about topics that went deeper, such as what we believe about God or how we could be more whole. I now know my friends far better." All the groups said that they wanted to continue. I arranged materials for them, such as Ron Wolfson's book *The Seven Questions You're Asked in Heaven* (Jewish Lights Publishing). Some groups said that they would take turns bringing in articles to discuss. Most said that they would shift to monthly meetings.

I was uncertain if I could find continued success without a new book. At the same time, I knew that Saddleback did not produce a new book each year, rather just booklets that fostered group learning and conversation. Pastor Rick Warren's *The Purpose Driven Life*, which sold over thirty-five million copies, emerged from a small-groups campaign, but the book only came after the community had actively explored the topic. I consulted again with Pastor Steve Gladen about a second year's campaign. He challenged me, "The key question for a religious community is why?, which Pastor Rick has answered: 'To lead a life of purpose.' Before taking on other topics, consider addressing why Judaism matters."

I prepared a booklet with the title "Leading a Life of Significance: Why Judaism Matters" and prepared short videos to go with each week's topic. The six units worked off two acronyms VET and WIT: (1) Values—Priorities for Character Development, (2) Extended Family—A Chosen People, (3) Torah—Sacred Text, (4) Worship Texts, (5) Israel—A National Jewish Home, and (6) *Tikkun Olam*—Healing the World. The launch was again set for Kol Nidre, using Rosh Hashanah as an opportunity to build excitement and for choosing sermon topics that linked with the campaign (https://www.cbi18. org/sermons/2016/10/). The back of the booklet featured eleven different *tikkun olam* projects in our community, with contact information. The concluding event, the sixth session, was a community-wide Mitzvah-Making Day, which began with brunch at the synagogue. I delivered a presentation on why service in the larger community was central to Judaism, and people had the opportunity to spend the afternoon in helping projects. I was deeply satisfied by the reactions once again, with members sharing how much they had enjoyed deepening friendships and exploring the grassroots, communal caregiving.

In this second campaign we had over sixty active groups, fewer than the first year. Clearly the excitement of getting a copy of the "rabbi's book," combined with the novelty of small groups, drew an increased audience. At the same time, sixty groups translated into close to three hundred participants, which was deeply satisfying.

Conversations about why Judaism matters had enriched participants' Jewish connection and brought them closer to their friends.
I gained the assurance that I could write a booklet, rather than an
entire book, as the foundation of small-groups activity. I also learned
that while some groups would meet weekly, others would take longer; and that for a manageable commitment, five sessions was about
right. The success of the second year motivated me to write another
booklet over this summer in anticipation of year three.

The topic of year three is "Born to Love: Why, How, and With
Whom?" I knew that "love" is among the most successful topics for
Saddleback Church. I acquired their book and watched the accom-
panying sermons. At the same time, I decided to start from scratch,
because I wanted to use rabbinic sources as the commentary of the
relevant biblical passages. The five units are as follows: (1) Defin-
ing Terms; (2) Love of Family; (3) Love Your Neighbor, the Stranger,
and Yourself; (4) God as Beloved Source of Love; (5) Born to Love (a
summation). For each topic I provided a variety of questions. I rec-
ommended midweek discussion with a *hevruta*, and on the practical
level, I encouraged participants to keep a gratitude journal in which
to record specific loving acts, individually and in some cases as a
group. In implementing this current campaign, I invited "mentors"
to meet in my home to provide guidance on implementation. Each
of the mentors had already hosted a group and agreed to reach out
to motivate others to do so. Getting hosts to sign up is the key, but
flexibility also adds to success. Beginning the first year, our school
educator, Rabbi Robin Foonberg, had held a Tuesday lunch session at the synagogue, which led to a large and diverse group. We
sought to expand on such synagogue-based gatherings and to use
our website to match people with groups.

Rabbi Lawrence Kushner instructed me when I was on the cusp
of becoming a rabbi, "Judge your success as an educator by how
much your congregants teach each other." Through the years I
have encouraged ongoing learning with congregational teachers to
focus on reading Hebrew, Torah, Talmud, and the Prophets. Those
have largely been sustained by the same core of devoted participants. Small groups have greatly expanded those numbers and the

diversity of congregational learners. The book and booklets have given Jewish content and context to conversations that matter and are deeply satisfying for participants. Through small groups my congregants have deepened their understanding of Judaism, themselves, and their bonds with friends. I am a believer: my congregants will prioritize time for five group sessions if the material and the topic are meaningful.

I invite you to use the materials that I have prepared for the small groups in my community. (See our "For Further Learning" section for a link.)

Takeaways

Once you know the ways in which you'll organize the members of small groups, you will need to decide what the small groups will do together. Some ideas that we have seen work are shared interest groups, discussion groups, support groups, social justice groups, and living in Jewish time groups.

Our Next Steps

What do we want our groups to do?

Shared Interest Groups

_____
_____
_____
_____

Discussion and Learning Groups

_____
_____
_____
_____

Support Groups

_____
_____
_____
_____

Social Justice Groups

_____
_____
_____
_____

Living in Jewish Time Groups

_____
_____
_____
_____

Forming Small Groups

Just as there are a number of different organizing principles you can use to bring groups together (geography, demography, availability, affinity), there are many different ways to form your groups.

"Matchmaking" by Clergy and Staff Is Not Necessary or Sustainable

At Central Synagogue, we began our small-groups initiative by hand-picking members to join our pilot groups. These groups were successful overall, but it quickly became clear that forming groups in this way has its downsides. First, while it is possible to handpick eight groups, it is impossible to form fifty or one hundred groups this way. It simply takes too much staff time and necessarily results in group membership being limited to the "usual suspects" who are most known to the clergy and staff. Given that one goal of our initiative is to engage those who may not be on the radar, we decided it was not a sustainable model long term. Second, this method led to members feeling that our small groups were exclusive and to some members feeling hurt when they were not picked.

We began experimenting with alternative means of group formation, including matching events to which everyone was invited. Having spoken to members of groups that were formed in both ways, we learned something unexpected: members of handpicked groups attribute part of the success of their group to the particular mix of people; members of randomly assigned groups attribute their success to the diversity of membership and to building relationships with people whom they otherwise would never have met. There also appears to be no difference in the percentage of groups who choose to continue past their initial commitment. Based on these results, we recommend against spending too much staff

133

time handpicking group members. Better to spend that time recruiting and training excellent leaders.

Ways to Attract Group Members

Depending on the needs of your community, you might try one or more of the following models:

> *Matching events.* If you are trying to start a large number of groups at the same time—whether as part of a campaign or just a large enrollment push—you might consider holding an in-person matching event, to give your members a taste of what groups are like and help them discern which groups fit their needs and interests.
>
> *Launching parties.* At The Temple, we ran a very simple experiment. At the beginning of the year during religious school, when we knew that people would be walking through the front foyer, we simply placed chairs along the walls with group names on signs (and balloons tied to the backs of chairs to draw attention). Next to each chair stood that group's leader, there to describe what the group did and how it worked. In this manner, we filled one whole group, and many other groups picked up people.
>
> When Central Synagogue started its *mussar* groups, it sent out a congregation-wide invitation to a "Taste of *Mussar*" event. Prior to the event we identified five leaders, who were then trained to lead these types of groups. At the event, we explained the approach of *mussar* and invited everyone to take part in a half-hour discussion using the kinds of texts and questions that people would encounter if they were to join a *mussar* group. At the end of the event, we handed out cards listing the group leaders, along with the days and times their groups would meet. Participants who were interested in joining a group then ranked the groups in which they were interested in order of preference. Staff then assigned participants based on these preferences. The benefits of this approach: (a) it was open to anyone in the congregation who was interested in participating; (b) it ensured that people who signed up for groups knew what they were getting into; and (c) it resulted in diverse group

membership, as the only thing the members had in common (other than their interest in the subject matter) was the day and time that they were free.

Leaders need followers. If you decide to form affinity-based groups, you may be inundated with ideas from members about different kinds of groups they would like to start. It can be difficult for some people to gauge how widely shared are their personal passions, and it is disappointing to create a group only to have no one join. Therefore a good rule of thumb for affinity groups is to ask the potential leader to find at least two other people who would join their group. If the leader can round up at least two other people, this is an indication that there is some shared interest and that the leader is the sort of person that others are happy to follow. If the leader cannot whip up interest from at least two other people in their underwater basket weaving group, that's a sign that it is unlikely to take off. You might instead brainstorm with them about other interests or demographic groups that would garner more interest. You also know that this person may need a little extra help finding a group to join, during which time they can make the two friends it would take to start a new group! For learning- and discussion-based groups, we recommend that there be at least eight members for the group to start. In this case, you may need to use a matching event or online sign-up to fill the group rather than asking your leaders to fill them on their own.

Online signups. For the reasons discussed above, it is advisable to minimize the amount of staff time and involvement in forming groups. (Of course, after groups have formed, there may be times when a clergy or staff member will recommend a particular group to a potential new participant). One way for staff to get out of the way while maintaining access to group lists and contact information—is to use an online signup platform. There are a number of options, most designed specifically for small church groups. The platforms designed by GroupVitals and ChurchGroupsHQ, for example, allow potential participants to see a list of groups (including how many spots are left in each), along with information about the days and times the groups meet, their locations, and other details. Users can filter the listings by location, day, time, and other specifications and sign up instantly. Leaders can then email their groups directly from the webpage. Whether online signups make sense for your community will depend in part on how comfortable your members are navigating online resources.

Organization-wide publicity. In order to continue to highlight these various groups, it's important to use high-attendance events and seasons for publicity. Put flyers on the seats before High Holy Day services or at JCC open houses, mention group formations during announcements at services for a few months in the fall, honor group leaders and coaches with *aliyot* during services—people should become familiar with the small-groups effort and hopefully be inspired to get involved. At The Temple, we even made stickers for our coaches and group leaders to wear that read "Want to Get Engaged? Ask Me for More Information!" We hoped that using these eye-catching stickers would help raise visibility about the engagement efforts.

In addition, because synagogues and JCCs can organize groups according to neighborhood, you can use available database and email systems to invite people to join neighborhood groups. You can even subdivide neighborhoods into life age and stages. The more you help people feel that a given group is perfect for them, the more people you will motivate to check out a group.

On-Ramps, Off-Ramps, and Commitment In-Between

Securing a firm and bounded commitment from group members is important to the health of any group. First, it is difficult to build community if you never know who is going to show up to a given group meeting. Second, many members are concerned about what will happen if they don't like their group. They need reassurance that they are not signing their life away by trying something new.

One way to address both concerns is to create clear temporal on-ramps and off-ramps for your groups. Members should know that they are committing to show up regularly for a certain period of time—whether it's six weeks or one year—and that at the end of that period they can freely decide whether to continue. It's important to stress to group members and leaders that while enforcing expectations of attendance is fair game during a given "season," once the season is over, there is no moral weight attached to deciding whether to continue on.

Setting Ground Rules

One essential tool for any kind of group will be a set of ground rules, or a *brit* (covenant). These rules should be agreed upon when the group first meets and should be reviewed periodically. In fact, some groups review the "headlines" of their *brit* at every meeting, as a way to separate the "holy" environment of their group time from everyday interactions.

Here's an example of a *brit* from Temple Emanu-El in Dallas, Texas, and their small-groups initiative called Sh'ma Emanu-El:

Brit for Small Groups

ACCOUNTABILITY

I'll show up to our agreed upon times: (weekly, biweekly, triweekly, monthly). I'll let the group leader know the (good) reason I will be absent. I will also be punctual and respect everyone's time.

PRESENCE

When we're together, I'll be present and mindful. I will listen and share. Life (and our mobile devices) offers many distractions, but I will stay present and engaged.

CONFIDENTIALITY

I'll maintain complete confidentiality. What I hear and say stays here.

VULNERABILITY

I'll stretch myself to be as open and honest as possible with my perspectives and experiences in order to create a safe environment that might encourage others to take risks as well.

RESPECT

I will remember that all of us are here for a common purpose, and I will respect and acknowledge everyone in my group.

NO FIXING, ADVISING, SAVING, OR SETTING STRAIGHT

I will give each person the gift of true attention without trying to "solve their problem." No advice unless it's asked.

LISTENING

I understand that some of us are talkers, while some of us are quieter. I'll be aware not to dominate discussions and to balance how much I'm talking with how much I'm listening.

CURIOSITY

Judaism is a religion of exploration; of big questions more than answers. I will get the most out of my group by being open to our discussions and the people around me.

OWNERSHIP

This is our Sh'ma Emanuel Group. This is our community to create. While we have guidelines and suggestions, it is ours to shape and form. We will get out of it what we put into it.

You may emphasize to your leaders that if the dynamic in their group begins to stray from the expectations in their *brit*, they can always return to it as a way to keep the group on track.

Measuring Success

How will you know if your groups are working? It is important to build in mechanisms to measure success. But all the data in the world will not help if you don't know what you want to measure. As we suggested earlier, the most important thing to do when planning a small-groups initiative is to be sure you and your lay leaders understand the purpose of these groups. When your goals are clear, it is easier to determine what you need to measure.

At Central Synagogue, our goal is for groups to help our members connect more deeply to one another, to the Central Synagogue community, to Jewish tradition, and to God. Thus when we survey group members (at the end of every group experience—whether it be a year for ongoing groups or the end of a shorter "campaign") we ask them to rate the extent to which their group experience has increased those connections. (See our website, www.relationaljudaismhandbook.com, for a sample survey.)

Once you have determined what to measure, there are a number of ways to measure success:

> *Regular check-ins with leaders.* It is a good idea to check in periodically with your group leaders, not only to offer support in terms of facilitation and interpersonal issues but also to see whether their groups are meeting the goals you have set for them. Are members building relationships? Are they choosing to meet outside of the group? Is the group taking ownership of its experience? Are there any members who might be interested in growing into leadership roles? These conversations are also a great source of stories, which can be used to explain the power of groups to your board and other leadership.
>
> *Surveys.* End-of-year or end-of-campaign surveys are good tools for measuring success over time. Just be sure you know what you want to know!

Database. Keeping track of group membership in your congregation's membership database can help you determine how many new members have joined groups, what other activities your group members have engaged in, how participation has grown over time, and more.

Group self-assessment. We encourage groups to evaluate themselves. How are they doing at following their ground rules? How is the group functioning as an engine for relationship building? For congregations that seek a "balanced group," you may also want them to do a more formal assessment to determine where they can improve their balance.

Spotlight on Best Practice

The core team of lay leaders at Temple Emanu-El explains how their groups use a group assessment tool to measure their group's health. (A copy of the tool can be found at our website, www.relationaljudaismhandbook.com.)

The group assessment tool was designed to help each Sh'ma group periodically assess the status of the group in terms of adherence to the group and individual goals and needs. Groups have thus far been asked to complete the evaluation yearly. The tool has proved to be helpful in two ways:

1. It has allowed the leadership an opportunity to understand how groups are functioning. For example, are groups meeting regularly and using the curriculum provided? What is the measure of satisfaction with the group experience?

2. It has enabled groups that have used the tool to evaluate their satisfaction regarding the group and either sustain the status quo or institute changes. The evaluation tool has given every group member the opportunity to have a voice within the context of the group dynamics.

The process for the group evaluations has been as follows: The group facilitator emails the evaluation tool to group members in advance of the meeting. Group members then subsequently share their thoughts regarding the questions. Ideally, the facilitator then collates the information received and emails the final product to the leadership team. Some groups choose to complete the process entirely by email.

Case Study

Rabbi Asher Knight, senior rabbi, Temple Beth El, Charlotte, North Carolina; former associate rabbi, Temple Emanu-El, Dallas, Texas

In 2012 Temple Emanu-El was preparing to lay new physical foundations. We were in the midst of a $38 million capital campaign to construct a new and renewed building that would include usable spaces for us to encounter the values of Judaism in relationship with one another. Rabbi David Stern, Temple Emanu-El's senior rabbi, called this the "architecture of possibility." But building spaces are not "community." The possibility was ours to fulfill, ours to create the human foundations and lived Jewish experiences that will support our renewed congregational environments, our homes, and our lives.

Listening was our first step. Why? Because we didn't assume that we knew what was on the minds of the temple's members. We didn't assume to know what was central and important in each other's lives. Each member of our congregation has desires and interests. Each member of our congregation faces the dynamics of modern society in similar and different ways. And each of us is a central element to the living faith that we build together.

I worked closely with Mike Sims, then a Temple Emanu-El vice president; Diana Einstein, our director of community connections; and a team of lay leaders that included leaders from Just Congregations Committee (Congregationally Based Community Organizing), our lay leadership training and development committee, and our membership services committee. The group worked collaboratively to create a listening campaign in our congregation that helped us uncover the troubling truths and enlightening visions about our community. We trained over two hundred facilitators to conduct conversations, take notes, and listen deeply to the diverse voices of our congregants. Over the year, 1,170 temple members met in members' homes in over seventy-five Havdalah parties and at large events where we divided into small-group conversations led by our facilitators.

The experience helped us discover these troubling truths and enlightening visions about our community. Some members didn't realize that they lived on the same block with other temple members. Parents and grandparents lamented that their children didn't have deep relationships with other Jewish kids. People were frustrated with surface-level friendships with other adults. Some people spoke about serving on committees at the temple and feeling as if no one knew them. We heard sadness that people felt imprisoned and fragmented by the broader secular culture.

We also heard a sense of possibility and optimism. People raved about the small-groups gatherings in each other's homes. They also spoke about moments of sacred connection. Members wanted to connect with other Jews and build relationships that add substance, support, and meaning to their lives. Jews with deep spiritual practices and Jews who are as secular as they come told us that they wanted a paradigm shift in congregational life. We heard that people were ready to build face-to-face connections in a digital age and slow down in a culture that often rewards us for speeding up. We heard that people needed friends who can be relied upon during the ups and downs of life. People were inspired because the experience of the listening campaign was an invitation to share their unique gifts and insights with others. We heard that people were seeking opportunities to grow and to become the best within themselves. Best of all, the entire process was lay led. While our clergy each attended one Havdalah party, none of our clergy led a group. The leaders proved to themselves that they could create Jewish small-groups listening and learning experiences that weren't dependent on clergy facilitation.

The idea to create the small groups developed directly out of our conversations. Our members desired smaller settings in which to grow and share in the lived experience of being Jews. In truth, we need both the large and small gathering moments: to pray, celebrate, and learn from our tradition and to experience our Jewish values in personal and relatable smaller settings, where we are seen for who we are, and where we see others for who they are.

The Vision for Groups at Temple Emanu-El

After the listening campaign, our leadership team began a learning process about small groups in church settings. The Christian literature describes three congregational models: the church with small groups; the church of small groups; and the church itself is small groups. Translated into Jewish language, we explored the three options:

A temple with small groups would be a synagogue where small groups are an important program and members are encouraged to consider this option as a means of connecting to the synagogue, meeting some people, and teaching whatever the groups might be studying. The temple might list the group in a program or have an occasional announcement reminding the synagogue that the small groups exist. There may be little public information or affirmation of the groups. Groups start and end as people form them.

A temple of small groups means that small groups pervade congregational life. There would be a wide range of kinds and sizes of groups. This approach sees the value of a small-groups community as an essential aspect of membership (it may, however, take a while to fully get there). Every member is encouraged to connect with others for a group experience on a regular basis. A temple of small groups sees small groups as a vital vehicle for spiritual formation, and leadership development is core to its practice. This requires staff time toward building groups. The temple would need to allot, over time, an intentional and significant amount of resources toward leadership development, essential staffing, training, and materials for leaders.

A temple that is small groups is similar to the aforementioned temple of small groups but tends to be even more dogmatic. A temple that is small groups would make membership in a small group a requirement of membership in the synagogue.

	Temple *with* Groups	Temple *of* Groups	Temple *Is* Groups
Purpose	Help people find a place in the temple	Core element of temple community	Primary expression of the congregation
Group Membership	Not required for temple membership	Not required, but strongly pushed as being a key element of membership	Required
Use of Curriculum	Chosen by the leader of the small group	Recommended by staff, leader of small group, or chosen by the group	Designated by staff
Temple Authority over Group	Low	Middle	High
Temple Monitoring of Groups	Low	Middle (significant emphasis in monitoring leaders)	High

The Sh'ma Emanu-El team determined that the congregation should aim to become a temple of small groups. We recognized that real cultural change would take many years to fully realize, and in the meantime, we would likely feel like a congregation with small groups. Nevertheless, we determined to aim high and realize a cultural shift. By doing so, we expressed a vision of community and individual transformation that would constantly and consistently encourage members to be in small groups, which we called "Sh'ma Groups." We also developed a small-groups vision statement:

SH'MA EMANU-EL VISION STATEMENT

Imagine hundreds of temple members gathering regularly in small groups to learn and laugh, to rest and rejuvenate, and to deepen connections to one another, to the temple, to the Jewish people, and to the rhythms of Jewish time and life. Sh'ma Emanu-El will help the temple realize this future of a connected, committed membership through the formation of small groups, which will:

• Focus on the lives and significant concerns of our members.

• Organize around shared interests, life stages, and geographies.

• Feature shared Jewish experiences, learning, and celebration.

• Be self-led by lay leaders working in a group dynamic.

Establishing Best Principles for Sh'ma Groups

Sh'ma Groups are regular, small-groups gatherings of five to eighteen members in people's homes. They are led by trained guides and use common learning materials developed by clergy and partners. Some Sh'ma Groups are geographic in nature; others connect around common interests, life stages, and affinities. All Sh'ma Groups engage in meaningful Jewish conversation and respect the diversity of opinions and ideas of each individual. Activities include monthly meetings (minimally) in members' homes, leadership trainings, opportunities for celebration and recognition, and integration into the larger congregation. Sh'ma Emanu-El is designed to be scalable, replicable, and a sustainable model for congregational learning, engagement, and leadership development. The core team established guidelines and expectations of "small-groups" best practices:

• Meet regularly in a home or in an agreed upon setting that is conducive to creating a safe space.

• Agree to and observe a covenant *brit* with each other.

- Create meaningful relationships.

- Have meaningful discussion of provided materials.

- Have regular attendance by the majority of its members.

- Invite everyone to share.

- Create safe spaces where members are "present" for each other.

- Embrace everyone present.

- Have fun and look for joyful opportunities.

- Participate in acts of justice.

- Celebrate Shabbat, holidays, and life cycles together.

- Attend temple programs or larger gatherings together.

- Support group members in times of need and celebrate in times of joy.

- Communicate outside of meetings.

- Encourage shared responsibilities.

- Provide feedback to coaches and the Sh'ma Emanu-El team.

How Sh'ma Groups Fit into Temple Emanu-El

We believe that there is a direct connection between the large gatherings of temple life and the intimate gatherings in Sh'ma Groups. Sh'ma Groups are about the lived experience of being Jewish. Shabbat worship, holiday celebrations, lifelong learning, and social justice will enhance and deepen the Sh'ma Group experience. Likewise, the strength of the Sh'ma Group can help lead to personal transformation that will enliven and enrich all of temple life.

Sh'ma Groups intentionally relate to the core values of Temple Emanu-El: learning, prayer, community, *tikkun olam*, and peoplehood. We believe it is critical to balance these values within every Sh'ma Group.

Talmud Torah: *Learning*. We affirm the power of Jewish learning to create and deepen Jewish identity and commitment. Learning brings Jewish values to our daily lives, nurtures spiritual experiences, anchors and challenges us to reach out to a world in need.

T'fillah: *Prayer*. We celebrate the potential of prayer to help us reach out to God, root ourselves in community, and affirm the most deeply held values of our people and our faith.

Kehilah: *Community*. Community means a sense of warm welcome, meaningful relationships, and mutual responsibility. We celebrate our identity as a multigenerational community. We envision the relationship between congregants, rabbis, and staff as a partnership based upon mutual respect, shared Jewish commitment, and ongoing Jewish growth.

Tikkun Olam: *World Repair*. We emphasize the ethical ideals of social justice at the core of the Jewish tradition. We have a covenantal obligation to engage in the ongoing task of world repair.

Am Yisrael: *Peoplehood*. We exist in vital relationship to the Jewish people in Israel and throughout the world. We acknowledge our responsibility in promoting pluralism in the Jewish world.

Temple Emanu-El is a vibrant Jewish community that strives to be a place of sacred encounter, where learning, prayer, and deeds change our understanding of ourselves, our world, and our responsibilities in it. For us, community means a sense of warm welcome, meaningful relationships, and mutual responsibility. We seek to bring Jewish learning and values to our daily lives, to nurture spiritual practices, and to build an exciting and relevant Judaism that elevates our souls and challenges us to make an impact on a world in need. Thus Sh'ma Groups are about personal and communal transformation. Sh'ma Groups understand that balancing the temple's core Jewish values is the key to a healthy group. Not every core value needs to occur when a Sh'ma Group meets. Over time, the groups should try to seek balance and depth as they engage in holistic Jewish living.

Launching Sh'ma Groups

Our team set an initial goal of eighteen small groups. We invited everyone who participated in the listening campaign to a reporting event, so we could share what we learned from the listening process and the vision for small groups at Temple Emanu-El. We asked the members of the congregation who attended the reporting event to consider facilitating a small group. Over sixty people stepped forward to train to become small-groups leaders.

We then created a small-groups facilitator training, a small-groups manual, and assigned each small-groups facilitator a coach from the core team that had established the vision for Sh'ma Emanu-El. Some small-groups facilitators had a group of friends whom they wanted to invite into a predetermined group. Some small-groups facilitators wanted to meet new people and were open to inviting people to join. We created multiple matching events that modeled small-groups discussion and learning, led by the facilitators. We asked the facilitators to create signs about their intended group (affinity, neighborhood, and the like). Then we invited participants to spend time meeting the facilitators, learning about the different small groups, and inviting them to sign up for the small group that interested them the most. We were honestly surprised at how well these matching events worked. In some cases, where members could not find a group that matched their interests, we invited them to become facilitators, supporting them to establish their own groups. We launched fifty-five Sh'ma Groups with over six hundred members participating, initially. We far surpassed our initial goals. Since then, we have had continued growth and trained new small-groups facilitators and coaches, which has allowed the congregation to scale and expand toward the vision of becoming a synagogue of small groups.

Takeaways

There are many ways to get people into your small groups, including matching events, launching parties, asking leaders to start with two friends already committed to the idea, online signups, and organization-wide publicity.

People are more likely to sign up if they know in advance how to get into a small group, how to get out of a small group, and what the commitment will be in between.

It's important to set ground rules for the group at its outset. These agreements will serve as guardrails for the quality of the groups' experience.

You will need to decide what success means for your community and find ways to measure your progress.

Our Next Steps

What are the next three things we need to do to help people start their groups?

_____

_____

_____

_____

How will we know we have been successful?

_____

_____

_____

_____

The Importance of
Lay Leadership

Small groups are lay led by design. If you are in a community that is used to deferring to rabbis and staff as "experts" in Jewish life, you should be prepared to remind your people frequently that having members lead is a feature and not a bug. Why? First, small groups are a great way to develop lay leadership, and the best way to create leaders is to allow them to lead. Second, one goal of small groups is to give members a sense of authentic ownership over their Jewish lives. The moment a rabbi or other "expert" steps into the room, our lay members tend to forget about the life's worth of Torah they brought into the room and revert to old habits of deferring to authority. Finally, having clergy or staff lead groups is simply not a model that can grow to meet the needs of a given organization; if the organization would like a large percentage of the community to get involved, the clergy and professional staff are only able to support so many groups before they reach a limit.

Building Your Core Team

Ideally, before you get too far down the road, you will create a core team, a group of lay leaders who are intimately involved in different aspects of creating and developing your Relational Engagement Campaign. Sometimes these are the same people with whom you conduct the listening campaign. In other cases, you'll find them through the campaign itself. These people will serve as your ambassadors and problem solvers, your visionaries and your detail people—basically whatever gaps you need to fill in your organization's leadership. You will rely on these people to build the capacity of small groups and spread the word about their benefits.

They may continue to serve as group leaders and coaches as your small-groups initiative grows.

Empowering Your Members to Lead

Depending on the leadership culture of your community, the limiting factor on the number of groups you can create may be the number of members you have who are willing and able to lead them. Resist the temptation to meet demand for group participation by creating groups run by staff or clergy. Instead, consider what the barriers to leadership are and address those directly:

> *"I don't know enough."* The most common reason our members resist becoming leaders is that they are insecure about their level of Jewish knowledge. Remind them that small groups are *not* classes, and they are not teachers. Instead, the point is for every person to share the Torah of their own lives; they are merely facilitators. Assure them that any Jewish content will be provided, translated, and clearly explained.

> *"My apartment is too small/messy/far away."* Depending on where you are located, it may or may not be safe to assume that most of your members could easily host ten to fifteen people in their homes. Some of your most natural leaders may live in tiny apartments or may simply be too self-conscious to comfortably act as host. They will often ask if they can meet at the building instead. We recommend that you resist this solution for two reasons. First, it is unlikely that you will be able to make this kind of accommodation for all your groups, and it is best to structure your groups in a way that is sustainable and scalable. Second, there is something about meeting in a person's home that invites a level of warmth and intimacy that is difficult to achieve around a conference table or in a nursery-school classroom. The goal of small groups is to get people to build an intimate community, and it is just more difficult to do in an institutional setting. Instead, you can assure them that they can ask someone else in their group to host or even rotate hosting responsibilities among the group's members.

Of course, there may be reasons to make exceptions to this general rule. For example, if you have a group of people in their twenties and thirties who are living in a city with a high cost of living, there may not be anyone in the group with an apartment big enough to fit everyone. In that case, you might offer to find a space for them to meet. Or in a synagogue setting, you may have a group that wants to meet on Friday nights just before services (or Saturday after Shabbat morning services). You may decide that the benefit of having such a group worship together outweighs the downsides of meeting on premises. In cases such as these, though, you might recommend that at least a few times a year, they meet offsite for dinner or some other social event.

"I don't have time." This one merits serious consideration. If you think the task just seems too overwhelming, you may point out that responsibility for hosting the group can be separated from the tasks of facilitating conversation, providing refreshments, and other responsibilities. But you do need leaders who are committed to regular preparation and follow-through. If you or they are unsure, you might recommend that they begin by joining a group to get a sense of what is involved and return to the question of leadership later.

Shared leadership is also an option. This is a basic principle that we use on all levels, from running the synagogue to small groups sharing small leadership tasks with their group members.

Training Your Leaders

The amount of training your leaders will require depends on the nature of the group they are leading. A leader of a content-driven group focused on *mussar*, the Jewish tradition of ethical development, will require some orientation to the subject matter and approach of that discipline. The leader of an affinity-based group of theater lovers will require less formal training. Depending on how you roll out your groups, you may opt to have periodic training sessions for groups of leaders or conduct less formal orientations on a rolling basis.

In designing your leader training or orientation, consider what your leaders need to know in order to advance the core purposes of your small-groups initiative, create an environment conducive to sharing personal stories, and appropriately manage difficult group dynamics. Keep in mind that ideally your leaders will have regular check-ins with staff members or lay coaches who can help them troubleshoot issues as they come up. The initial training need not cover every possible scenario; the goal is to give your leaders a sense of what a well-functioning group looks like so that they can begin with a greater sense of confidence and reach out for help if needed.

Developing Small-Group Coaches

Who are these coaches to whom we keep referring? Organizations working toward a culture of small groups will eventually want to recruit and train a group of leaders to act as coaches, with each coach supporting two or more small-group leaders. At The Temple, we rely heavily on our coaches, a group that evolved out of the initial leadership of the listening campaign and into serving as coaches to small-groups leaders, who help launch groups, trou-bleshoot where neces-sary, and create a feedback loop to the professional staff so that we can address issues as they arise. These coaches meet every four to six weeks, as this group is the backbone of the whole system. Why go to so much trouble to add another layer of leadership? As your number of groups begins to grow, there will not be enough staff to support each group sufficiently. You will need to lean on vol-unteers to help support your groups. Like an upside-down pyramid, we see group

INDIVIDUAL TEMPLE MEMBER
Attends their group and shares the joys and responsibilities

SUPPORTED BY:

GROUP LEADER
Organizes and guides the group

SUPPORTED BY:

COACH
Acts as a sounding board and coach for up to four group leaders

SUPPORTED BY:

TEMPLE CLERGY, STAFF, AND CORE TEAM
Designs the overall initiative and supports coaches, group leaders, and individual temple members

members as the foundation of what we do—their experience is the most important part of our work. We see the role of the group leaders as basically supporting group members, the roles of coaches as supporting group leaders, and the role of Temple staff as supporting coaches.

Our coaches help us care for the group leaders who care for their group members. Nothing would work well without this layer of leadership contributing their time and caring to our group leaders.

To care for our groups and their leaders well, coaches are tasked with the following responsibilities:

> *Launching groups.* Coaches help groups get started by offering ideas for getting people into their groups, including using their own networks of friends and acquaintances at the organization. They can also offer advice on the Internet-based meeting tools that are recommended. Coaches share ideas on how to talk with the group initially about the *brit* and how to hold the group members accountable to their commitments.

> *Ongoing support.* Coaches help the leader keep an eye on the group's health by troubleshooting tricky group dynamics when needed and holding the group leaders accountable to their original commitments. They also offer recommendations for ways to keep the group lively and interesting.

> *Connecting groups to the larger organization.* Coaches feed pertinent information back to the organization's leadership (with the permission of group members and group leaders), such that they are aware of developing issues in the lives of their members and can respond to them accordingly. This response would include addressing a complaint registered against the organization in a timely and loving fashion or supporting a member in their illness or grief, about which the organization may not have otherwise known.

> *Leadership development.* Coaches develop group leaders with the goal of identifying and promoting great new leaders into fellow coaching positions as well as board and committee positions outside of the small groups.

Fresh Leadership for Your Organization

As was mentioned above, we recommend establishing a core team, a group of the organization's members that helps guide the direction and promotion of small-groups culture within your organization or synagogue. We recommend that this core team ultimately be populated mostly by your coaches. Coaches become the most expert of all people in small groups and how they work best; why not leverage that knowledge and experience as the team of people who also guide the direction overall? They also feel the most invested in its success, as they are face-to-face with group leaders most often, giving them the most up-to-date information about the groups, and yet they also have a big-picture view of the ways that small groups are impacting the culture of the organization. Lastly, coaches need to be in regular conversation with one another so that they can share best practices and support one another in their work. For these reasons, we recommend the core team meet at least once every four to six weeks. They become a small group of their own and often bond with one another in a very similar way.

As a part of the core team, these special leaders may have additional responsibilities. They can help with research on small groups within the Jewish world and beyond. They help with the recruitment of new group leaders and offer ideas on how to best accomplish this within the organization. They develop strategies for bringing more of your organization's members into small groups—after all, they *are* your organization's members! For these reasons, it's important that your coaches and core team represent the diversity of people you anticipate participating in small groups.

Not every person on the core team must also be a coach. For example, at The Temple, the core team is co-chaired each year by our executive vice president and our membership chair, so that each new Temple president and membership committee chair understands small groups deeply and continues to cultivate small-groups culture within all aspects of the organization. For instance, our current Temple president served as our core team co-chair for two years and has now made participation in small groups a part of the board's annual commitment. The rest of the core team is a combination of board members and involved lay leaders, though this is a great place for the stellar lay person who may not currently be heavily involved but for whom this could be a great entry into Temple leadership.

For instance, some of our best coaches have been empty nesters who were once very involved when their children were in religious school but now need to define their relationship to the synagogue anew. This commitment feels serious enough that they know they are legitimately needed but not so intensive that they can't still enjoy other hobbies.

One trend that we've noticed over the past few years is that our greatest group leaders encourage group members to start their own groups. This does two things: (1) It allows new groups to form with enthusiastic new leaders who have had transformative small-groups experiences already. (2) It allows for a natural next step for the original group leader, who can now become a coach for the new groups. Who better to coach and encourage a new group than the leader of the original group and a dear friend, no less! In this way, we are watching people who were relatively uninvolved become more involved at The Temple and more engaged with Temple leadership. Some of our first group leaders are now not only coaches but also moving into our mainstream leadership development program and onto the Board of Trustees. Small groups have helped us expand the pipeline into leadership beyond the traditional ways organizations find leaders. These new leaders understand the organization's evolving culture, feel connected to the organization and its other members with fresh energy, and will likely bring interesting perspectives and experiences based on their relational orientation.

We are still learning how best to use our coaches. For instance, some coaches find that groups only need coaching in the first few months after their launch, though we also find that when groups get into a bind, it's great to have a coach to offer advice, encouragement, or even the recommendation to end the group. Other groups that are in their second or third year need very little coaching. As a result, we reconfigure our coaching structure such that some coaches are experts at getting groups off the ground, while others specialize in routine group maintenance.

Leadership Commitment

Just like group members, small-groups leaders and coaches also need clear on-ramp and off-ramp options. This may be one of the most difficult parts of any initiative. We love to hang on to great leaders because it makes us feel that our program is more secure. It is difficult to find new leaders and get them up to speed. But we always say that we would rather them leave happy than burned out; that we care more deeply about their well-being than any single volunteer role; and that when this is no longer fun for them, they should take a break. Most leaders and coaches make a yearlong commitment and then have the option of re-upping for more years.

We also ask for an intangible commitment: the willingness to stick with a group even when the people seem difficult or the group itself seems to be imploding. Such occurrences do happen, though it is rare. We need leaders and coaches who are willing to rise above any person or petty offense, who can see the big picture even while being stuck in a chain of emails that may become insensitive or blaming, and who can approach all these situations with compassion and patience. While we as clergy or senior leadership may want to shield and protect our volunteers from this side of our work, it is sometimes beneficial for our leaders and coaches to walk with people through these difficult moments. Sometimes we get unexpected results. During one such moment in a group at The Temple, the coach came away not only feeling more sympathetic to the senior leadership as she imagined how often they encountered this kind of situation, but she also found an unexpected connection to the difficult person in the encounter. She had assumed all kinds of things about the person who had acted out, but because of our training around deep listening and compassion, she discovered a new side to this person and helped to reshape the person's attitude to fit better with the group. Everyone won!

Tips for Leaders: Managing Group Dynamics

As in any social setting, it is possible for small groups to be dominated by one or more people. Still, people are not always aware that they are making the facilitation of a group difficult. It happens at least once or twice a year that a group includes a member who takes up too much time or unloads all their emotional baggage on the group such that it turns into a therapy session. Compiled by Temple Emanu-El in Dallas, Texas, here are four examples of small-group "hijacker" behaviors and how group leaders can address them.

The Talking Hijacker

This is the person who answers every question before anyone else can respond. While most of the members of the small group are still pondering the question, the talking hijacker is spurting out a response. Though you may be grateful for the liveliness and contributions, the talking hijacker leaves the group with a sense that no one else has a chance to respond. Instead of drawing other people out, the talking hijacker makes people want to withdraw. What needs to be said after it feels like everything has already been said?

Taking Control from the Talking Hijacker

First, try to pull the person aside one-to-one. Thank the person for contributing, but be honest about the need for others to contribute. Encourage the person to only respond to every other or every third question and to keep responses brief. Or encourage the person to allow two or three other people to share before sharing. If the talking hijacker still can't help him- or herself, you may need to structure your discussions differently. Set up this ground rule for the next session: you'll be calling on specific people to respond to questions. This will encourage the quieter person while deterring the talkative one.

The Emotional Hijacker

This small-group member shows up every week with an emotional crisis. Before you know it, the majority of the gathering is spent trying to unravel the problem, and the majority of time and energy is spent on the emotional hijacker.

Taking Control from the Emotional Hijacker

One way to deal with an emotional hijacker is to take the person out to coffee or lunch. Once this person has space to share everything going on in life, he or she may not need as much of the small group's time to share. Spending more one-to-one time may also allow you to better understand the person's needs. Depending on the situation, you may be able to suggest a visit with a clergy or staff member. At the next gathering, if the person tries to hijack the group with another crisis, reemphasize the *brit* and remind the small group that the purpose of the meeting needs to focus on the learning at hand. This will allow you to get through the material and still allow the person to share within a more limited time constraint.

The Backseat Driver Hijacker

This hijacker gives you constant directions on how to best guide the group. The backseat driver assumes he or she has the best approach to guiding and frequently mentions past leadership positions. The other members don't know who to listen to: you or the hijacker.

Taking Control from the Backseat Driver Hijacker

Talking directly with the backseat driver will take courage, but it's the quickest way to get results. Sift through his or her comments to see if you can glean anything helpful. Sometimes there will be good suggestions that can benefit the group. If so, mention these helpful suggestions in your conversation, which will keep the atmosphere positive. Tell how you appreciate his or her willingness to share leadership skills, and then politely ask the backseat driver to stop doing so at the small-group meetings. Let the backseat driver know that sharing these ideas during the meeting promotes conflict in the group. Affirm the hijacker by asking for input (at a one-to-one meeting) when you feel you need it and by offering to listen to suggestions outside of meetings. At the same time, confirm that you are leading in a way that suits your personality and leadership style, noting that it may be different from the hijacker's. If the hijacker makes another comment in a small-group meeting, respond by saying, "Let's talk about that suggestion outside of our gathering."

The Late Hijacker

Without fail, this person walks into the Temple Connect Group meeting late. You've spent twenty minutes building momentum toward a specific point, and right before you ask the most important question the late hijacker bursts in. The entrance disrupts the group, and you can't get the group's attention again. The momentum and focus are lost.

Taking Control from the Late Hijacker

Approach the late hijacker privately and encourage this person to make a better effort to be on time. Explain how it's hard to get the group refocused once everybody is distracted. If the person can't get there any earlier, encourage them to enter more quietly and sensitively.

There are likely other kinds of hijackers one might encounter in small-group life; we have just tried to outline some common ones here. But no matter the type, it can be challenging to confront a fellow member with critique. The opportunity, though, is to ask open-ended questions and get to know someone you might not usually spend the time getting to know.

Beta Mode as a New Norm

We reminded participants at almost every leader training that we are still at the beginning of creating something different inside of a synagogue. We hope that this notion gets our leaders and coaches excited about being a part of a bigger picture that will allow the efforts to ripple into the future, but we also believe in instilling an ethic of experimentation. With as much at stake in synagogue life as there is, we nonetheless believe that core to the process of small groups is a sense that we are constantly in beta mode, testing our hypotheses and making changes and adjustments as needed. Our world today changes much too quickly to rely on any one major new initiative with a major rollout and a process set in stone. Instead, we start new ideas as pilots, test the process on a small group of people first, make tweaks, and then roll it out to a larger and larger group. In this way, the small-groups work is constantly evolving, even as our main goals remain the same.

One huge help has been the participating synagogue's partnership with Union for Reform Judaism's Community of Practice: Small Groups Cohort. Through the leadership of Lila Foldes and Rabbi Esther Lederman, we learned with a cohort of other synagogues doing this work, such that we could benefit from each other's thinking and piloting. We have shared best practices, curricula, and, most importantly, encouragement and motivation. Having other communities in a cohort meant for sharing ideas and materials makes all the difference, especially after the first year or two when the novelty is in danger of wearing off and the harder, long-term work settles in.

Case Study

Rabbi K'vod Wieder, rabbi, Temple Beth El of South Orange County, Aliso Viejo, California

At Temple Beth El of South Orange County, our board and leadership led our congregation through a series of focus meetings to determine what our priorities should be over the next five years. Top on the list was "building relationships." Through his book *Relational Judaism*, Ron Wolfson helped us turn our attention to the reality that meaningful experiences in Jewish community occur through our connections with each other and that we need to make opportunities for those connections a priority for our synagogues.

When my colleague and friend Rabbi Elie Spitz invited me to meet with the folks at Saddleback Church to learn more about small groups, and when I read *Small Groups with Purpose*, written by Saddleback small-groups pastor Steven Gladen, this model inspired me as a vehicle for creating a more relational community as a whole, not just another programmatic offering. While the engine to get people involved in small groups is a program, called a "campaign," the overall intention is for the relationships that people build through the campaign to endure beyond it.

At Temple Beth El, our first campaign was a series of six small group meetings in people's homes to discuss "How Our Relationships Can Help Us Live More Fully." For each meeting, one person chose to host, which simply meant opening their home, playing a video, serving a snack, and creating space for a discussion. My co-rabbinic partner Rabbi Rachel Kort and I prepared six videos where we spoke about different aspects of the topic and then had a discussion booklet, which supplemented our talk with Jewish texts and questions to stimulate discussion. We strove to make the questions not just intellectual but also personal, so that people had the opportunity to know each other better.

For our second year, our topic is "Discovering Peace through Embracing Uncertainty." It features four videos of us speaking about different aspects of the topic and a discussion booklet. This topic was drawn from Estelle Frankel's book *The Wisdom of Not Knowing*, which we invite people to read to deepen their engagement with the topic, but reading the book is not necessary to participation in the group.

A few points that are important to the success of our small-groups campaign:

1. We chose topics that every person can relate to, that hit at the heart of what it means to be human. While we will use Jewish wisdom and teachings to provide our tradition's perspective on the topic, we do not lead with the Jewish content; we lead with the human content.

2. Since we do not have professional group facilitation for our forty-plus groups, we needed to create a structure where a group of people could have a successful experience. Creating the videos allows us as rabbis to provide the content that engages people and roots the conversation in Jewish tradition. We also encourage people to use the think/pair/share model in order to make sure that everyone has a chance to speak and be heard. Whenever a discussion question is posed, group members first take some quiet time to think about the topic. Then they pair up with another person to share their responses and be heard, and then they come back to the big group to engage in discussion.

3. In order for people to be willing to sign up and be a host, they need to know how little is asked of them. They need no expertise and no preparation. The materials help with their confidence, but we also have engaged a group of congregants at

the beginning of the campaign as community leaders—people who have some experience in group facilitation who will be mentors and be present for questions or challenges hosts may face. Each community leader is assigned a few hosts, and they check in with them periodically to offer support.

At the end of the small-groups campaign period (six to eight weeks), we invite all participants to a Shabbat dinner at the synagogue to share experiences and be inspired. At our first culmination dinner, the overwhelming feedback from the participants was that they made meaningful connections with congregants they did not know and were able to know their friends on a deeper level.

Also at the end of the campaign period, we give congregants other options and opportunities to continue with their small groups. For those who enjoy intellectual discussion, we propose a subsequent book with questions to continue their conversations. We give congregants opportunities for social action projects with their small groups. We propose attending events at the synagogue with their small group, such as our annual fundraising gala, comedy night, or second-night Passover seder. These opportunities allow congregants to connect with the larger synagogue community under the safety of their small group with whom they already feel comfortable. We have also created a "Bringing Home Shabbat" Friday night, where we do not hold services and instead give people Shabbat table materials for meeting in their homes. Congregants can meet with existing small groups or form new ones for this Friday evening experience.

Participants do not have to continue in their small group at the conclusion of the campaign. People are more likely to sign up when they are not committing their social life away to a group they don't know. They are more willing to experiment with a new group of people if they have the easy option to leave after a fixed time period. Sometimes groups coalesce and want to stay together. They turn into a *havurah* of sorts. However, we find that even people who had great group experiences in the first campaign period want to try a new group and meet new people for the next one.

We are noticing a culture change here at Temple Beth El. Not only are people making themselves available for these small-groups opportunities, but they are also willing to expand their circles, make room for new people, and make themselves available to people they don't know. From my perspective, this is the environment that we want to create in our synagogue communities. Torah is something that needs to be discovered in relationship, in community. Our tradition is not based on the insight of one holy person like a Jesus or a Buddha. Torah was given at Sinai—we stand together as an entire community, "as one people, with one heart," as Rashi teaches. When I witness our congregation coming together in different configurations to learn and share, open and welcoming to each other, I know we are fulfilling the purpose for which we were created.

Takeaways

Small groups are lay led by design. So the quality of the training and support for your leaders is paramount. Among the most important aspects is building a strong core team to help you oversee the entire effort. These key members may also serve as coaches to your small-groups leaders. You will also want to train your group leaders, helping them overcome perceived barriers to leadership and giving them concrete tools to help them lead.

By creating a broad system with many ways for members to get involved, you will also create new pipelines for leadership that will offer your community more trained and willing leaders interested in getting involved in other parts of your organization.

You might consider the following questions:

What should the qualifications be to become a small-groups leader? A coach?

What do you want them to get out of the experience?

You will want to make sure they are comfortable with the basics of group facilitation. Do you have experts in group facilitation in your community who might be able to help with training?

Our Next Steps

1. Who would be great group leaders and great coaches for our small-groups initiative?

_____

_____

2. What do we need in order to train and support them?

_____

_____

_____

Grand-Scale Relationship-Building Strategies

Small groups are not the only way to encourage your members to connect to one another. The possibilities for relational programming are endless, and your choices will depend on the particular needs and resources of your community. Here we highlight just a few ideas to spur your imagination.

Age and Stage–Based Medium Groups

At The Temple, we developed "Age and Stage" groups: eight medium-sized groups of twenty-five to fifty people that enable people to get to know one another in their own demographic. The Age and Stage initiative divides participants in the following ways:

Young Families (families with children ages five and younger)

K through Second Grade Families

Third through Fifth Grade Families

Post–B'nai Mitzvah families (which include sixth through twelfth graders)

Young Professionals (postcollege, pre-children)

Kulanu (meaning literally "All of Us," which encompasses our families without children, singles over forty years old, empty nesters, early retirees)

Sages (seventy-two years old and older)

Many families include people in different Age and Stage groups; they self-select which group they would like to be included in. Leaders include one staff member who oversees the initiative and two or three *roshim* ("heads" or "leads")—lay people in each demographic. They program for their peers—social events, learning events, social action events—and take on the role of host at all events. They make sure that people are mingling and talking, and they keep an eye out for the people standing alone to make sure they are included to the degree they feel comfortable. The *roshim* also play an integral role in our welcoming new members. When new members join, they get phone calls and emails from a range of people, including the senior rabbi, executive director, president, and others, depending on their potential interests. (For example, when an interfaith couple joins The Temple, our membership coordinator sends an email to the chair of our Interfaith Committee, who then reaches out on behalf of the committee to invite them to their next event or even just a conversation about learning to navigate the complexities that sometimes arise for these valued families.) Most importantly, though, they get a phone call from their Age and Stage *rosh*, asking them to coffee, answering questions, and making connections that are more easily made with others in the same demographic.

Age and Stage groups allow people to get to know one another at their own pace and level of commitment. One can attend one or all the Age and Stage events in a year, with nothing more asked of them. People enjoy the events because they are planned by their peers, and they love attending because they know that they will meet nice people. From the synagogue's perspective, we see these groups as on-ramps into small groups.

Spotlight on Best Practice

I (LM) have seen our Age and Stage initiative work like magic as an on-ramp into life at The Temple. There was one woman who had been a Temple member for years and could identify a couple of High Holy Day friends, but she has not been an active participant in The Temple for years. Shortly after losing her husband, she decided it was time to see how The Temple might help ward off the too-quiet weekends. She was shy but finally got enough courage to attend a Kulanu event. There she was welcomed warmly by the *rosh* and introduced to new people. She immediately felt included. She met the leader of a Temple Connect group, who recruited her to join his group, Gourmet Cooking. Over the next few months, she joined two groups, and her calendar was quickly filled. But more than that, she says that she is now surrounded by a group of caring and loving people with whom she comes to services and for whom she now cares a great deal. She would have never found these soul mates in her same age and stage had we not provided an easy way to meet them.

We realize that small groups may not be for every person. While we try to keep the bar of entry as low as possible, our members may not have the time to invest or the inclination to commit to a group of unknown individuals, no matter how much they love a given affinity. But they may still desire to connect with new people in a low-key, relaxed setting.

Spotlight on Best Practice

I (RW) and my wife, Susie, were invited by our children, Havi and Dave, to accompany our grandchildren, Ellie and Gabe, on a Disney Cruise Line seven-day excursion in the Caribbean that turned into a remarkable experience in relational engagement. In her online research into blogs about Disney cruises, Havi had discovered something called "fish exchanges," an initiative by Disney cruise veterans to create small groups among the four thousand passengers on the cruise ship *Disney Fantasy*.

Before you begin to imagine real fish being exchanged between passengers, permit me to explain. Attached to each cabin door on a Disney ship is a metal clip in the shape of a fish that acts as a kind of letter holder for notes and flyers from the activities staff. When you return to your cabin after evening programs, there are usually envelopes with notes from the cruise director, a schedule for the next day's activities, and personalized reminders of upcoming reservations in restaurants or appointments in the spa, all placed in the "fish" on your door.

On one of the early Disney cruises through the Panama Canal in 2005, Debbie Chitester, a passenger, gave her friends handmade receptacles—think felt mailboxes—to hang from the fish clips as a kind of "extender" in which to collect these notes. Before long, the idea emerged to place small gifts in the extenders—and *voila*—thus was born the idea of the fish exchange.

Here's how it works: Passengers organize Facebook pages for their specific cruise sailing date. Our cruise page ultimately had more than four hundred individuals in the group. Someone, usually a veteran fish exchanger, organizes the four hundred into small groups of ten to twelve cabins. Our small group was called "The Dead Men Tell No Tales Group 10." About a month before the cruise, we received a spreadsheet that listed the cabin number, the names of the adults and names and ages of the children in the cabin, a few words about each person's favorite Disney characters, special celebrations, any allergies, and an email address. Then you begin to create or buy small gifts to give to each person or family in your small group.

Since Susie is one of the world's greatest gift givers—always searching for just the right gift and card—she took on this task as if preparing for Hanukkah. For example, she saw that Chad and Kim Burrus in Cabin 10526 loved the classic Disney film *Lady and the Tramp*. She went online and discovered a company that cuts out single frames from 35mm prints of old Disney movies and creates bookmarks with them. Susie knew this would be a creative and sensational gift for these folks we had never met. But, importantly, we knew something personal about them that would help us find a memorable gift. Other gifts were things such as Disney sticker books Susie found at the dollar store. All told, there were forty individual gifts, each beautifully wrapped with their names and our names attached. We actually shipped two boxes of these gifts to the Disney cruise terminal a week before departure.

Then we needed a "fish extender." Well, it turns out that creative folks on Etsy will make a personalized one for you, complete with pockets for each person in the family. We simply hung ours on the fish clip when we arrived on board, and sure enough, before the first night was over, we had gifts placed in our extender. Susie dispatched me to distribute our gifts to each of the eleven cabins on the first night, although we received our gifts on different days of the cruise, always delighting us when we returned to the cabin. Havi reports that Ellie and Gabe could not wait to run back to their cabin to see what surprises were in their extender pockets. We had a few extra sticker books that Havi suggested we anonymously place in any cabin that had a fish extender, a practice known as "pixie-dusting."

We did meet some of our group members while delivering the gifts and a few others at an announced gathering in one of the ship's lounges on the first afternoon of the cruise, but there were so many parallel activities at any one moment, it was nearly impossible to gather the entire group at one time. Interestingly, the fish exchanges were developed by the passengers, not Disney, as a way for them to "add to the magic," as one blogger put it.

I, of course, immediately thought of ways this concept could be used in Jewish organizations. Imagine a synagogue or JCC encouraging members to form small groups for exchanging *mishloach manot* at Purim or a gift exchange at Hanukkah, perhaps by zip code, a good example of groups organized by geography. It could be a terrific and fun way for strangers to engage each other.

Spotlight on Best Practice

Havi Wolfson Hall, LCSW, child and adolescent therapist, Parents Place, Palo Alto, California

When my husband, Dave, and I moved to the Silicon Valley, we were eager to find a warm and welcoming community for us and for our children. At first it was difficult, but then I remembered how my grandfather, Abe, had found his community at the JCC in Omaha, Nebraska. So we enrolled our daughter, Ellie, and our son, Gabe, in the preschool of the Oshman Family Jewish Community Center (OFJCC) in Palo Alto, California, and we found what we were looking for, mostly due to an early childhood educator who understood the power of small groups.

Her name is Shuly Paret, the director of the "Mommy and Me" program at OFJCC, which she calls "Yad b'Yad" (Hand in Hand). When I first expressed interest, Shuly immediately called on the phone to invite me for coffee and a tour during which she listened empathetically to our story and concerns, and guided us to the class that was right for our toddlers. With enthusiasm and passion, she encouraged us to join her one-and-a-half-hour class where her "mommies and babies" enjoy wonderful crafts, activities, stories, holiday celebrations, and a very special Kabbalat Shabbat every week.

What makes Shuly truly exceptional is not only her warm embrace of the children at the front gates of the preschool but also her warm embrace of the group she lovingly calls her "Beautiful Mamas." I expected the sharing of parenting tips. But I did not anticipate Shuly's insistence that we Mamas gather together for experiences outside the classroom. She helped us organize Shabbat dinners, a weekend retreat for our families, and nudged us Mamas to get together for a "Girl's Night Out." The result of the sharing in class and these experiences created connections between the Mamas that resulted in our own very tight small group that is still going strong, years after our children have graduated the preschool.

We Mamas go to concerts, take trips, run 10K races, and organize an annual camping expedition for our families. We continue to celebrate our children's birthdays—and our own birthdays!—even though we now have our kids in different elementary schools. We celebrate many of the Jewish holidays together. We have truly become BFFs, best friends forever.

For this, we have Shuly and the Jewish Community Center to thank. To this day, when we visit the preschool to see younger siblings, there is Shuly at the front gate, with her infectious smile and open arms as our children run to her squealing her name: "SHULY!" And we, her Beautiful Mamas, we exchange hugs of gratitude with her for launching our small group we have grown to love and depend on.

Spotlight on Best Practice

Melissa Balaban, founder and executive director, IKAR, Los Angeles, California

The Megillah reminds us that everything we know to be true can change in a heartbeat. Laughter turns to tears, grief turns to celebration. On Purim we respond to life's preciousness and capriciousness with both abject silliness and a renewed commitment to social connectedness and social transformation; we send sweet gifts (*mishloach manot*) to family and friends and give generously to the poor (*matanot l'evyonim*). At IKAR, we create *mishloach manot* to evoke how both precious and precarious life is.

In the past, our themes have included the following:

Life turns upside down. Everything we know to be true can turn on its head, in an instant, so embrace life's messiness and impermanence with love, gratitude, and a renewed commitment to social transformation.

Honoring everything and its shadow side.

Getting to gratitude: one hundred blessings a day.

Embracing spiritual mobility in times of unpredictability to cultivate humility, patience, and generosity in their place.

The four things that matter most: Please forgive me. I forgive you. Thank you. I love you.

IKAR staff and volunteers carefully curate, create, and assemble over nine hundred packages based on the above themes to send to our members, friends, donors, and colleagues around the country and internationally.

For those in Los Angeles, we devised a strategy to ensure that each package is delivered to everyone's door. Since IKAR members and friends are spread throughout Los Angeles County, we use Google Custom Maps and then Route4Me to group our local members and friends into neighborhood clusters and then easily navigable routes. We recruit dozens of volunteers, at least one in each neighborhood, to personally deliver each package. This creates a sense of community and alerts community members to meet fellow IKARites who may live on the same street. It also inspires them to deepen their relationships with their fellow IKARite neighbors by having neighborhood Shabbat dinners and other social activities.

Technology

We would be remiss if we did not mention the potential that technology holds in helping us connect with one another. While even the most tech-savvy among us would admit that face-to-face interaction must serve as the basis of our connections, technology affords us the luxury of continuing to strengthen and deepen relationships beyond real life. We have seen Facebook groups and Google groups used to help group members keep up with their shared calendars, pictures, events, and each other, as group members reflect together on past meetings and look forward to the next one. Central Synagogue's religious school has an active Facebook group through which the synagogue can send announcements but also so that parents can share photos of their children enjoying their learning and one another.

Organizations use customer relational management (CRM) programs to keep track of anniversaries, birthdays, and *yahrzeit*; our Relational Engagement Campaign may lead us to ask ourselves, "How can we wish each member a happy birthday?" or "Does my database provide each member the ability to reach out to one another on their own?" Technology can be used to determine meeting dates and times. Doodle.com has been especially helpful and simple to use in this regard, and there are a few free websites from which one can choose. We can also use video conferencing technology to facilitate face-to-face meetings when in-person meetings may be too onerous or impossible for any number of reasons. We like Zoom, which comes with a fee but is reliable and relatively straightforward to use.

At The Temple, one group of young professionals met in person three times over the seven-week course of the counting of the Omer, but they met each week in between via video conferencing. They reported feeling so close to one another with this combination of in-person and online meeting that one woman felt comfortable enough to come out as a lesbian for the first time, another woman could not wait to tell this group of her engagement, and another woman found incredible support when her father died unexpectedly. The group would not have been possible without the use of technology, as even the leader of the group traveled for work on a regular basis and would not have been able to host or attend in person. Technology can be daunting for any of us less native to it but it holds enormous possibilities if we keep an open mind and if it serves our communities without burdening them with yet another app to check.

A synagogue leader asks me (RW): "What about the uses of technology? And Facebook? What do you think of our live-streaming worship services? Isn't it a double-edged sword? On the one hand, there are people who truly cannot get to the synagogue on a Friday night. On the other hand, why come at all if I can watch the service at home in my pajamas?"

My answer: "Look, my daughter, Havi, an expert in what she calls 'e-healthy relationships,' has convinced me that Facebook is a real community. Facebook friends are there for each other, not just to share the photos of what they ate or where they traveled. They are there when a friend is ill or a parent dies or a birthday is celebrated. Watching a service online can be wonderful, but—let's be honest—if you wanted to experience a concert with a favorite artist, there is a big difference from watching it on a screen and being there live. Same thing with worship services. Because at a great worship service or a great program at the JCC, you not only have the learning and the affect, but you also have the social component, especially if you've done a good job creating connections between your members. Even shopping malls that are competing against Amazon are looking for value-added experiences that you cannot get online—playgrounds for the kids, destination restaurants, all sorts of immersive experiences. In the era of Facebook, Netflix, and Amazon, the value offer of a Jewish institution—synagogue, JCC, Federation, Hillel, school, or other organization—must be face-to-face relationships with people who care about you and for you and will be there with you in good times and bad."

Case Study

Rachel Gildiner, executive director, GatherDC

GatherDC is exclusively dedicated to connecting Jewish people in their twenties and thirties to each other, to DC Jewish life, and to a sustainable adult Jewish identity wherever they go next. We partner with and support other Jewish organizations targeting millennials and work to enhance the overall eco-system of Jewish millennial engagement, leading to a stronger and more vibrant DC Jewish community. With over six thousand personal "touches" across the city, and deepening these relationships each day, we are committed to helping every Jewish twenty- and thirty-something find their Jewish people, place, and path.

We profoundly believe that a lasting community is built and strengthened through meaningful, authentic one-to-one relationships. We spend our days delving deep into the art and science of relationship-based engagement as the fundamental way to create and sustain a rich Jewish community for millennials in DC and beyond.

Through our experience, we find that many organizations, when caught in the ambitious, arduous, and sincere quest to create strong Jewish communities, risk losing site of the core building blocks to a vibrant community—people. We acknowledge and empathize with the reality of this risk due to the vast time, financial resources, and energy that go into building individual relationships. However, our work evidently demonstrates the extraordinary success that a tenacious focus on relationship building can have on the present—and future—of Jewish life for people in their twenties and thirties.

As we define it, relationship-based engagement sets aside the traditional, top-down approach to Jewish community and builds a system of engagement composed of multiple, equal networks of personal connections that your organization helps foster. It is the act of reaching others, getting to know them in small or one-to-one settings, and connecting with them on the basis of their interests, ambitions, and passions. This type of engagement seeks to understand each member of our community and helps them discover offerings and experiences that meet them where they are. Each step of the way, the personal relationship is prioritized over the program.

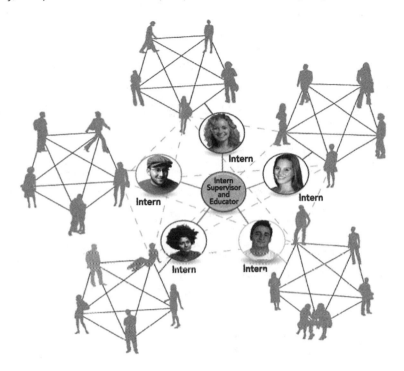

For example, when Jeremy Lustig arrived in DC at the age of twenty-three, he felt overwhelmed by the Jewish offerings and unsure about where to find his new Jewish home. Nostalgic for college, lonely in a journey to find new friends, and lost in such a big city, finding his place and people in Jewish DC seemed like an impossible task. Then he noticed a Facebook advertisement that spoke to him: "Questioning your Jewish identity? Want to get out of DC for a week and meet others searching for their place in Jewish life? Apply for GatherDC's Beyond the Tent retreat to start exploring your Jewish self." With seemingly nothing to lose, he immediately applied for Beyond the Tent, an immersive GatherDC weekend retreat that brings together forty DC-area young adults to think critically about their personal Jewish identity, meet close friends, and find a place to belong in the Jewish community. On this retreat, Jeremy was not just an addition to the attendance roster but rather a person with incredible insight to offer and a vivacious personality to share. By the program's making time for Jeremy to have in-depth conversations with the other participants and ensuring the staff spent energy getting to know him on a personal basis, Jeremy left the retreat having made incredible friends with fellow attendees and GatherDC staff, solidifying a welcoming space for him to belong in the Jewish community.

After the retreat, GatherDC staff made sure to follow up with Jeremy and other Beyond the Tent alumni on a regular basis, making them feel cared about as a valued individual in Jewish DC. GatherDC staff reached out with emails referring to inside jokes or valuable learning material based on discussions had on the retreat. Our staff asked Jeremy to meet for coffee and continued to build an intentional one-to-one relationship with him over the years. GatherDC's investment in the personal relationship helped Jeremy find his home in Washington. He explains, "Today, I attend weekly learning sessions with Rabbi Aaron Potek (GatherDC's community rabbi), served as a facilitator on a later Beyond the Tent retreat, and just led a GatherDC Jewish spirituality camping trip to Shenandoah National Park. Through GatherDC, I've met most of my friends, and gained the foundation to be a leader in the community."

GatherDC strongly believes that any organization can adopt core relationship-based practices that will deeply engage the members of the Jewish community they serve, just like Jeremy. The challenges and successes of our work have led us to adhere to the following best practices surrounding individual relationship building. We encourage you to try out a few—or all—of these in your journey toward a people-first engagement model.

Always start with people first. Ask "Who," not "What." Who is this experience for? Who will likely not attend? How do we know this will serve our community? Who can we think of who would be perfect to attend?

- *Pro Tip:* Have your organization invest in a network/community mapping process. Map the different communities and segments of people you serve and who you don't currently reach but would like to. How are these individuals connected to one another, and who are your influencers who are connected to multiple groups? (GatherDC has a workshop by request to guide you through this process.)

Meet them where they are physically, emotionally, and Jewishly. Leave your agenda at the door. Engagement is *not* recruitment.

- *Pro Tip:* After mapping, make an effort to reach those networks out of your building and at times of day when those people are available.

- *Pro Tip:* Don't have a prescribed way in mind that you think they should connect. Ask questions, listen, be open to deeply listening to their stories and hearing their own questions and experiences. Understand that you may walk out of the conversation realizing they would be a great fit for something or somewhere else, and then help them connect to that.

Programs are a means to an end, not an end in themselves. The goal for Jewish programming should be to build meaningful relationships with and among attendees. The goal should not be solely to have a high number of attendees.

- *Pro Tip:* Assign (and train!) one or more staff members or volunteers as greeters and engagers/schmoozers. This person(s) will spend the entire event greeting people warmly, making sure that no one is alone, and fostering connections between and among attendees.

- *Pro Tip:* Let attendees know who the event greeter/schmoozer will be leading up to the event by putting the person's name and/or photo on pre-event communications and offering to connect with them in advance of the event itself.

Make big communities feel smaller.

- *Pro Tip:* Even at larger events, create space for attendees to have in-depth discussion with one another in pairs or small groups.

- *Pro Tip:* When appropriate, always include name tags to ease introductions and recognition. If possible, have your greeter be able to attach faces to names so they recognize and can greet people by name when they arrive.

Follow-up after every interaction is even more important than any program itself. Focus your energy on building a replicable communications and personal outreach strategy to stay in touch with event attendees for the future. Attendees should feel valued, cared about, and missed when you don't see them.

- *Pro Tip:* Follow-up strategies can include phone calls, personal emails mentioning something specific you spoke about, coffee dates, early invites to future events, sharing photos from the event on social media, and so forth. Constant contact and mass communications are one part, but include individual and personal reach-outs on a regular basis as well.

- *Pro Tip:* Survey attendees after events to understand their thoughts and suggestions, then implement them! Always stay cognizant of unique, alternative ways to enrich programming so offerings reflect what the attendees want.

Assign and train a staff member or volunteer at your organization to be responsible for relationship building year-round.

- *Pro Tip:* This person should *not* be in a stewardship or development role.

Every part of your organization must reflect the people-first model of engagement. From the website navigation to the social media tone to the email strategy to the event icebreakers—a relationship-based way of thinking must infuse each aspect of your work.

- *Pro Tip:* When creating a social media post or writing an email from your organization, read it from your constituents' point of view before sharing. Ensure it comes across as welcoming, relatable, and engaging.

Make Jewish content relevant, authentic, and accessible. Jewish adults are trying to answer questions of meaning that have potential implications for their everyday lives: Who am I? What do I value and believe? What does community mean and look like to me? How do I live a life independent from my parents? What is my relationship with Judaism, and why does it matter to me?

- *Pro Tip:* Don't run away from depth. Jewish people in their twenties and thirties don't "show up" for many reasons, including inaccessibility of programs and lack of overt value propositions. Start each program from the question of "Why" instead of assuming that there is inherent value in a program simply because it brings Jewish people together. Education is in itself an engagement tool.

The work of your organization must always maintain the big picture—building strong, vibrant Jewish communities—front of mind. Your organization must see itself as a part of the collective whole of local and national Jewish organizations. Consider ways to work together synergistically to achieve a greater shared goal, even if you each approach that work differently. Your success should be each other's success.

- *Pro Tip:* Consider hosting regular, collaborative professional learning opportunities together to share best practices and explore ways to partner with one another.

Investing in people will take time, financial resources, energy, and staff. Put it at the top of your strategic plan this coming year. It is worth it!

As a part of our commitment to a people-first model, we encourage you to reach out to GatherDC's executive director Rachel Gildiner (rachelg@gatherdc.org), if you have questions about these concepts, would like additional training resources, or simply want to brainstorm ideas.

End Note

> What really matters is that we care about the people we
> seek to engage. When we genuinely care about people,
> we will not only welcome them; we will listen to their
> stories, we will share ours, and we will join together to build
> a Jewish community that enriches our lives.
>
> *Relational Judaism*, pages 4–5

I (RW) believe Jewish communal life is not about programs, marketing, branding, labels, logos, clever titles, websites, or smartphone apps.
After fifty years of teaching in the Jewish community, I have come to
an understanding about the essence of Judaism and, by extension, the
essential challenge and opportunity of engaging our people: *it's all about
relationships.*

Since *Relational Judaism* was published in 2013, I have been heart-
ened by the extraordinary response of Jewish community leaders, both lay
and professional. Many boards, clergy, and executives have read the book
and discussed the ideas together. They have asked for a "handbook"—a
step-by-step guide to creating and implementing a Relational Engagement
Campaign—and this is a first effort to create one. How fortunate that so
many Jewish organizations have taken the early first steps to experiment
with twenty-first-century engagement strategies and how wonderful that
they have shared their best practices and case studies with us. And how
wonderful it is for me to have partnered with two exceptional rabbis,
Lydia Medwin and Nicole Auerbach, who are on the front lines of the
small-groups movement in Jewish organizational life.

All three of us believe deeply in the power of relationships to transform the Jewish community. We have seen and lived what the Psalmist taught—"How good and how pleasing it is when we all live *yachad*—in relationship together" (133:1). For it is in our relationships that we find each other and discover the essence of Judaism and the presence of God.

When you have implemented the ideas presented in this book, you will experience the blessings of close personal relationships within a Jewish community. You will discover that Judaism can indeed offer you a path to a life of meaning, purpose, belonging, and blessing.

We stand ready to help. You don't have to do this alone. We have created a website for *The Relational Judaism Handbook*—relationaljudaismhandbook.com—where you will find sample testimonials, engagement resources, and training guides. We also invite you to share strategies and ideas. We encourage you to find a Relational Engagement Campaign *hevruta*—a colleague with whom you can share your successes and challenges. And we are happy to correspond with you via email:

Ron: ronwolfson1234@gmail.com

Lydia: lydia.medwin@gmail.com

Nicole: nicole@auerbach.net

Now the task is to join together with others to engage them into relationship with you and your leadership, with each other, and with a twenty-first-century Relational Judaism that can transform our lives.

Kadimah! Go forth! God bless you!

Ron, Nicole, and Lydia

For Further Learning

For additional materials, please visit relationaljudaismhandbook.com. If you would like to explore site visits, individualized consulting, or other presentations for help in taking the next steps toward your own Relational Engagement Campaign, email us at rjhandbook@gmail.com.

Books

Block, Peter. *Community: The Structure of Belonging*. Oakland, CA: Berrett-Koehler, 2009.

Disney Institute, with Theodore Kinni. *Be Our Guest: Perfecting the Art of Customer Service*. New York: Disney Editions, 2011.

Donahue, Bill, and Russ Robinson. *Building a Life-Changing Small Group Ministry: A Strategic Guide for Leading Group Life in Your Church*. Grand Rapids, MI: Zondervan, 2012.

Donahue, Bill, and Russ Robinson. *Walking the Small Group Tightrope: Meeting the Challenges Every Group Faces*. Grand Rapids, MI: Zondervan, 2003.

Gladen, Steve. *Small Groups with Purpose: How to Create Healthy Communities*. Grand Rapids, MI: Baker Books, 2013.

Gladen, Steve. *Leading Small Groups with Purpose: Everything You Need to Lead a Healthy Group*. Grand Rapids, MI: Baker Books, 2013.

Michelli, Joseph. *The New Gold Standard: 5 Leadership Principles for Creating a Legendary Customer Service Experience Courtesy of the Ritz-Carlton Hotel Company*. New York: McGraw Hill Education, 2008.

Schwarz, Sid. *Finding a Spiritual Home: How a New Generation of Jews Can Transform the American Synagogue*. Woodstock, VT: Jewish Lights Publishing, 2000.

Spector, Robert, and Patrick D. McCarthy. *The Nordstrom Way to Customer Service Excellence*. New York: Wiley, 2012.

Spitz, Elie Kaplan. *Increasing Wholeness: Jewish Wisdom and Guided Meditations to Strengthen and Calm Body, Heart, Mind and Soul*. Woodstock, VT: Jewish Lights Publishing, 2015.

Turkle, Sherry. *Alone Together: Why We Expect More from Technology and Less from Each Other*. Revised ed. New York: Basic Books, 2017.

Uram, Mike. *Next Generation Judaism: How College Students and Hillel Can Help Reinvent Jewish Organizations*. Woodstock, VT: Jewish Lights Publishing, 2016.

Warren, Rick. *The Purpose-Driven Church*. Grand Rapids, MI: Zondervan, 2002.

Weinzweig, Ari. *Zingerman's Guide to Giving Great Service*. New York: Hyperion, 2004.

Wolfson, Ron. *Relational Judaism: Using the Power of Relationships to Transform the Jewish Community*. Woodstock, VT: Jewish Lights Publishing, 2013.

Wolfson, Ron. *The Seven Questions You're Asked in Heaven: Reviewing and Renewing Your Life on Earth*. Woodstock, VT: Jewish Lights Publishing, 2009.

Wolfson, Ron. *The Spirituality of Welcoming: How to Transform Your Synagogue into a Sacred Community*. Woodstock, VT: Jewish Lights Publishing, 2006.

Online Resources

Ask Big Questions

www.askbigquestions.org

Ask Big Questions c/o Hillel International
800 8th St. NW
Washington, DC 20001

Email: info@askbigquestions.org

A national initiative dedicated to improving civic learning and engagement through reflective conversations about questions that matter to everyone.

Ben Franklin Meets Pirkei Avot

www.benfranklincircles.org/jewish-toolkit

Ben Franklin Circles
Bronfman Center for Jewish Life
92nd Street Y
1395 Lexington Avenue
New York, NY 10128

Email form at https://benfranklincircles.org/connect

A project of 92Y, Ben Franklin Circles are secular "small groups" that bring people together to explore thirteen key virtues embraced by Benjamin Franklin. Their "Ben Franklin Meets Pirkei Avot" materials pair teachings of Franklin with those of the Jewish sages, offering an accessible entry point to small-groups discussion about Jewish and American ethics and values.

Central Syngaogue CORE Groups Resource Bank

www.centralsynagogue.org/engage/adult_engagement/core-groups/core-groups-resource-bank

Central Synagogue
123 East 55th St.
New York, NY 10022

Email: adultengagement@censyn.org

Central Synagogue has created and collected a wide range of discussion guides for small groups. All are free to use (with attribution).

Congregation B'nai Israel: Small Group Learning Resources

https://www.cbi18.org/small-group-learning/

Congregation B'nai Israel
2111 Bryan Ave.
Tustin, CA 92782

Email: cbi18@cbi18.org

Rabbi Elie Spitz (whose case study is featured in this book) has collected learning materials and other resources (including promotional materials) from Congregation B'nai Israel's small-groups initiative on CBI's website. These offer helpful examples of how to communicate the power of small groups to your organization.

"Relational Judaism" on Facebook

www.facebook.com/relationaljudaism

Ron Wolfson posts useful articles, videos, and links related to Relational Judaism online on Facebook. Follow him at the link above.

The Temple in Atlanta's Relational Question Bank

www.the-temple.org/relational-question-bank

The Temple
1589 Peachtree St. NE
Atlanta, GA 30309

Email: lmedwin@the-temple.org

This page offers a collection of "relational questions," which can be sent out to leaders of small groups to use during their meetings. These are a great way to invite members of "affinity" groups to get to know one another on a deeper level.

Notes

Shadow Baby

Also by Alison McGhee

Rainlight

Shadow Baby

by Alison McGhee

Picador USA
New York

www.picadorusa.com

Picador® is a U.S. registered trademark and is used by
St. Martin's Press under license from Pan Books Limited.

For information on Picador USA Reading Group Guides, as well as ordering,
please contact the Trade Marketing department at St. Martin's Press.
Phone: 1-800-221-7945 extension 763
Fax: 212-677-7456
E-mail: trademarketing@stmartins.com

Design by Susan Maksuta

ISBN 0-312-27529-3

First published in the United States by Harmony Books,
a member of the Crown Publishing Group, Random House, Inc.

First Picador USA Edition: July 2001

10 9 8 7 6 5 4 3 2 1

Dedication

This book is dedicated to Don and Gaby and Laurel and Holly and Doug, and to the sweet memories of Christine McGhee and Marty Walsh.

Acknowledgments

For lending her keen writer's eye to this book in its forma-
tive phase, not to mention every other draft I sent her way,
I thank fiction writer and friend Julie Schumacher.

My gratitude to Tom and Kitty Latané, of T&C Latané
Metalworking in Pepin, Wisconsin, for their generosity in
sharing with me a bit of their artistry in the ancient craft of
metalworking.

Devotion and thanks to Bill O'Brien, my lantern in
the darkness, for always being open to the possibility of
beauty, and to Ellen Harris Swiggett for the constancy of
her friendship.

Profound thanks to Shaye Areheart, editor extraordinaire,
and Doug Stewart, friend and agent, believers both in the art
of possibility.

PART ONE

In all metalworking operations, the workpiece is permanently deformed, sometimes very severely. A major object of metalworking theories is to permit prediction of the amount of deformation, and the forces required to produce this.

From *An Introduction to the Principles of Metalworking*

CHAPTER ONE

Now that the old man is gone, I think about him much of the time. I remember the first night I ever saw him. It was March, a year and a half ago. I was watching skiers pole through Nine Mile Woods on the Adirondack Ski Trail, black shapes moving through the trees like shadows or bats flying low. I watched from the churchhouse as my mother, Tamar, and the rest of the choir practiced in the Twin Churches sanctuary.

That was my habit back then. I was an observer and a watcher.

When the choir director lifted her arm for the first bar of the first hymn, I left and walked through the passageway that leads from the sanctuary to the churchhouse. The light that comes through stained-glass windows when the moon rises is a dark light. It makes the colors of stained glass bleed into each other in the shadows. A long time ago one of the Miller boys shot his BB gun through a corner of the stained-glass window in the back, near the kitchen. No one ever fixed it. The custodian cut a tiny piece of clear glass and puttied it into

the broken place. I may be the only person in the town of
Sterns, New York, who still remembers that there is one
stained-glass window in a corner of the Twin Churches
churchhouse that is missing a tiny piece of its original whole.

It's gone. It will never return.

That first night, the first time I ever saw the old man, I
dragged a folding chair over to that window and stood on it so
I could look through the tiny clear piece of patch-glass onto
the sloping banks of the Nine Mile Woods. Down below you
can see Nine Mile Creek, black and glittery. You would never
want to fall into it even though it's only a few feet deep.

I watched the old man in the woods that night. He held fire
in his bare hands. That's what it looked like at first, before I
realized it was an extralong fireplace match. Tamar and I do
not have a fireplace but still, I know what an extralong fireplace match looks like. I watched the old man for what
seemed like two hours, as long as the choir took to practice.
The moonlight turned him into a shadow amongst the trees,
until a small flame lit up a few feet from the ground. The
small flame rose in the air and swung from side to side,
swinging slower and slower until it stopped. Then I saw that it
was a lantern, hung in a tree. An old-time kind of lantern,
with candlelight flickering through pierced-tin patterns. I
knew about that kind of lantern. It was a pioneer lantern.

You might wonder how I knew about lanterns. You might
wonder how a mere girl of eleven would have in-depth knowledge of pierced-tin pioneer lanterns.

Let me tell you that a girl of eleven is capable of far more
than is dreamt of in most universes.

To the casual passerby a girl like me is just a girl. But a girl
of eleven is more than the sum of her age. Although it is not

often stated, she is already living in her twelfth year; she has entered into the future.

The first night I saw him the old man was lighting up the woods for the skiers. First one lantern hung swinging in the tree, then another flame hung a few trees farther down. I stood on my folding chair and peeked through the clear patch-glass on the stained-glass window. Three lanterns lit, and four. Six, seven, eight. Nine, and the old man was done. I watched his shadow move back to the toboggan he had used to drag the lanterns into Nine Mile Woods. He picked up the toboggan rope, he put something under his arm, and he walked through the woods to Nine Mile Trailer Park, pulling the toboggan behind him. The dark shapes of skiers flitted past. The old man kept walking.

I watched from my folding chair inside the churchhouse. In the light from the lanterns I could see each skier saluting the old man as he walked out of the woods. A pole high in the air, then they were gliding on past.

He never waved back.

I pressed my nose against the clear patch of glass and then the folding chair collapsed under me and I crashed to the floor. My elbow hurt so much that despite myself I cried. I dragged over another chair and climbed up again. But by then the old man was gone.

The old man lived in Sterns and I live in North Sterns. A lot of us in North Sterns live in the woods. You could call a girl like me a woods girl. That could be a name for someone like me, who lives in the woods but who could not be considered a pioneer. Pioneer children lived in days gone by.

I started at Sterns Elementary, I am now in Sterns Middle, and in three years I will be at Sterns High. So has, and does, and will everyone else in my class. CJ Wilson, for example. CJ Wilson's bullet-shaped head, his scabbed fingers, the words that come leaking from his mouth, I have known all my life. Were it not for CJ Wilson, and the boys who surround him, I might have been a different kind of person in school. I might have been quicker to talk, faster to raise my hand. I might have been picked first for field hockey. I might have walked down the middle of the hallway instead of close to the lockers. I might have been known as a chattery girl. I might have had a nickname.

Who's to say? Who's to know?

Jackie Phillips wet her pants in kindergarten. We were in gym class. Jumping jacks. I looked to my right, where Jackie Phillips was jumping kitty-corner from me, and saw a puddle below her on the polished gym floor. A dark stain on her blue shorts.

Six years later, what do the students of Sterns Middle School think of when they think about Jackie Phillips? Do they think, Captain of Mathletics, Vice-President of 4-H, science lab partner of Bernie missing-his-right-thumb Hauser, Jackie Phillips whose hair turns green in summer from the chlorine at Camroden Pool, Jackie Phillips who's allergic to strawberries?

They might. But they will also think: Jackie Phillips wet her pants in kindergarten while everyone was doing jumping jacks. That's the way it is.

Does everyone look at me and think, Clara Winter who loathes and despises snow and cold, who lives with her mother The Fearsome Tamar in North Sterns, whose eyes can look green or gray or blue, depending, who has never met her father or her grandfather, who has represented Sterns Elementary at every state spelling bee since first grade, whose hair could be called auburn, who loves books about days gone by? Clara Winter who saw that Jackie had wet her pants in gym class and so stopped jumping jacks and ran out of line and tried but failed to wipe up the spill surreptitiously with a used tissue before anyone else would notice? Is that what they think?

They do, and they do not.

The eyes, they know. That I live with my mother Tamar in North Sterns, they know. The spelling, they know. The fact that I, as a kindergartner, got Jackie Phillips's puddle all over my fingers from trying to wipe it up, they know. These are the things they know.

You see how much is left out.

Some may not even know about Tamar. Tamar is what I call my mother, but only when she's not around. I tried it once in front of her.

"Good morning, Tamar," I said. "Any Cheerios left?"

She gave me a look.

"Clara Winter, what the hell are you up to now? Is this another of your weird word things?"

I tried to look ingenuous, which is a word I believe to be a perfect word. Only certain words fit my personal category of perfection. What makes the word *ingenuous* perfect is the way the "g" slides into the "enuous."

"What? What do you mean, Tamar?"

She couldn't stop laughing. That was the last time I did that. To her face I call her Ma mostly, because that's what pioneer girls called their mothers. That's what Laura Ingalls

Wilder called her mother. I'm the only girl I know who calls her mother Ma.

You might wonder why a girl of eleven would be interested in an old man. You might think that a girl of eleven would have time only for her fellow sixth-graders. You might assume that the life of an old man who lived alone in a trailer in the Nine Mile Trailer Park in Sterns would hold no interest for an eleven-year-old child.

You would be wrong.

After the first night, when the old man lit lanterns in Nine Mile Woods, I saw him everywhere in Sterns. I saw him in Jewell's Grocery buying noodles and a quart of milk when I was there buying a lime popsicle. I stood behind him in the checkout line and observed his movements. The old man gave Mr. Jewell forty-five cents—five pennies, one quarter, one dime, and one nickel—and Mr. Jewell gave him a Persian doughnut. The old man reached into his pocket and took out another penny, which he dropped into Mr. Jewell's "Take a Penny, Leave a Penny" cup.

"Thank you, Mr. Kominsky," Mr. Jewell said. "And what can I do for you, Miss Clara?"

I waited until the old man had walked out of Jewell's and down the sidewalk toward Nine Mile Trailer Park.

"I would like to know Mr. Kominsky's first name," I said.

"Mr. Kominsky's name is George," Mr. Jewell said.

"Thank you."

I left Jewell's and walked across the street to Crystal's Diner, where Tamar was waiting for me.

"There is an old man who lives in the Nine Mile Trailer Park who will soon become my friend," I told her. "That is my prediction."

Tamar sucked her straw full of milkshake, then suspended the straw above her mouth and let it drip in. That's a habit of hers.

"Well, far be it from me to argue with a Clara Winter prediction," Tamar said.

That's Tamar. That's a Tamar remark. Tamar's mother died when she was eighteen years old. On Tamar's seventeenth birthday, her mother gave her a black and red and orange lumberjacket that Tamar still wears despite the fact that the seams are ripping, the zipper keeps breaking, and moths have eaten holes in the wool.

When I first spoke to the old man, I told him that my last name was winter, which I always keep in small letters in my mind, so it doesn't gain in importance. Winter is something that should be lowercase, in my opinion. Winter is to be feared. Winter is to be endured. That's what I believe to be true.

"Hello," I said. "I'm Clara winter. I was wondering if I could do my oral history project with you."

No answer. He stood there behind his screen door, looking at me.

"It's for my sixth-grade project."

No answer.

"I'm eleven."

Why did I say that? Why did I tell him I was eleven?

"I saw you lighting lanterns. You like lanterns."

Babbling! But when I mentioned the lanterns, he let me in. Interview an elderly person, they said, find out all about their lives. It's called an oral history. The minute they assigned the oral history project I knew that I would interview the old man. I wanted to listen while he told me about lanterns. I wanted him to be my friend. I wanted my prediction to come true.

"I'll do Georg Kominsky," I said. "He lives in the Nine Mile Trailer Park."

I had already found his name in the telephone book. *Georg,* not George. He wasn't on the approved list. They had a list of Sterns residents who had been oral historied in the past.

"He's an immigrant," I said. "He's old."

Was he? I didn't know, but they love old immigrants. The old man was also a plus because Tamar, my mother, goes to choir practice every Wednesday night at the Twin Churches, exactly opposite Nine Mile Trailer Park.

"I've never been in a trailer before," I said when the old man let me in.

I took the liberty of walking around. It was a very narrow place. I had the feeling that if the old man, who was tall, laid down on his back crosswise, he might not fit without having to crumple up a little. Each end of the trailer was curved.

"Sir, is this what being on a boat's like?" I asked the old man.

Already I was getting used to him not talking. I liked the sound of my voice in his trailer. There was something echoey about it.

"I've always wondered what life on a boat was like," I said. "The smallness of it."

I walked straight to the end of the trailer, past the tiny kitchen with the miniature refrigerator and the miniature sink, past the little room with the sliding curtain-door that had a bed built onto a wall platform and drawers built into the opposite wall, into the tiny bathroom at the end that had a miniature shower, an ivory toilet, and a dark-green sink.

"I like your dark-green sink. It's unique. It's a one-of-a-kind sink, just like your house is a one-of-a-kind house."

"It's not a house," the old man said. "It's a trailer."

"Why do you think they're called trailers?"

That's when I first learned the trick of how to get the old man to talk. Just keep talking and once in a while throw a question in. He wouldn't answer and he wouldn't answer, and then he would answer.

"Do you want something to drink?" I said. "I can make you something to drink. I brought a selection of various beverages for you. Tea, instant coffee with instant creamer, and hot chocolate."

I had little bags of everything.

"I could make you some hot chocolate," I said. "It would be my pleasure. Miniature marshmallows already mixed in."

It was the end of March in the Adirondacks that night. We sat at his kitchen table and he stirred his coffee. Around and around he stirred. This is the kind of thing I think about, now that the old man is gone. I submerged all the miniature marshmallows in my hot chocolate until they disappeared. They dissolved. They were no more. You could say I killed them.

"Let me ask you a question," I said. "Say you're on death row. How would you rather die: electric chair or lethal injection?"

That used to be one of my favorite questions. I used to ask it of everyone I met. The old man stirred his coffee.

"If you had to choose, that is," I said.

"Did they tell you to ask that question for the oral history?"

"Yes."

He kept on stirring.

"Actually, no," I said.

There was something about the old man. Even though it was my habit then to tell untruths, around the old man I couldn't.

"This would be for my own personal information," I said.

"Well then," he said. "Let me think about it."

I had hoped for an immediate answer. But immediate answers were not forthcoming from the old man. That was one of his traits.

The Adirondack Ski Club created the ski trail from Utica to Old Forge, fifty miles of cross-country skiing. The night I first observed the old man, they had just finished the portion that wound its way through Nine Mile Woods and up through Sterns. Would you find me skiing on that trail? Would you find me out on a winter night, a scarf wrapped around my face, poling my way through the snow?

You would not.

I had a feeling that the old man knew the power of winter. How did I know that? Because when I told him why I spell my last name with a lowercase w, he nodded. He did not question. I used to love that about the old man.

The first night I ever met the old man, sitting at his kitchen table, I read a book report aloud. You might think that seems like a strange thing to do. You might think, Tamar is right, Clara Winter is indeed an odd child. But still, there we sat, me reading, him listening.

They like us to read a book and do a book report on it once every two weeks. "Now that you're in sixth grade," they say. "Time to develop your critical faculties." Etcetera. I scoff at this. Their definition of a book and my definition of a book do not coincide. "Fifty-page minimum," they say.

What kind of book is only fifty pages long? A comic book?

It hurts me to see a book report. It's painful to me. Book reports are to books what (a) brown sugar and water boiled together until thick is to true maple syrup from Adirondack sugar maples, (b) lukewarm reconstituted nonfat powdered milk is to whipped cream, and (c) a drawing of a roller coaster is to a roller-coaster ride. Give me a *real* assignment, I say.

I like to read books one after another. *Immerse*—another perfect word—myself in a book and then *immerse* myself in the next book, and just keep going until there aren't any more books left to swim in. That's why I hate it when authors die. I cannot stand it. There will be no more books forthcoming from that person. Their future books died with them. In the past I have found a series of books and loved it so much that all I wanted to do was read and read and read those books for the rest of my life. Then I would find out that the author was dead. Had in fact been dead for many a year. This has happened to me several times.

You can see how much it would hurt me to write a book report every two weeks. I could do such a thing only to a book I hated. And why would I read a book I hated? Self-torture?

My only option is to make them up.

Besides, there're not too many unread-by-Clara-winter books left in the school library. It's a strange feeling, to walk down a row of books with your head bent so you can read the titles, and recognize most of them. *Amelia Earhart: American Aviator. Alexander Graham Bell: Inventor of the Telephone. George Washington Carver: American Botanist.* I like biographies. I like the early childhoods of famous people. Sometimes they're what you'd expect them to be, sometimes they're not.

I like reading between the lines of famous early childhoods.

My favorites are pioneers. Winter explorers. The kinds of pioneers who bore the burden of snow and ice, who faced the cold head-on. Winter is to be feared. But who thinks about that now? Everyone thinks we've conquered winter. Houses with heat, cars with heat, stores and schools with heat. They forget what it used to be like. They can't begin to imagine what it was like for the pioneers, with one small fire in an unchinked cabin, or how cold it must have been in the Indians' winter camps.

Imagine it.

We are close to death every winter day. What if the furnace went out and the electricity went out and the phone line went out and the blizzard raged so hard that the road was a pure whiteness, and you slowly burned up everything wood in the house, and then twisted newspaper into tight rolls and burned them like fast-burning logs, and then started in on your summer clothes and the sheets and towels and mattress stuffing and anything else that could possibly burn, and finally, even, tore all your books apart and burnt the pages, all the time jumping up and down to stay warm, dancing even, with all your winter clothes on? It wouldn't matter. You would die. No one thinks about things like that. They all feel so safe.

Not me.

"Would you like to read my fake book report?" I said. "I have it here in my backpack. It was completed just this afternoon."

The old man stirred his coffee with the handle of his spoon. He did not use the *bowl* of the spoon, as I have seen it referred to in books but never, not once, in real life.

"It concerns winter," I said.

"You read it to me," he said.

The Winter Without End, by Lathrop E. Douglas. New York: Crabtree Publishers, Inc., 1958. You need to make up a title that sounds possible and an author that doesn't sound impossible. I always put down a year from long ago, just in case they check. They'd never check, but still. You could always say, "Oh, you couldn't find it? That's because it's out of print." They'd be impressed that you knew what out of print meant.

"Ready?" I said.

"Ready."

It was the longest winter that Sarah Martin had ever known. Growing up on the Great Plains, she had known many a stark December, many an endless January, and the bitter winds of February were not unfamiliar to her. She was a child of winter. But that winter—the winter of 1879—Sarah knew true cold.

The potatoes had long since run out, as had the cabbages and carrots buried in sand in the root cellar. The meager fire was kept alive with twists of hay. When the first blizzard came, followed every few days by another, Sarah's parents had been trapped in town. It was up to Sarah Martin to keep her baby brother alive and warm until the spring thaw, when her parents could return to the homestead.

The true test of Sarah Martin's character comes when her baby brother wanders into the cold in the dead of night. Sarah blames herself for this; she was too busy twisting hay sticks in a corner of the cabin to notice that he had slipped from his pallet next to the fire and squeezed his way outside. "He's only two years old," thinks Sarah. "How long can a tiny child survive out-side in this bitter cold?"

Will Sarah Martin be able to find her little brother in time? Will she be able to rescue him from a fate so horrible that she cannot bear to think about it?

Did Sarah Martin have the foresight to dig a snow tunnel from the house to the pole barn where Bessie and Snowball are stabled? Or is there nothing beyond the cabin door for her beloved brother but blowing snow, bitter wind, and a winter without end?

Will Sarah have to face the responsibility of her brother's death?

Will her baby brother be forgotten by everyone but her?

Will she miss him her whole life long?

Read the book and find out.

I live in North Sterns, in the Adirondack Mountains. Winter loves these mountains. Snow is attracted to them. Snow craves falling here. Snow falls on the young and the old, the quick and the dead, the CJ Wilsons and the Clara winters.

"Well?" I said to the old man after I read him my fake book report. "What do you think?"

He stirred his coffee so that it slopped into the saucer.

"What happened?" he said. "How does the story turn out?"

"Read the book and find out," I said.

Most of the time I give my book reports a happy ending. The teachers expect that. An unhappy ending would raise alarm bells in their minds. That's because most books for children have happy endings. Few end in tragedy. Few contain irredeemable loss.

You might wonder why a girl of eleven would want to be around an old man seven times her age. You might wonder why she craved his presence, what she was hoping to find in Georg Kominsky. You might wonder if she found it.

"Tell me how the story ends," the old man said when I finished reading the fake book report. "I would like to know what happens."

So would I.

CHAPTER TWO

S oon after I met him, I told the old man about my missing
lantern earring. I was making toast for myself and mixing
up the coffee in his mug. You had to put a saucer underneath it.
That's how he drank his coffee. He poured the milk in and then
he stirred and stirred and stirred with the handle of his spoon
until it slopped into the saucer, and then and only then would
he take his first sip. I soon learned that about the old man.

"My lantern earring has met a tragic end," I said.

Tragic is a good word. It would be a good name too, with
that soft middle "g," except it's not a name. You couldn't
name a baby Tragic. That would be a travesty, which is also a
beautiful-sounding word. Travis is the closest you could come
to that one.

"My earring shall not see the light of day again," I said.
"Swallowed by the snow like Jonah was swallowed by the
whale."

It was my favorite pair of earrings, tiny silver lanterns like
the kind pioneers used to light their way in the barn at chore-
time. They were a gift for my tenth birthday, before I ever met

the old man. Once in a while Tamar used to give me earrings, but only tool earrings, in keeping with her theory that work makes you strong. I used to have a set of hammer earrings, a set of pickaxes, a pair of scissors, all made of silver. But I lost one of each set. That's what happens when you wear clip-on earrings. They disappear. I would never have lost my lantern if Tamar had let me pierce my ears. The one fell off, to be lost forever in the snow.

"Two more years before Tamar will let me pierce my ears," I told the old man. "A veritable lifetime." *Veritable* belongs to me. It's one of my words. I like the way all the syllables after the "ver" go mumbling into each other.

"Two years is not a lifetime," the old man said.

"Nay sir, but it is 730 days. If it's not a leap year."

That's one of my talents. I can add extremely quickly in my head. Let me tell you a secret. As long as people believe you're an extremely fast adder, it doesn't matter if you make a mistake. No one notices. I've gotten by quite a few times like that.

Even as I told the old man about it, gravity may have been pulling my silver earring down to the earth, the little lantern dropping crystal by crystal deeper and deeper into the six feet of snow piled beside the entrance to the old man's trailer park, which is where I lost it. Maybe it would rest on the frozen crust of the ground until the end of April. When spring finally came and all the snow melted, maybe then it would be carried away by flooding, swept into Nine Mile Creek, and from there into the Utica Wetlands, to sink into the swampy mud without a trace.

"Ne'er to be seen again," I said to the old man.

It all comes back to snow and cold.

• • •

The old man planned to make me a replacement for my lost lantern earring. He had the ability to do that because he used to be a metalworker. There were many things about the old man that no one ever knew. They were all inside him. People thought he was a silent man, but they were wrong.

"Please tell me about your occupation."

That was a question I asked him in the beginning, when I was still doing his oral history. It was straight from the oral history list they gave us. Did they not trust us to come up with our own questions?

"Metalworker."

I wrote all his responses down on my roll of green adding-machine paper from Jewell's Grocery: 3/$1. Mr. Jewell keeps them in a bin up near the register, things that are a little cracked, a little broken, maybe not wanted. Things that they think people aren't going to want, that's what goes in the bin. Like adding-machine paper: who's going to want green?

Sometimes I think of it as my bin.

"I lost my lantern earring," I told him. "I knew something was wrong. There was just a feeling, like something was missing that should be there. The unbalancing. That lantern earring was heavy."

I showed him the one earring that was left.

"Early American," he said.

"Maybe."

"No maybe," he said. "That's a traditional American copper or tin lantern pattern."

"It's sterling silver," I said. "It was my tenth birthday present from Tamar."

He examined it. He tossed it from hand to hand for a little while.

"Paul Revere," I said, when I saw that he had stopped talking again.

Paul Revere was an early American man. I figured it might get him back on the talking track. I used to do that sometimes, let a name or a word drop into the air in front of the old man's quiet face.

"I read his biography," I said. "I took it out of the school library."

There's a Paul Revereware factory right in Rome, just fifteen miles from Sterns. The factory has a galloping red neon horse on the front of it. At night it's very bright.

"It took Paul Revere a long time to get his first silver pitcher made small the way he wanted," I said. "He couldn't get the proportions right. He had to figure out how to reduce and enlarge proportions without destroying the inherently graceful line of the original silver pitcher."

I like to talk like that, which is the way certain books are written.

"Do most eleven-year-olds talk like you?" the old man said.

"Nay sir, I think not."

Pioneers may have talked like that. It's hard to know. They didn't have tape recordings back then. It's all speculation, how they really talked. That's why I started writing down the story of the old man's life, because he didn't talk to anyone else and there was no one else to listen anyway. There needed to be a record of his life. That is what I believed to be true.

"Do not forget, however, that I am not merely eleven," I said. "I am even now in my twelfth year."

He smiled. No one else would have noticed but me, because I'm the only one who knew the looks on the old man's face well enough to tell what was a smile and what was a grimace.

"I used to make lanterns," he said. "Like your earring but big. Tin, mostly."

"Tin?" I said. "Tin."

Not a good sound, tin. Too short. Too abrupt. Too *tinny*.

"How about aluminum?" I said.

"What do you mean, how about aluminum?"

"Like soda cans. Like tinfoil."

"There is possibility in aluminum too," he said.

Possibility. A five-syllable word. If every finger is a syllable, possibility uses one entire hand neatly and nicely. It takes a tin-smith, someone who knows sheet metal, to see the possibility in aluminum. After the old man said that I started seeing possibilities myself. I looked up aluminum and tin in the library. You can find out a great deal from one half hour well spent at a library. I tested the old man after I had done my research.

"What sort of metal is tin, and is it commonly used by itself?" I said.

"Soft, white, and no."

"What metal, when combined with tin, forms bronze?" I said.

"Copper."

"Tell me the melting point of tin."

"450. About."

He knew his stuff. The old man really knew his stuff when it came to sheet metal. That's why he had the capability of making me a matching lantern for my one remaining silver earring.

"I learned how to make real lanterns that look like your earring when I was a child," the old man said. "Decorative tin lanterns."

There are people who would not have understood the old man when he said "decorative." There are people who would have gotten twisted up in the old man's pronunciation, gotten lost in the vowels and consonants, given up in despair.

Not me. I understood the old man. We were *compadres.*

The old man's father may have been a metalworker too, with a forge in a shed near their thatched hut. That's how I picture the old man when he was a boy, living with his mother and his father in a thatched hut with an open cookstove in it. Walls made of turf bricks. Every few years the old man's father repaired the thatched roof, or even tore all the thatch off and started again. Their hut was on a street with many other neighboring huts. Horses and wagons clopped up and down the rutted muddy road. No cars. All day Georg's father worked in his forge, pumping air at the fire to keep it hot, banging and pounding on metal things such as horseshoes and anvils.

Georg's father was the town blacksmith. After school, which lasted only half a day, Georg would come immediately home, eat the bread and butter that his mother had ready for him, and go directly to the forge. It was from his father that Georg learned all he knew about metalworking. Georg's father was a stern but kind teacher. He wanted his son to grow to love working with metal as much as he, the father, loved it.

"For a skilled metalworker there is always a job," he told his son Georg. "Learn the trade well and you will never go hungry."

Georg's father sometimes did favors for his friends, straightening a horseshoe or bent nails without charging. He was known in the village as a generous and honest man. A beggar could always find a hot meal at the home of Georg's mother and father. From his father Georg learned the tools of the metalworking trade and much more. When school was out for the summer they worked together from sunup to sundown, then they would put away their tools for the night and go next door, where Georg's mother had dinner and tea waiting for them. Glasses of hot tea, strong and plain for Georg's father, half-milk for Georg.

In this way Georg learned, without haste, the ways of metalworking.

His particular gift for decorative metalworking was discovered early, when he would take the scraps of sheet metal left over from one of his father's projects and turn them into beautiful and useful objects, such as miniature lanterns, cookie cutters, and candleholders. Anything that could be made from sheet metal, Georg could make and make decoratively. Friends and villagers soon noticed the unusually beautiful lanterns and candleholders coming from Georg's father's forge. When it was discovered that it was not his father, but Georg himself, who was the artisan, word quickly spread.

"He has the touch," they said.

The old villagers nodded knowingly. They had seen this kind of talent before, but rarely. Rarely, a child is born with the knowledge of past lives still in his fingertips. They believed that Georg was such a child, that he had lived a life before as a forger, as a craftsman, as an artist. In this life, the skills from the previous blended in his fingertips, allowing him to produce useful objects of great beauty.

Georg was known for his precision, his vision, and the way that everything he created was made to be used. He was destined to be a metalworker. It was the fate he was born into.

Is that a true story? It may well be. Who am I to say?

I started collecting aluminum cans for the old man. I still have them. There may be a use for them yet. There is possibility in them. When you have your eye out for them, they're everywhere. Aluminum cans can be found crushed on the sidewalk, placed upright against buildings, and in every large garbage can you walk past and most small trash cans as well. Almost every car contains the possibility of an empty aluminum can, rolling back and forth underneath one of the seats. You can find an aluminum can, drained of soda, stuck behind a stack of Wonder bread in the Bread/Cereal aisle at Jewell's. Not paid for, no doubt.

We started out as interviewer and interviewee, but that changed. There were things the old man and I knew about each other. After a while, I just visited him, *compadre* to *compadre*. I used to write down his life because much of the time he was in a dark lantern world. You could see it in his face. Somewhere, there might still be a person who wants to know about the old man's life. Somewhere, someone who doesn't know he's gone might still be looking for the old man.

"When we left we had a lantern with us," the old man told me that night.

"When you left where?"

"Our country."

"What country?"

"It doesn't exist anymore. This was a long time ago. This was before the war. It was snowing."

I wrote that down: *snowing.* I could tell it had been snowing hard by the look on the old man's face. His eyes were squinted the way eyes get when snow is driving into them. There are those who see beauty in snow. They like its whiteness, the way it shuts out sound. My mother Tamar is one of them.

"It covers the good and the evil," she says. "Everything is equal in the snow."

Every September Tamar lifts her face to the sky and breathes in to the bottom of her lungs. "Smell it, Clara," she says. "A September blue sky, and the smell of autumn leaves. There is nothing better in this world."

Nay sir, I think not.

Now that the old man is gone, I wish I had asked him about my chickens. That's one of my regrets.

My chickens used to live in the broken-down barn across the field by the pine trees. They lived there, scrabbling in the dark, maybe flying up to the posts they roosted on. They were there every morning, waiting for the feed and water to be flung at them through the bars. They may have plotted to kill me.

It's possible. It's entirely possible.

"Do you believe that chickens are inherently vicious?"

That's a question that I want to ask someone. Who can you talk to about insane chickens? Not Tamar.

Those chickens, they started out so cute. I got them last June, when it was warm, a few months after I met the old man. They came in a wooden box, Rhode Island Reds, two roosters and twenty-three hens. Peeping yellow fuzzy balls. They crowded against each other and sipped up chick feed with their sweet baby beaks. Tamar penned off a corner of the broken-down barn for them. I put in my old dollhouse to amuse them.

"Now don't go making pets out of those things," Tamar warned me. "You know you're going to end up killing and eating some of them."

"Don't worry, Ma," said I. "I'm not even going to name them."

I read somewhere that if you didn't name your animals you wouldn't care about them. That was not a worry anyway. Those chickens grew up mean. The cocks jumped on my back every morning and every night. They dug into my skin through my shirt and pecked my head. Horny yellow beaks pierced my scalp and made my hair streaky with little lines of blood. Tamar did not go out to the broken-down barn. She spent a morning out there fixing up the pen, then she said: "This is your project, Clara. You're eleven now. These chickens are your first grown-up project, you think of them that way."

Is an eleven-year-old a grown-up? What would my father have thought of the grown-up project idea?

I do have a father. Everyone has a father. It's a law of nature. But I couldn't tell that to Tamar. *He doesn't exist,* she said. *You don't have a father.*

Chickens were not my idea. An animal of any kind would not have been my idea of a grown-up project. It's true that I wanted a grown-up project. It's true that I had complained to Tamar about not being given credit for no longer being a child. But chickens were not the answer I had envisioned.

"Tell me about my grandfather, and when you're done, tell me about my father," I said to Tamar a few months before the chickens arrived.

Hope springs eternal. It was my hope that if I occasionally, without warning, sprang the words—*grandfather, father*—on Tamar, she would be so startled that answers would spring unbidden to her lips.

"Nope and nope."

That was her response. That was a Tamarian answer.

"I'm an adult now," I said.

"You're eleven."

"In many cultures that would be considered nigh to adulthood."

"Nigh but no cigar," Tamar said.

She smiled. She liked the sound of that. I left her in the kitchen with a can of tomato soup and her can opener. I left her neither laughing nor chuckling. It could be said that when I left the kitchen after being told that I was nigh but no cigar, Tamar was *chortling*.

Three months later the chickens appeared.

In the beginning I tried to walk into the barn tall and stern, like I was in command. I carried the feed bucket in my left hand and the water bucket in my right, swinging them from side to side so that the water sloshed. Still, they attacked.

"Get off of me!" I yelled. "Get off of me, you devil-chickens!"

Then I tried to look like a man. I made my voice deep. I intoned.

"Get the H away from me."

Sometimes I even said the word. Get the HELL away. But

it didn't make any difference. The cocks just looked at me with their beady eyes and didn't move.

I named the meanest one CJ Wilson.

Why didn't I tell the old man about the real CJ Wilson either? I could have told him. He would have listened. You might think that I knew all the old man's secrets and he knew all mine. You would be wrong. Even now I wonder what secrets I never found out about the old man.

The first day of school last September, CJ Wilson corrected the teacher when she said his name at roll call: Charles Junior Wilson.

"It's CJ," he said. "Don't call me Charles Junior."

Winter comes right after Wilson.

"Clara Winter," said the teacher.

"It's Clara *winter*," I said.

"That's what I *said*."

She gave me a look. She was impatient. I could tell. After school CJ grabbed my leg as I walked past him on the school bus.

"Nice skirt," he said. "Nice skirt, Clara *Wipe*."

Then he flipped my skirt up so that my underwear showed. He hated me because Tamar is the Justice of the Peace of the Town of North Sterns and CJ's father had to come to her court at our house. Drunk driving.

"Good-bye and good riddance," Tamar said when CJ's father was gone. She was sitting at the kitchen table, which is her courtroom. Being JP is a part-time job. It takes about five hours a month to be JP of the Town of North Sterns. Tamar holds court wearing jeans and a T-shirt. She doesn't have a gavel. She says they're not essential.

"How are those chickens of yours?" she said.

"Fine."

"You getting any more eggs?"

"No."

There had only been a few that I could see, a few laid right by the gate so I could reach in quick and grab them.

"Well, look around good for them. That feed isn't free, you know."

"I know."

I couldn't even get near the pen. I stood four or five feet away, with the CJ Wilson chicken hissing from the dollhouse. I tossed the feed in a sudden jerk, aiming for the trough. The hens fought and gobbled for the bits of corn. While they were scrabbling I scooped up any eggs that I could see. Only one or two each time were close enough for me to grab through the bars. Where any others might be, I didn't know.

Laura Ingalls Wilder would not have feared my chickens.

Laura Ingalls Wilder was a snow lover. Laura was a true pioneer girl. Laura is the reason I call Tamar Ma to her face, because Ma is what pioneer girls called their mothers. I used to love Laura Ingalls Wilder when I was a child. When I started reading about Indians, I had to revise my initial impression of Laura. It was hard to do that. I loved Laura so much. At first I tried to defend her: it was way back then, they didn't know. Then I had to admit it: the pioneers were awful to the Indians.

"The pioneers were awful to the Indians," I said to the old man after we had become *compadres.*

"Yes," the old man said.

We were sitting at his kitchen table that had cigarette burn marks in it from the previous owner. The old man had found the kitchen table set out for the trash on scavenging night. I made some more toast. I spread it extremely thickly with margarine. I was embarrassed to have the old man see how much margarine I put on toast. I only did it when I was visiting him. He didn't seem to notice.

Tamar would never allow me to put so much margarine on toast. She has an eagle eye for that sort of thing.

"The problem is that I still love her," I said. "I love Laura."

"And what's the problem?"

"She was mean. She was awful to the Indians."

"An entire nation was awful to the Indians," he said. "They invaded their land, they pushed them onto reservations, they tried to kill them off."

"Yes. That's right. That's my point exactly."

"But still, you love her."

"Yes. That's my other point," I said. "My other exact point."

"It's the same point," he said.

I wrote that down. It had the ring of wisdom, although I didn't understand it. That used to happen to me when I was with the old man, not understanding something but knowing it was important. Being on the verge. That's how it felt. I used to write down the things he said. I kept track.

Are young chickens capable of hatred? Is it possible for an eleven-year-old girl to be killed by a flock of young chickens?

I would like to know.

I feel in my gut that the old man would have known what to do about my chickens. I should have told the old man about the chickens. There were things the old man knew that you would not have suspected he knew and chickens may well have been one of those things. After he was gone I researched

31

chickens in the school library. Researching is one of my talents. There was nothing about a tendency toward violence in poultry. Feed, growth patterns, eggs, fryers versus roasters, and so on.

Violence? Nothing.

When CJ Wilson flipped my skirt up the first day of school he turned to the other boys and laughed. Some were embarrassed, some looked surprised. Some laughed along with CJ.

That's what happens when you're eleven. You say good-bye to the kids in your class in June, when school lets out. Maybe you'll see them a couple of times over the summer, maybe not. But in September, the day after Labor Day, you know you'll see them again. School will resume. Life will go on. You'll slide your tray through the cafeteria line: tiny fluted paper cups of applesauce, sloppy joe on hamburger buns. You know that nothing will have changed.

You're wrong.

You get on the bus the day after Labor Day and you're wearing new school clothes. New underwear, polka dot. CJ Wilson flips your skirt up and everything's changed. You never saw it coming.

CHAPTER THREE

The story of my birth is an astounding one. I was born during a February blizzard in a truck tipped sideways into a ditch on Glass Factory Road. My grandfather was trying to get Tamar to Utica Memorial in time for the delivery, but there was no such luck. Astonishingly, a midwife came walking by the stuck truck just at the critical moment.

The midwife was trying to get to Clearview Heights, the road on the hills above Utica where she lived with her husband and young child. She had to take Glass Factory, because it's the only road that intersects with Clearview Heights. The midwife, whose name was Angelica Rose Beaudoin, was driving her car and it broke down in the middle of that blizzard. Bravely, Angelica Rose laced her boots up and tied them into double knots. She rummaged in the back seat for the emergency road kit that her husband had put together for her in a recycled coffee can. In it, the young midwife found some chocolate bars, some change for a pay phone, extra mittens, a space blanket, and a pair of earmuffs. She put on the earmuffs. She wrapped the space blanket around her body, underneath her parka, for extra insulation. She put the extra pair of mittens on over the mittens she was already wearing.

I love thinking about Angelica Rose Beaudoin, the young midwife. Angelica Rose had not been a midwife for long. She had trained for emergency births but had not actually had to deliver a baby outside of the hospital or a home. Never in a blizzard.

Angelica Rose set off, keeping track of where she was by the telephone poles she could barely see through the driving snow. Up the steep hills and down she went, trudging her way toward Clearview Heights and home. Darkness was all about her, and the snow felt like stinging bees on her face. Her feet made no sound in the powdery snow. Unbeknownst to the snow, or to the frozen ground beneath it, the young midwife was thinking about a baby, her own baby, who had been born without ears. Within his tiny skull, Angelica Rose's child had the means of hearing, but with no passage to the outside world her son lived in an unknown world. Sound came to him as if from underwater. His mother's voice floated past his round baby-fuzzed head as if in a bubble. What her baby heard was not what was heard by her. What her baby heard was his own, his own to make sense of, his own to understand. Already, his mother could see a difference in the way her child inclined his head to speech.

Angelica Rose trudged through the snow and thought about things that were missing, things that were broken and could not be fixed.

Then, from the heart of the blizzard, the midwife heard a muffled cry.

Angelica Rose cocked her head and listened again, to make sure she wasn't imagining it. The cry came again.

Help!

It was my grandfather, calling for help through a hairline crack in the driver's side window. He didn't want to leave my mother and search for help, but hoping against hope that someone would pass by, he kept calling out the window into the storm. *Heeeeeeeelp*, he called, once every couple of minutes, while Tamar twisted in the seat next to him.

"Helloooooo!"

That was the sound of the midwife's voice, responding to the person in need. My grandfather heard her voice. Disbelieving, he cranked open the window, struggled out into the snow and found the midwife, her head turning this way and that, listening for that lone cry of help.

"Come on! My daughter's having a baby!"

That was what my grandfather said. Angelica Rose Beaudoin said not another word. She had been trained for this moment. She nodded, started beating her mittened hands together to warm them, and followed my grandfather to the truck in the ditch. As she stumbled after him she summoned all her medical training and ordered her mind as to what needed to be done. They found Tamar in agony on the front seat.

The midwife pushed her way in and cradled Tamar's head. She spoke soothingly and quietly to Tamar, to calm Tamar's fears and prepare her for what was to happen.

The old man listened carefully to the story. Already he knew of my fear and loathing of snow and cold. Blizzards especially. I could tell the old man was listening carefully because the more carefully he listened, the more he tilted his head. His head was semihorizontal. That used to happen sometimes, when I was telling a story and the old man was listening.

"And then my twin sister was born, and I was next," I said. "And that's the story in a nutshell. That's all she wrote."

"You have a twin sister?" the old man said.

"Indeed I do."

"Does she live with you?"

"She lives with me in a way," I said. "In a certain manner of speaking, she lives with me."

"In a certain manner of speaking?"

"In a sense," I said. "In a sense my twin sister lives with me."

He looked at me.

"Do you want me to heat some more water for coffee?" I asked.

"All right," the old man said.

I got up and filled the old man's teakettle with water and put it on to boil. I looked out the window over the old man's kitchen sink toward the Twin Churches. An hour had already gone by. Tamar and the choir would be winding down in another forty-five minutes.

Often I have wondered about Angelica Rose Beaudoin, where she is now, if she ever remembers me and my baby sister. Angelica Rose was extremely grateful that her husband had thought to put earmuffs into the emergency blizzard road kit, because she had only a hat that didn't cover her ears. You have to be vigilant about exposed extremities in an upstate New York blizzard. Extremities are the first to go.

And what became of her child, her hearing but uneared child? I wonder about that too.

I brought the old man more coffee.

"Where is she?"

"Who? Angelica Rose Beaudoin?"

"No. Your twin sister."

"I only wish I knew," I said.

My baby sister is the reason why I hate my last name. It's a name of cold and ice and snow. People who look at me see a girl named Clara Winter. They don't ever think about the significance of my last name, and if they do, they see a world of whiteness. Blowing snow, drifting fields of white. Maybe some of them see the darkness of trees, winter branches reaching into an empty sky. Maybe others picture the Adirondacks in January, the green of evergreens so dark that it could be mistaken for black.

I spell my last name with a lowercase w, but I'm the only one who knows that a lowercase w is a rejection of winter, an acknowledgment of what winter really is and how it can kill.

"What do you mean?" the old man said. He gazed at me with his head nearly horizontal. "You said that she lives with you."

"What I mean is that the entire story I just told you is a lie," I said.

The old man took a drink of coffee, which he drank only after it was almost cold. He looked at me. I looked at him. Words hung in the air between us, heavy and dark. We sat that way until Tamar drove up and honked her secret Tamar honk, two shorts and an extralong: *beep-beep, beeeeeeeeeeeeeeeeep.*

I dreamed about the old man that night. It was silent. Lights flickered. People I didn't know were coming through the woods from far away bringing lights that were lanterns, lanterns for the old man.

I woke up and thought, I may not be a metalworker but I can still make lanterns. I could bring lanterns for the old man.

Why not? I went down to the closet in the kitchen where we hang the can bag. It's a plastic Jewell's Grocery bag and we throw tin cans into it. It was the middle of the night. I didn't want to wake Tamar so I used the flashlight that I keep under my bed in case of emergency. But the bag came tumbling down and all the cans spilled and Tamar came rushing down the stairs holding her baseball bat with both hands.

"What the hell's going on, Clara?"

"I was getting a snack," I lied. "Then I bumped into the closet and all the cans spilled."

She thunked her baseball bat on the floor a few times.

"I'm sorry," I said.

"Pick up this mess and go back to bed," she said. "You've got school tomorrow and your chickens to feed beforehand."

I picked them all up. Next morning after Tamar was gone, before the bus came, and after I fed my chickens I cleaned out the biggest cans, the ones that Italian plum tomatoes come in. Plum tomato cans don't need much washing. A swish or two and they're done. No grease, that's why.

I was determined to make lanterns for the old man. It was a semifixation. That's what Tamar would have called it, had she known about my desire.

"Another semifixation on the part of my daughter," she would have said.

Tamar often talks that way, as if someone else is in the kitchen. In real life Tamar puts on and scrapes off huge orange flower decals on Dairylea milk trucks on an as-needed basis. Decals are always needed, though, so Tamar's job is full-time. She leans extension ladders against the sides of the milk tank trucks and climbs up to the top and scrapes and peels all day long. In winter she scrapes and peels inside a giant semi-heated milk truck garage in Utica. They assign Tamar to the decal work because she doesn't mind heights. She's fearless. She's known for it. The JP job is a sideline. Speeding, drunk driving, boundary disputes: these are the usual cases. The oldest Miller boy, for growing marijuana in the middle of his father's biggest cornfield.

Once in a while there's a wedding.

The old man used to make lanterns when he was a child, in his country that he would not tell me the name of because he said it didn't exist anymore. I am older than the old man was when he learned the art of metalworking. If he could do it, so can I, I thought.

It was hard work, puncturing the sides of those tomato cans. The church key didn't want to do a good job. A few of the cans buckled under the pressure. I strung twine through the holes to hang the lanterns by. After school I bought some burgundy-colored votive candles at Jewell's from the reject bin.

"Burgundy votive candles," Mr. Jewell said. "An unusual item for an unusual girl."

He smiled at me.

"And what do you plan to do with these burgundy votive candles?" he asked. "Or is that a secret?"

"Secret."

"I thought as much. Would you care for a Persian, Miss Winter?"

I could hear the capital W in the way he said my name. No one but me knows it's lowercase. He reached for the box of Persians that he and his friend Spooner Hughes were eating from. "Fresh," he said. "Made them myself."

"Thank you."

The secret to a good Persian doughnut is extra glaze. Also, they double the amount of cinnamon. Mr. Jewell told me that once.

I hung the plum tomato can lanterns in the old man's weeping willow tree. It's hard to hang can lanterns in a weeping willow. The branches bend. With a scratching sound, they scrape across the top of hard shiny snow, old snow, the kind of snow you find in the middle of a cold snap in March. I had to choose the thickest branches of the weeping willow; otherwise the lanterns dragged the branches down too far and made the tree look sad.

It was going to be a surprise for the old man. I knew he wasn't in the trailer because I had stood on the cinder block outside the little window by the built-in bed and seen that he was not there. Also, I had jumped up and down at the curved end of the trailer and seen that he was not sitting in his tiny curved-wall kitchen.

Each can that I hung I put a lighted burgundy votive candle into. I didn't hang them too high. I was only eleven. I wasn't that tall.

The can lanterns swung in the branches of the weeping willow tree.

The neighbor lady from the greenish trailer three trailers down from the old man's opened her door. She had a scarf tied around her head. She was leaning out her door with slippers on. I could see her mouth moving but I closed my ears to the sound of her voice. Then she came out with a pair of big boots on. They were not tied. They were men's.

The sound of the neighbor lady's voice seeped in anyway.

"Miss? What, may I ask, are you doing?"

"It's a surprise for the old man."

"You mean George?"

You could hear that she didn't know his real name. *Georg.*

"Old tomato cans hung in his tree?" she said. "That's your surprise?"

"It's a secret. You won't get the full visual effect until night-fall," I said. "Then you'll see."

She raised her eyebrows. Then she backed into her trailer and shut the door. Finally they were all hung. Where was the old man? He could have walked into Sterns. It was only one-quarter of a mile, which is not a far distance. He could have been doing his shopping at Jewell's. He went there once a week and always bought the same things: elbow macaroni, spaghetti sauce, three cans of tuna, one quart of milk, canned peaches in heavy syrup, a package of Fig Newtons, two loaves of bread, one container of whipped margarine, and two boxes of frozen peas. That used to last him a week, even with me there on Wednesday nights, eating toast.

Sometimes he put tuna in his spaghetti sauce before he poured it over his bowl of elbow macaroni. I saw him do that on a semiregular basis.

Tamar was at choir practice. The stained-glass windows all lit up. It was pitch dark when I finished tying all the cans into the tree.

Still no old man.

The neighbor lady stuck her head out the door again and watched me for a few minutes. She didn't say anything. I walked around the trailer park three times. There's a road that goes around the whole thing. Around and around I went, so my feet wouldn't freeze. Keep stamping and walking, that's the way to keep the circulation going. When the feet of the pioneers froze they stripped off their boots and socks and rubbed them with snow in front of a roaring fire. It was extremely painful. The pioneers lost fingers and toes.

Winter kills.

The third time I walked around the trailer park road I came upon the cans in the weeping willow and they looked different. Things change. You think they won't. You don't plan on things ever changing, but then you take a walk around a trailer park and you come back around, and things are different. You've moved into the future, even a little bit, and things don't look the same.

I saw that the cans were not lanterns. I did not have the skill of the old man. I could not work with metal; I could not make something beautiful out of a plum tomato can. I had not yet become the old man's apprentice. My lanterns were just old tomato cans, stuck in a tree whose branches were too spindly to support them. It took me only a few minutes to cut them all down with the Swiss army knife I carry in case of emergency. When I turned around, there was the old man, watching, standing there with a plastic Jewell's bag hanging from each hand.

"I brought you a sugar cookie from Jewell's," he said. "It's the kind of sugar cookie I ate when I was a child."

"In your country that doesn't exist anymore?" I said.

"That's right."

The old man did not say, What were you doing, stringing plum tomato cans in a tree? That was the difference between the old man and Tamar. She would have said, What the hell are you up to now, Clara Winter? She would have said, I have a strange child.

The old man was late that night because he wanted to offer me a treat. He wanted to have a sugar cookie waiting for me when I came to visit him. He didn't say that, but I could tell. That's what I believe to be true.

"When we got to Ellis Island, they almost wouldn't let me in," the old man said one night after we had become *compadres*.

"Why not?"

"Retarded. They thought I was retarded."

"But you weren't."

I tried to picture the old man as a kid. A skinny boy body floated into my mind. A skinny boy body with an old man's face.

"Why would they think you were special ed if you weren't?"

"My nose," he said. "I used to draw in the air with my nose. If you look down the corners of your eyes you can see the outline of your nose. Pretend that the end of it is a pen. Draw something in the air."

"Noses don't draw," I said. "Noses can run but they can't draw. Ha! Get it?"

I tried it. He was right. My nose made a nice invisible line. *C, L, A, R, A.* I wrote my name in invisible capital letters. Then I wrote my last name: *w, i, n, t, e, r.*

"I was tracing the outline of the American flag on Ellis Island," the old man said. "With my nose. That's why they thought I was retarded."

"Tell me about your family of origin," I said.

That's a term they told us to use in the oral histories. Your family of origin is the one you started out with.

"Georg, who is myself."

I knew the first time I heard his name to leave the "e" off. It's one of my skills. Clara Winter, you have an inborn sense of spelling, my fifth-grade teacher told me.

"My parents. Eli, my young brother."

"Do you have relatives back where you came from?"

"Where I came from does not exist," the old man said. "It used to be one country. Now it's another country."

"But there's got to be people related to you there."

"I am the last of my line."

That was one sentence that I wrote down in its entirety: *I am the last of my line.* It had the ring of truth.

"Tell me about being an immigrant," I said to the old man. "Tell me about leaving your country."

It's my belief that the old man could be called a pioneer.

"I held the lantern," the old man said. "That was my job."

I wrote it down.

"It was dark. I held it pointed in back of me so that my brother Eli could see his way. If I didn't look at the light from the lantern, the moon was light enough for me. You can't let your eyes get used to an abundance of light, that's the trick."

An abundance of light.

My roll of green adding-machine paper kept spooling out. It didn't seem to matter to him. That was the secret with the old man: get him talking and keep him going. That was how I discovered the nuances of his life.

"So I got to Ellis Island," he said.

"And what then?"

You had to keep him talking when he started, otherwise all was lost.

"And then nothing," he said. "It was all over then, the woods and the lantern and the walking. I lost two toes. They almost didn't let me in because of the nose-writing. They thought I was retarded."

"Special ed," I said.

"Retarded."

"And then what?"

"And then I started work. Metalwork. I am a metalworker."

That was something I knew. He didn't know that for two hours on a March night, a girl of eleven had spied on him through a piece of patched glass, had watched him hang lantern after lantern in the trees. I said nothing.

He stirred his coffee until it slopped into his saucer. I spread some more margarine on my one last bite of toast. I didn't want him to see how thick I was spreading it so I held it beneath the rim of the table. I was getting addicted to thickly spread margarine. There's something about the taste. It's cool. It slides around your mouth.

"Did your brother write with his nose, too? Did the Ellis Island guys think he was retarded, too?"

But the old man was done talking. *Finis.* I could tell. I could always tell, with the old man. He stirred his coffee until it slopped into the saucer, and then I drank my hot chocolate and ate my toast and he waited until his coffee was cold and then he drank it, and then we sat until the clock said I had six minutes. It was time for me to go. Tamar would be driving up to the curb by the Nine Mile Trailer Park sign in exactly six minutes. That's how long it took her to get from choir practice to the trailer park, including saying good-bye to her friends and starting the car. Tamar is never late.

"Bye," I said.

He didn't say good-bye. I knew he wouldn't. He was in his dark lantern world. I shut the door tight behind me so the snow wouldn't drift inside and make a tiny pile by his door, like sawdust. Tamar drove up on the dot, eating a miniature ice cream sandwich from the front freezer case at Jewell's. Even in the dead of winter she loves them. They're only a quarter each.

CHAPTER FOUR

I used to wonder why my chickens turned mean. Lack of sunshine, maybe. The corner of the broken-down barn where Tamar built the pen was dark. No windows. It was a big pen but nothing in it was interesting, not even my old doll-house, the rusty one that the younger Miller boys wrecked years ago when they held their Final Battle of the G.I. Joes.

One day the January after I got the chickens, I went in with the feed and water. It was hard to see at first because the snow was so bright outside, the barn so dark inside. The CJ Wilson chicken was sitting in the dollhouse. Right in the living room where the winning G.I. Joe busted through the floor. He stared at me. He didn't blink his nasty beady eyes.

See, he was saying to me. This is my house. There are my women.

I looked in the corner and saw the other cock lying dead. Pecked to death by the CJ Wilson chicken. I took the barn shovel and scooped up the carcass, carried it out to the pasture and flung it into the weeds. Then I went back into the house, washed my hands, scraped the bottoms of my boots, and got on the bus when Tiny pulled up to the driveway.

That was the first day that I knew I was in for a long haul with my chickens. Next to the chicken problem, the real CJ Wilson momentarily faded in importance. When he got on the bus there must have been a look on my face because he said not a word, just pointed out the window as Tiny pulled away from his trailer.

"You see that car?" said CJ to the North Sterns boys. "You see it?"

An old white Camaro with rust spots was parked in a snowdrift in CJ's unplowed driveway.

"Yeah," said one of the boys.

"That's mine," said CJ. "My dad, he's saving that for me. For when I get my license. He's going to fix it up and give it to me on my sixteenth birthday."

The boys nodded.

"It's a Camaro. He's saving it for me. Hey, Wipe! Your chickenshit mother got a car for you?"

I said nothing. I never said anything to CJ.

"Didn't think so," CJ said.

Occasionally I used to think about writing a fake book report about a boy named, for example, CJ Wilson. In the morning, when the chickens squawked and pecked, when I brought them their food and water in two buckets, with the snow packing down into my boots, I thought about CJ. I thought about the fake book report I could write about CJ, disguising his name to protect the innocent although he isn't innocent.

But I've never written a word.

"My dad used to be a professional wrestler," CJ said on the bus one day. "His name was Chucky Luck. He had his own show on TV."

CJ screwed his mouth up and squinted his eyes, punching his arms straight ahead of him like pistons. Grunting like a pig.

"Yeah right!" said one of the boys. "How come I never heard of it?"

"Before you were born, asshole," said CJ. "He doesn't do it anymore."

"Well if it was before I was born Tiny must have seen it. Tiny, you seen it?" asked the boy.

Tiny shoved down another handful of M&Ms and laughed the way he does, which sounds like a cough.

"See?" said CJ. "Tiny's heard of Chucky Luck."

All those boys live out on the border of North Sterns. Sometimes they used to yell to me.

"Come sit by your boyfriend, Clara," they yelled. "Come sit on CJ's lap."

The first time they did that I didn't get off at my stop. Tiny went right on by when I didn't come lurching up the aisle to wait by the door. I sank down in my seat and peered over the bottom of the window, watching the boys get off. Each one at his own trailer. The bus dropped off its last passenger, Bonita Rae Farwell, and turned around in Ray Farwell's rutted pasture-track. Tiny squinted in his rearview mirror. He reached into his M&M bag and tossed down another handful.

"What in the H you doing back there, Clara Winter?"

"I'm sorry, Tiny. I forgot to get off."

"Well what were you thinking, Clara?"

"I don't know. I guess I was reading and I missed the stop."

"Now I gotta go back all the way to North Sterns to let you off. We all know you got a brain in that head of yours, little girl, you use it now."

"I'm sorry, Tiny."

Tiny revved the engine so I could feel it throb under my feet. I watched Tiny's hand go back and forth from the bag to his mouth. When I got off he smiled at me. Little pointy black teeth.

You would not have known it to look at him, but the old man was a hero. In his life, he was a savior of babies, treed cats, and victims of natural disaster. In large and small ways and always for the better, the old man changed the lives of those who encountered him. I used to sit across from the old man at his cigarette-burned kitchen table and picture him as a young man, doing his heroic deeds.

The old man, as a young man, once saved a baby from drowning. Back where the old man came from, in his country that doesn't exist anymore, natural disasters were not a rarity. Spring floods, winter storms, summer tornadoes: these were the realities of the old-man-as-a-young-man's life.

Once, when the old man was only eleven, a spring flood came that was worse than the village had ever known. Flood legends that went back hundreds of years in the life of the village did not begin to match the enormity of what the old man and the villagers were seeing. The dikes, which were constructed of flower-patterned flour sacks stuffed with sand, gave way. Angry gray water foaming with yellow spume and filled with debris and broken dishes spewed over the top of the banks and exploded through the streets of the town.

"Georg! Climb to the roof!"

That was Georg's mother calling to him, frantic that her son be safe in the face of the water that threatened to overtake him. Georg, heeding his mother's cry, swiftly climbed the wooden peg ladder that leaned against the loft of the hut in which he lived with his parents.

"Where is Papa?" he shouted to his mother as he climbed.

"Still in the forge!" his mother called back.

Clutching her apron filled with the family's most treasured possessions—a Bible, three silver forks, the white baby dress that Georg, and later his brother Eli had been christened in—Georg's mother climbed after him. Together they huddled on the thatched roof of their cottage, holding hands and silently praying.

Remember, the old man was only eleven.

The roar of the water drowned out almost all other sound. For hours Georg and his mother crouched on the thatch, made slippery by the rain that accompanied the flood. The sky was dark and heavy with water. All around them the people of the village, neighbors they had known all their lives, huddled on their own roofs. On one, an old woman had managed to shove her pig through a hole in the thatch. She tethered him to the chimney with a rope and knelt next to him as he squealed and tried to push away the leash with his snout.

"Where, is, Papa?" Georg called again. Even though his mother was next to him, holding his hand, he had to yell because the noise of the thunder and rain and racing water drowned out sound.

His mother looked at him and said nothing. She shook her head.

"Pray," she said.

Then Georg's sharp ears heard a cry that was not of the wind or water. So faintly that he could not be sure he'd actually heard it, the cry of a newborn came drifting past. Borne on the wind of the storm, the cry was gone almost before it came. In the next moment it came again, and then again.

There's a baby out there, Georg thought.

He looked at his mother, her eyes closed tight against the driving rain and the tears that were blinding her. Across the street now filled by raging floodwaters, the old woman had put her arms around her pig and was holding it as if it were a child. The infant's cry came again, and young Georg felt his heart contract. He crouched and scanned the surrounding huts. *Where was the child?* The cry came again, and it was then that he saw her. Wrapped in a yellow blanket, placed in the forked limb of a black locust tree, as if someone in great haste had tried to do the one thing she could think of to save her child. Georg knew that it was up to him and him alone to bring the child to safety. Who else was there? Who else had heard the child's cry?

His mother had buried her head in her hands by then. Unseeing, unhearing, she was lost in a chanted prayer for Georg's father, still at the forge.

Quickly, before he lost his courage, Georg scrambled back into the loft and then down the peg ladder into the kitchen. Water had reached the halfway mark of the wall, and Georg lost his footing. Before he was swept under and out the door, he managed to take off his boots and soaked tunic. Then he was in the water, and part of the flood.

Getting across the street, which had become a torrent of water and debris, took many minutes. Every time he was swept under the surface of the frantic water, Georg held his breath and struggled to find his footing, struggled to the top again, gasped in a great lungful of air and shook the water from his eyes.

The baby cried, and cried again. Led by the thin wail of the baby's fear and sorrow, Georg found himself at the scarred trunk of the black locust, fighting to stay upright. Above him the faded yellow of the blanket hung suspended in the crotch of the tree. A tattered corner dangled in front of his reaching fingertips. The baby's cry was the cry of all babies, lost and alone and bereft. *If I could just reach that baby, if I could just—*

Do you see how it happens? Can you feel it growing inside your own heart? An old man tilts his shoulder in a certain way, or rubs his eye, and then it all comes over you. The yellow blanket, the raging floodwaters, a boy's mother crouched on a thatched roof crying for her lost husband. It all comes tumbling out.

The real story of my birth is that there was no midwife.

Angelica Rose Beaudoin, American Midwife, never lived or breathed. She never delivered two twin girls in a truck in the ditch in the middle of winter. She never stayed with my grandfather and Tamar, sharing her chocolate bars and telling jokes and stories, making sure Tamar was resting and recovering and not bleeding to death, until the Glass Factory Road snowplow came through. It never happened.

There was only Tamar and my grandfather and me: me crying, Tamar half-passed-out and bleeding, my grandfather not knowing what to do with my baby sister who lay wrapped in a scrap of blanket on the seat between them.

That's what I see when I think of the story of my birth. That's why I prefer to think about Angelica Rose Beaudoin, the brave young midwife.

Had there been an Angelica Rose Beaudoin, she would have seen immediately what the problem was. A trained midwife would have known what to do. She would have breathed life into my sister, rubbed her tiny chest, warmed her until she was a living being. The midwife would have stripped off the space blanket her husband had packed for her in the recycled coffee can emergency road kit, wrapped my sister up in it and handed her to my grandfather, who would have cradled her and rocked her.

Then I would have been born. I would have been strong and healthy, screaming from the first. *A healthy baby girl*, the midwife would have said to Tamar. *Two healthy baby girls.* A story with a happy ending, the kind of sixth-grade fake book report that my teachers would give me an A on.

It was the dead of winter, a February blizzard. Tamar couldn't get to the hospital, that was the whole problem. Her father was driving her in his truck. This was in the days before four-wheel drive. That's what Tamar said the one time I heard her talking to the choir director about it on the phone. She said, "Now there's four-wheel drive. That would have made all the difference." She had me and my twin sister in a ditch halfway to the hospital in Utica. Tamar couldn't hold us in. When babies want to be born they will be born. Nothing can stop them.

"We were born before four-wheel drive," I said.

The old man nodded.

"The problem is that they never should have taken Glass Factory," I said. "In a blizzard you never take Glass Factory. You take Route 12. You get to the hospital sooner. You don't wait until the last minute. You don't take Glass Factory hoping to save half a mile, hoping that some midwife will just happen to be passing by in the middle of a blizzard."

I had a twin sister. I think about her all the time.

If she were alive, people would talk about us in a different way. It would be "Tamar and her girls," "Miss Winter and the twins," "Tamar Winter and her daughters." Tamar refused to name my sister when she was born dead. Bad luck, she said. But what I believe to be true is that all babies should have a name. When I think about my sister, there is no name attached to my thoughts. She is nameless. All I see in my mind is _____, which I have changed to Baby Girl.

Tamar never told me about my sister. If it had not been for the choir director, I would still be living my life knowing that something was missing but not knowing that something was my twin sister.

"Your mother has a beautiful voice," the choir director said to me when I was nine years old, before I met the old man, when I used to have to sit in the sanctuary listening to the choir practice.

"Do you have a beautiful voice, too?" she asked me.

"Mediocre," I said, which is true.

"Imagine if you had a beautiful voice and your poor dead twin had had a beautiful voice," the choir director said. "The Twin Churches would have soared with the angelic voices of the three Winter women."

That's how the choir director talks.

"That poor baby," the choir director said. "She never had a chance, did she?"

I shook my head. I said nothing. I waited for more, but none was forthcoming. Even though I was only nine at the time and Tamar had never mentioned a word, I knew that what the choir director said was true. I had a twin. I could feel it in my bones.

My baby sister was dead, my chickens wanted to kill me, and the old man came from a country that doesn't exist anymore. Those were the kinds of secrets that I used to write down on my spool of green adding-machine paper, on Wednesday night when I visited the old man in his trailer. Soon I had unspooled enough paper to make several curls. Enough to hang to the floor.

I wish now that I had told the old man about CJ Wilson and the other boys and Tiny and the chickens. I wish that one cold night when my chickens were just beginning to be mean, and Tamar was at choir practice, and I had made the old man his coffee and me my hot chocolate, and we were sitting at his kitchen table and I was eating my toast spread with an inordinate amount of margarine and he was stirring his coffee with the handle of his spoon, I had told the old man everything.

Tamar says I'm crazy. Tamar says, That baby was dead before she was born. Tamar says, Give up.

But my sister was alive before she was dead, wasn't she? She grew the same as me, swimming around in a little water world. We knew each other. We touched each other. We would have been together forever.

Winter killed my baby sister. Not only was she my twin sister; she was my identical twin. I can feel that in my bones, too. If it hadn't been a blizzard, and if the truck hadn't gone off the road into the ditch, and if the plow hadn't chosen to do Route 12 before Glass Factory Road, my mother, Tamar, and my grandfather would have gotten to the hospital on time and my twin sister and I would have been born in the hospital and my sister would have lived. This is what I believe to be true.

"My mother didn't name my sister," I told the old man after we were *compadres*. "She did not give her own child a name. Is that even a possibility?"

"Anything's a possibility," the old man said.

"But she buried her," I said. "You don't bury someone unless you think of her as someone. If she was someone enough to bury, she was someone enough to have a name."

"You don't know what was going through your mother's head."

"But her own child?"

"She was not *your* child, she was your sister," the old man said. "There's a difference."

My sister is stuck forever at the spot where she was born. She was born there and she died there, while I lived and grew. I'm still growing. There's no telling how tall I'll be when all's said and done.

Tamar doesn't have the memory to connect her September blue sky and the smell of autumn leaves with the coming snow and what it means. She pushes it out of her mind. She pretends there never was another baby. She pretends that I was the only one. You don't have a sister, she says, stop dragging her into conversation all the time.

"But what would you have named her?" I used to ask her.

I can't help it. I've got to know.

"I wouldn't have named her anything," Tamar says. "She was born *dead*. And that's the end of it."

"But what if?" I say. "What if? Just tell me. Just give her a name."

She doesn't answer. She never answers. She has condemned me forever to think of my sister as Blank.

"She wasn't ever alive!" Tamar says. "Get it through your head, Clara. *You never had a sister.*"

I did, though. She swam beside me for nine months. We might have held hands inside Tamar's womb. Our noses might have touched. She might have played a game with me, pushing me around with her tiny unborn foot.

If you have seen a death certificate, you know what a small piece of paper it is. If you have ever searched your mother's bureau drawer for something that would be proof of your twin sister's existence, you might have been surprised at how small and simple a death certificate is. You don't even have to put someone's name down on a death certificate. If the person who died was a baby, all you have to put is "Baby" and the baby's last name. For example, "Baby Girl Winter."

If only the snow hadn't been blowing horizontally the way it does in an upstate New York blizzard, if my grandfather had only been able to rock his truck out of the ditch. If only Tamar hadn't mistaken early labor pains for indigestion and started for Utica sooner, if only we had just managed to stay inside her belly instead of forcing our way out. If only Angelica Rose Beaudoin, American Midwife, had been a real person.

But that's a different story. That's the story I would have written myself: my twin sister and I alive together, each the other's half, one child under God indivisiblewithlibertyandjusticeforall. That's the kind of book report I would have written, if I had made up a book about me and my sister.

"I want my sister," I said. "I want Baby Girl Winter."

The old man said nothing. He got up and carried his coffee cup and the plate that my sugar cookie had been on to his miniature sink. He put the stopper in and squeezed one small squirt of dish soap into the sink, then ran hot water. I watched him do that the exact same way every single time I ever visited the old man.

CHAPTER FIVE

What sorts of books are placed by garbage cans on garbage night in the town of Sterns? Mainly they're old class books, the kind people carry around in boxes in their basements for twenty years and then one day think: *I will never again in my entire life open this book and there is no sense in its taking up valuable space in my basement*, and they throw them out. Right out by the garbage cans they put them, in cardboard boxes with the bottoms falling out.

Books should not ever be treated that way. It's a sin to treat a book that way. That's what I believe to be true.

The world of my childhood is behind me now. I am no longer a child and I have put away childish things. But childish things come back to haunt you. The destruction of books is something I would not have visited upon even my most hated enemy. Had you asked me, I would have termed myself incapable of such an act.

There it is, though: I was a book ripper.

It hurts me now to think about it. I can't remember the actual ripping as I was only a baby. At most, a very small child.

Tamar told me about it on a day when I came to her holding a library book that someone had written in in purple magic marker. Not only that, but the top corner of each page had been creased, folded over in a triangle as if every page was a bookmark. It had to be the same magic marker person. A maniac.

"How can someone do this?" I said to Tamar.

She was making split pea soup, the only item of food that she actually cooks from scratch. A soup I like to eat but hate the smell of while it's cooking.

"Ma? Look."

I showed her the book, each page corner worn and creased, purple magic marker underlining certain paragraphs.

"And the thing is, the paragraphs that this person underlined don't even stand out," I said. "There's not one thing special about any of these underlined paragraphs."

Tamar took a cursory look. How I love that word. There may not be anyone in the world who loves the word *cursory* as much as I do. That's how I am about certain words.

"See what I mean?"

"Doesn't look so bad to me," she said. "Considering how you used to rip books to pieces when you were a baby."

She dumped two cupfuls of tiny hard green peas into the giant pot she makes soup in. They sank to the bottom with a clattering sound. Immediately the boiling water in the pot stopped boiling. It settled down and became ferociously quiet, working hard to start boiling again. The quietness of the once-boiling water made it seem as if the water was too busy to make noise. *I mean business* is what is meant by that absence of sound.

"What are you talking about?" I said.

"You," she said. "Clara Winter, defender of books. You used to rip them to shreds. Drove me crazy."

The water in the pot began to hum in a sinister way. A low, gathering hum, bringing itself back to a boil as if getting ready to go off to war.

"Any kind of book," she said. "Your baby books, my books, books belonging to other people. You'd rip the cover to pieces, then you'd start on the insides. You were possessed."

She took a bite of honey toast, a big one right out of the folded-over middle. That's something about Tamar. She greatly prefers the soft middle of bread, but she would not admit it, nor would she ever not eat her crusts. On her deathbed, Tamar will be finishing her crusts. That's the kind of person she is.

"Little Clara rips books, I scream at little Clara, little Clara laughs," Tamar said. "That's the way it was."

I had my roll of green note-taking adding-machine paper ready in its paper holder. The old man made the paper holder out of tin for me. He followed directions by looking at the pictures in his book *Metalworking Made Easy*. It holds my roll of adding-machine paper perfectly. It keeps it taut and tight, ready for me to take notes on.

"Yup," Tamar said. "That's all she wrote."

That's all, I wrote.

Books? Books are sacred. Books are to me what the host is to the priest, the oasis to the desert wanderer, the arrival of winged seraphim to a dying man. That's the main reason why I can't write a book report. I can't stand what a book report does, boils a book down to a few sentences about plot. What about the words that make each book unique, an island unto itself, words like *cursory* and *ingenuous* and *immerse*? What about the *heart and soul*?

Plot? Who cares?

My plots are always interesting. They're just not real. After the last report I wrote, my teacher sent me a personal note: "Clara, you have an intuitive understanding of how to include just enough information about a book to make your report exciting, while not giving away the ending. I am intrigued now and I may just have to go read this book myself."

That's the danger. She wants to know the nonexistent ending to a nonexistent book. I know how she feels. After I finish making up a book report, I myself want to read the book. I myself feel as if the book is out there, searching for me, with an ending I don't know, a future waiting to be written.

The old man knew of my love of books. He used to gather them for me on scavenging nights. Another place to get books is garage sales, of which there are many in a Sterns summer, but the old man didn't do that. He didn't go places where there might be crowds of people. He was a loner, the old man. He preferred solitude to conviviality.

Conviviality. Six syllables. A word that would be hard to say were English not your mother tongue.

Some of the books the old man gathered for me were not to my taste. I said nothing, though. He chose them mostly for their pictures and photos. I could tell. They had personal meaning for him, the books that he chose. I always thanked the old man when he saved a book for me. Here's the kind of book that appealed to him: *Metalworking Made Easy*, by William J. Becker. 1942. The old man had *Metalworking Made Easy* open to the page that showed a picture of how to make a tin paper roller.

"This would be useful for you," the old man said. "You could put your roll of adding-machine paper in it and it would keep it taut."

That was thoughtful of him, to think of me and my adding-machine paper. Next time I came to visit, he had a paper roller waiting for me. He had made it out of some sheet metal that he cut with his tin snips and soldered together with his solder iron. It looked just like the one in the book.

If you know how to read, you know how forever. You can't unread. You can't ever look at a word and not know what that word is, precisely and permanently. You just can't do it. They should tell you that when you're a kid, that once you get into phonics you're into them for life.

"There's no backing out, kiddo," they should say.

Brainwashing. That's what it actually is.

The old man though, he was a different matter. The old man was seventy-seven years old. When I met him, he was exactly seven times as old as me. How I love numbers that are multiples of eleven. They are far more interesting than multiples of ten, which are what the structure of the world revolves around when you think about it.

Here's a secret about the old man: he did not know how to read.

A few months after I met the old man I had a dream. I was on Ellis Island. The old man was standing on the edge of a pier. He was wearing a coat with a round collar like in the olden days. He was a boy. He was seventeen years old. His nose was moving, lines and stars and rectangles. The shape of the American flag.

The old man had told me that he used to use the tip of his nose to write in the air as a child. He called it air-writing. In my dream, there was a certain look in the old-man-as-a-young-man's eyes. I woke up and I knew he couldn't read.

I proved it.

"I'm writing you a message in the air with my nose," I said.

This was one day after he told me about the air-writing.

"You see if you can figure it out," I said.

I wrote it in small letters: *bye.* That was the whole message, three small letters. It was time for me to go. Tamar didn't like to drive all the way in to the old man's trailer. She liked me to walk out to the entrance and meet her there. It's good for you, Clara, she used to say, the fresh air.

"Good," he said, after I wrote it in the air with my nose. "You're getting the hang of it."

"What did it say?" I said. "Did you really figure it out?"

"I did."

"But could you tell I was writing *bye*?"

"I could."

Nay sir, I think not.

I tested him again.

I wrote him a note and put it under his coffee cup when I brought it over to the table.

"What's this?" he said.

He pulled it out and looked at it.

"What do you think?" I said.

"Very good."

Why did I have to test him again? There wasn't any need to. How I wish I hadn't written what I wrote on that note: *I know you can't read.*

• • •

The old man remembered things in colors and sounds, not letters. Shapes he could hold in his head, and ideas, and memory was locked in him tighter than you can imagine. He had learned to form the words of his name. I watched him do it on the check he used to get every month. He made the letters by putting slashes here and slashes there: Georg Kominsky. You could tell he didn't know how to make real letters. Letters to the old man were only shapes and sticks and curves, actors strutting and fretting on a stage, signifying nothing.

Picture all that came into the old man's life that he never knew the meaning of: words and sentences and paragraphs and pages. Pages and pages and pages.

How many letters came to his trailer, and to all the places he may have lived before the trailer? How many people in this world sat down once late at night, lit a candle or turned on a lamp, and took pen in hand to write to the old man?

Dear Georg.

Dearest Georg.

My beloved Georg.

And nothing, nothing in return.

Picture the old man opening an envelope. Picture him recognizing the shapes of the writing, the twists and turns. Picture him looking at the lines and curves of the words. He could not make sense of the shapes. He could not turn lines and curves into meaning.

People who loved the old man may have thought he died. They may have thought, no news from America is not good news. Our Georg surely would have written by now. Something unimaginably awful must have befallen him.

The old man never let anyone know he couldn't read. He was too proud. I knew this about him. I could tell. I can always tell. It's one of my skills.

They almost didn't let him into Ellis Island because of his nose. The air-writing. Retardation, they thought, because of his nose going around and around and the look on his face because of his concentration. They almost chalked his coat with a white X, which meant they were going to send him back. It was only at the last minute that the old man realized why they were looking at him that way and he stopped tracing the flag in front of the Ellis Island building with his nose. He stood perfectly still and put a very intelligent look on his face. This is how I picture him, in his olden-days coat with the round collar and a dark hat, and boots that laced up high and were wearing through at the bottom, and one small satchel. That's what they called duffels back then: *satchels*. He stood straight. He looked intelligent. He willed them with all his might to let him in.

I've come this far, he willed them. *Let me in.*

The old man didn't speak English yet. He would have willed them in his own, lost language, without seeing the image of the words in his mind. Everything in his body would have been bent into the willing. *Let me in, let me in, let me in.*

The old man's little brother had known how to read. I know this because the old man told me.

"Eli was very good in school," he said to me once during the oral history.

Eli knew that his brother could not read, so Eli would do the reading for the both of them while Georg, the old man, would go out and get a job and support them both. That was the plan. The old man never told me that but still, I know. I believe it to be true.

But the old man came alone to America.

You could write a book report about the old man. You could use his real name and the true facts of his life. His life could be a historical biography, like Eli Whitney or Julia Ward Howe. His life could be boiled down to a two-page plot synopsis. You could include his boyhood in a country that doesn't exist anymore, his coming to America at age seventeen, his job as a metalworker, and how he ended up at Nine Mile Trailer Park in Sterns, New York. You could call the book report *Georg Kominsky: American Immigrant.*

That's a book report I would not write.

I decided to make a show of nonreading solidarity with the old man.

I cut the labels off all the cans in the can cupboard. When I was done, I had three dozen labelless cans. The big fat ones were plum tomato cans. They stood out. But all the others, the other thirty-one cans, were anonymous. No pictures, no words. No identifying characteristics.

The cans lined up nicely, stacked one on top of the other, nothing to tell them apart. I was in the dark. Helpless. Nothing I could do would reveal the meaning of these cans other than opening them up.

Tamar was not pleased.

"What the hell's going on here, Miss?" she said when she opened up the can cupboard. Tamar prefers to eat out of cans and jars. She likes food that comes in glass and tin packages. Sometimes she heats them up, sometimes she doesn't.

All the nameless cans shone in the overhead light. They were pretty, shining like that. Tamar crossed her arms and leaned against the counter. She had a look in her eyes.

"For school," I said. "They're doing a label drive."

She just looked at me.

"We each have to bring in three dozen labels."

She kept on looking.

"For reading," I said. "It's a literacy drive. Literacy is very important."

Still looking. She didn't budge. That's one of her skills.

"What's going on here, Clara?"

There was nothing I could say that would be true without giving away the old man's secret.

"I got going and I couldn't stop," I said.

Still she kept looking at me.

"Is there something you're not telling me?" she said.

"I got going and I couldn't stop," I said again. I kept seeing the words in my head: *I got going and I couldn't stop, I got going and I couldn't stop, I got going and I couldn't—*

"Stop," I said.

Tamar was taking all the cans out of the cupboard. She put them in a brown paper Jewell's Grocery bag and handed them over to me.

"They're yours, Clara," she said. "You can have a mystery food dinner party. I expect replacement cans to be in the can cupboard by Thursday evening."

No plan. No instructions. That's Tamar. She's a you made your bed, you lie in it kind of person. I watched her fix herself a bowl of Cheerios with a banana and raisins and sugar in it and eat it up. That was her dinner. It looked pretty good.

• • •

I took the Jewell's bag of unidentifiable cans down to the old man's the next night, which was Wednesday, choir practice night. Tamar didn't say anything when she dropped me off and saw me haul it out of the back seat. Three dozen cans is a lot. Heavy. Awkward. The bag split halfway down to the old man's house. The lady who lives two trailers down from the old man and wears men's winter boots pushed her living room curtain aside and watched me pick them up.

Did she come out to help? No.

I put a few cans in my jacket pocket and carried as many as I could in my arms and hands. Then I put them all down and put just one large can on top of my head. That's the way African women carry water, in jugs on top of their head. If they can do it, I can too. I tried walking that way. It's quite difficult. You can't look down with your whole head. You have to trust where you're going. Little steps.

The old man opened the door for me. He reached out and plucked the one can from my head. Then he handed me another Jewell's bag, plastic this time. He took another one and we went back to the cans lying in the snow. They shone in the light from the one Nine Mile Trailer Park streetlamp. I pretended the streetlamp was the moon, shining down on the cans.

"I brought dinner," I said. "It's a mystery dinner. We will have no idea what we're eating until we open up the cans."

One of the things about the old man was that he didn't question.

"All right," he said.

In the trailer I was going to make the old man close his eyes. I was going to wrap a dish towel around his head for a blindfold, then I realized it wouldn't matter. What was there to read? What was there to give away the secret? Everything was unknown. That was the whole point of the show of solidarity.

"Pick a can," I said. "Any can."

He picked one, then I picked one. Then he picked another one.

"Three," I said. "That should be good enough. With three we should get in at least two of the four basic food groups."

The old man got out his can opener.

"Can #1?" I said.

"Creamed corn," he said. "Can #1 is creamed corn."

"Can #2?"

"Corned beef hash, from the looks of it."

"#3?"

"Sauerkraut."

We heated up the food and ate it. The old man used a soup spoon to eat everything. No fork. The old man didn't like to waste utensils. Why use two when one will do? In solidarity, I used only a soup spoon, too. Things taste different when you don't use a fork.

"Not bad," I said.

The old man didn't say anything. He didn't usually say anything when he was eating. What he did was look down at his plate and eat steadily and quietly until all the food was gone. Then he picked up his plate and carried it over to his miniature sink and ran water on it.

My heart was not in the dinner. It didn't feel like a show of solidarity to me. Creamed corn, sauerkraut, and corned beef hash. It wasn't so bad. It was a regular dinner, just that we didn't know what we would be eating before we ate it. Nothing lost, nothing gained. No pain involved. What was the point?

• • •

It didn't use to be a shameful thing, not knowing how to read. In many countries of the world almost no one knew how to read. Take China. Only the rulers had enough time to learn how to read and write. That's what a book I read said. *Keep the workers down!* Make a written language so hard to learn that someone with no spare time would never be able to. Never write. Never read. Spend your life cutting stone for the rulers who lay around reading and writing their nearly impossible language.

That's what the book said.

It's an actual book. I didn't make it up.

Think of what the old man lost, not reading: jobs, because he couldn't read the want ads. Doctor appointments, because he couldn't read the reminder slip. Electricity and phone and gas and heat, turned off because he didn't read the bills. Packages sent to him, because he couldn't understand the post office pickup notice. Friends, because he didn't write back. Family, because they never heard from him again.

I thought of the old man as a young man, a boy of eleven, struggling across torrential floodwaters to save a baby wrapped in a yellow blanket, crying in the crook of a black locust tree.

"Clara?"

The old man was standing by the sink in his trailer. He held a dishcloth in his hand. He had rinsed and dried the nameless solidarity cans.

"Clara? Did you hear it?"

"Yes," I said. "Yes, I did hear it."

The old man gave me a look.

"And what did you hear?" he said.

"The baby."

"What baby?"

"The baby you saved in the flood," I said. "The baby in the yellow blanket."

The old man folded his dishcloth. He had a precise way of folding his dishcloth, and a precise way of hanging it on his oven door.

"I saved a baby in a yellow blanket?" he said.

"Yes."

I could hear that baby crying still, laid in the crotch of the black locust tree. What had happened to her mother? How could a baby come to be laid in a tree during the worst flood in the village's history? In my mind the young Georg struggled and fought his way across the raging current, bent on saving the helpless child.

"I was talking about the owl by Nine Mile Creek," he said. "You can hear it sometimes on a night like tonight."

I looked at him. It was hard to come back from the flood, hard to unimagine him as a boy.

"And this baby, what about this baby in the yellow blanket?" he said.

"Nothing," I said.

A single thought spun out of air turns into a baby in a yellow blanket, longing for its mother. But there was no baby in a yellow blanket. The old man never struggled through foaming water and tumbling debris to rescue a crying infant perched in the crotch of a black locust tree. That was my story, not the old man's story. None of it happened, none of it was real. Still, it's what I believed to be true.

Again he asked me:

"What happened to the baby in the yellow blanket?"

I wanted to say, *You tell me. You were the one who saved that baby's life.*

"That baby never existed," I said. "End of story."

The old man turned his hands palms up. That's something he used to do. He would turn them up and study each palm, tracing the lines. After a while of the old man studying his hands and waiting for me to talk, and me not talking, he went to his bedroom and brought me back a brown paper bag. Inside was a lantern, a regular-size pioneer lantern made of tin.

"To replace your missing earring," he said.

"This is not the sort of lantern I intended," I said. "You said you'd make me a lantern *earring.* This is a real lantern."

He had made it out of my leftover plum tomato cans, the ones I had strung in his weeping willow. You could still see the red tomato labeling on the inside of the lantern. He had punched holes into it in decorative patterns, like the kind of decorative patterns the pioneers used to make. I had seen these patterns in old library books. The old man had cut thin strips of aluminum from the cans and curled them into little curlicues and attached them to the top and bottom of the lantern for decoration. He had put a nail into the bottom of the lantern and spiked a candle on the nail. He had made a carrying handle for the lantern out of twisted wire.

"This is not an earring," I said.

"Lanterns should be useful as well as beautiful," the old man said.

I thought of my missing lantern earring, sinking ever deeper into the snow and mud. I imagined floodwaters sweeping it away, helpless in the torrent, down the Nine Mile Creek and into the Utica floodplain. Swamp gas enveloping my lovely earring in its evil vapors. Swamp worms curving around it, thinking it was some kind of treasure.

The old man took one of his furnace matches, gigantic long ones, and lit the candle. It was getting dark outside. Across Nine Mile Creek I could see the stained-glass windows of the church where Tamar and the other choir people were practicing. The old man put the lantern on the kitchen table and turned out all the lights. We sat there at his table looking at the lantern. He had punched winter into the lantern: snowflakes, stars, a snowman.

"I hate winter," I said. "I hate snow. Winter is what killed Baby Girl."

The old man turned the lantern around. On the other side he'd punched in summer: a sun with big rays, a flower, a robin. Across Nine Mile Creek the stained-glass windows went dark. Tamar would be driving up to the trailer park in exactly six minutes. She's never late.

"This is a pioneer lantern," the old man said. "For doing winter chores."

"But what I wanted was a new lantern earring for my one remaining lantern."

"It never would have been an exact match," he said. "It never would have been the original."

He turned the lantern around. Winter shone out at me. He turned it again, and it was summer. Outside the trailer it was pitch black. Tamar would be driving up in exactly three minutes. She would honk the horn and reach across to open up the door for me. It doesn't open from the outside anymore. The old man turned the lantern around and kept on turning it. The candle stayed steady. It was stuck firmly on its spike. Stars turned into sun, snowflakes into flowers, a snowman was a robin with a big fat worm. I stared at the turning lantern. I held my head straight and did not blink, trying hard to train my eyes to see the possibility of beauty.

CHAPTER SIX

T amar has a father, which means that I have a grandfather.
If A is Tamar, and B is her father, and C is me, the relationship is mathematically clear. He was in the truck when I
was born in the blizzard.

"He lives way up in the Adirondacks," Tamar said years
ago, when I first asked her about him and she forbade me to
mention him ever again. "Near the Vermont border. And
that's all you need to know."

Way up in the Adirondacks near the Vermont border
sounds like hermit territory to me. Is my grandfather a hermit? Why not? Nary a single visit to his only living granddaughter makes my grandfather a hermit in my book.

My grandfather lives in a tent in the middle of a primeval
forest in the Adirondacks. You may think that upstate New
York has no primeval forests left. You may think that there are
no primeval forests on the east coast of America, nor in the
middle west, nor on the west coast with the exception of the
ones in Oregon and Washington that everyone knows about.

You would be wrong.

There is a small primeval forest in the hermit country of upstate New York, just before the Vermont border. It is composed of old-growth trees, trees that are more than five hundred years old. These trees have existed since before the American Revolutionary War. They were here when Columbus sailed onto Plymouth Rock, if he actually did. They were here for the Civil War. The Green Mountain Boys snuck through this primeval forest on their way to fight the graycoats.

Am I telling the truth?

I very well may be.

Who would know?

Is there anyone who has inspected every square inch of the Adirondack Park? Have helicopters and airplanes and surveyors and bloodhounds straining at the leash and hikers and campers and forest rangers mapped out every square inch of the Empire State? Has every square inch been traversed and retraversed? Is there anyone alive who can say with absolute certainty: *"No. Not one square inch of Adirondack woods consists of primeval forest."*

Do you see what I mean?

The truth can be sought. The truth can be hunted down. The truth can be your one and only rule, but it is slippery. It hides. You think you've got it pinned down, but you don't.

When I first started imagining my grandfather up in the Adirondacks, I wondered what he lived on. Was he totally self-sufficient? Did he trap furs in the winter and barter them for essential supplies? Every hermit must have some essential supplies, such as matches, flour, cooking oil. A hammer, a hunting rifle, and ammunition. Candles. Cornmeal. Tobacco, for the pipe he smoked while hunched over his campfire in the dead of winter. My hermit grandfather knew the fearsome power of snow and cold.

I still think about my hermit grandfather. I still wonder about him.

Some would say that I made him up, that he never existed. But I can see him in my mind, walking silently through the woods on the breast of new-fallen snow. Doesn't that make him real in a way?

"Ma, is your father a hermit?"

I asked Tamar that, even though she had forbidden me ever to mention her father. Tamar looked at me.

"A hermit? My father, a hermit?"

"Yes. That is the question," I said.

"What possesses you, Clara? What goes through your brain?"

I said nothing. In the face of Tamar's derision my dream was already crumbling into dust and blowing away like sand in a Thebes desert storm. I wanted to hang on to my hermit. Already I loved him.

In certain snow conditions you can't see your hand in front of your face. Tamar and I were coming home from Boonville one winter day when I was nine. She was driving. It was whiteout conditions: snow blowing fast and furious, horizontal because of the wind. When you look out a window and you see snow blowing horizontally, it's instinct to turn your head sideways.

Horizontal snow is a world gone awry.

Tamar and I were a couple miles out of Boonville, heading south to North Sterns, when it turned from slanted to horizontal and intermittently to blizzard. It was only midafternoon. Everything was a fury of white.

"Do not dissolve, Clara," she said.

Tamar knows how I hate the snow.

She opened her window and stuck her head out. She slowed the car down but she didn't stop. It's better not to stop unless there's a parking lot or something. On a back road you have no idea where you're stopping. A plow, a sander—anything—can come up behind you on a back road in a blizzard and smash you to bits. That's the risk you run, stopping.

Tamar had her head stuck out the window. Snow was already clumping on her hair and her eyelashes. Her head was tilted and she squinted against the snow. I saw what she was doing. She was sighting her way by the telephone poles. She was going just fast enough to find the next one after the first one receded. From telephone pole to telephone pole, Tamar kept the car going.

"Hang tough, Clara," she yelled with her head out the window.

I hooked up my personal backup bungee cord belt system. I use it only in dire straits. Two bungee cords, one orange and one black. Emergency colors. One stretches from Tamar's headrest over my left shoulder and fastens onto the door handle. The other stretches from my headrest and fastens onto the stick shift. They cross in my middle and pinion me.

Tamar's head was out the window. She didn't see me hooking up the bungee cords. They're for extreme conditions only. Tamar hates them.

"Worse than useless," she said when I first devised the system. "Those bungees'll kill you before they'll save you from anything."

She unhooked the orange one and shook it in my face.

"You see this hook? Any kind of crash, even a fender bender, this thing'd come unhooked and slash your face up. Or gouge your eye out."

She let go of the hook and I hooked it up again. She could tell I was not going to be intimidated.

"You are an odd child, Clara Winter," she said. "You are truly strange."

But ever since that day south of Boonville, when she was sighting her way by the telephone poles, she hasn't said a word. She lets me hook up the bungees. They're only for when I feel extreme danger.

Sometimes Tamar's unarguability is useful. When we were driving in that blizzard and she was sighting her way along the road by the telephone poles, it was useful. I was bungeed in and chanting. If you chant when you're in grave danger, you can transport yourself into a world of safety. You just chant and chant and chant, the same thing over and over, until you feel yourself transported.

mm, mm, mm.

That's my chant. I don't want it to be anything that makes sense, because then I would focus on the sense I was making instead of the world of safety. It's all related to the ability to read. Are you beginning to see that? If you say something that makes sense, and you're a reader, the words scroll across the bottom of your mind and there you are. You're stuck. You're focusing on the meaning of the words, the shape of the letters, rather than the meaningless sound of the chant itself and the world of safety it's taking you into.

"Hold it together, Clara," Tamar yelled in from the window. She had one hand on the steering wheel and one hand on the

open window. I chanted and chanted but I was not transported. The bungee cords held me against the back of the seat
and I opened my eyes to watch Tamar's hand curled tight
around the steering wheel like a spider on a web.

Then we went into the ditch.

Immediately Tamar's head was back inside the car. She
rolled up her window and shook her head so that the caked
snow flew all over the dashboard. The snow on her eyelashes
started to melt and melted snow ran down her cheeks. She
reached across with her frozen hands and hooked her fingers
through my bungee cords.

"You will, not, fall, apart, Clara Winter," she said. "Hear
me?"

I could feel how cold her hand was even through my jacket,
sweater, turtleneck, and T-shirt.

"We are in the ditch," she said. "Being in the ditch is not the
end of the world."

She forgets. It *was* the end of the world for Baby Girl.

Tamar started to undo the bungees. Her fingers were so
cold that they didn't bend right. When she got them undone,
she undid the seatbelt.

"We're walking," she said. "Bundle up."

She was unarguable. I had to crawl over the hump and then
over her seat to get out, because the car was tilted into the
ditch. She was already marching ahead. The car was already
being snowed over. It was a true blizzard.

Did she think about my sister?

Did she blame herself? My grandfather? The snow?

On she marched. I ran to keep up.

"Wait," I screamed. The wind took my words and whipped
them away. I kept screaming out the word: *wait, wait,* but

Tamar's back kept getting away from me. I looked to my left. A telephone pole. You could barely see it through the driving snow. I looked for the next one. I couldn't see it. Then she was there, Tamar, standing in front of me.

"Keep, up," she yelled. "Do, you, hear, me? Keep, up. I do not plan to lose my daughter in a blizzard."

She puts it out of her mind. *You already did lose your daughter in a blizzard.* I couldn't say that to Tamar though. After I showed her Baby Girl Winter's death certificate, Tamar told me the bare minimum: the truck, the blizzard, the ditch. To her it was as if my baby sister never drew breath. Which is another of my questions: did my baby sister draw breath? Did her miniature lungs fill even once with frozen Adirondack air?

I saw that Tamar was wearing her loafers. She didn't even have her boots on.

"Ma? You don't have your boots on," I yelled.

I had to yell. That was the only way you could make yourself heard that day. She didn't say anything. She just kept marching. Her loafers were filled with snow. Packed with it. I did not allow myself to think of how cold her feet must be. In the pioneer days it was common to lose toes to frostbite. Pioneers were always getting lost in the snow. In the pioneer days blizzards were worse than they are now. Pioneers would often go out to the barn to milk their cow and then get lost on the way back to the cabin. The wind and snow drove so hard back in those days that they would walk right on past the cabin, just missing the log corner. They would walk right on into the wilderness. Lost pioneers would not be found until spring, when the snow melted. There they would be, curled up in a fetal position.

They say that death by freezing is not such a bad way to go.

Once you get cold enough you actually feel warm. This is what I have read.

I wonder what their last thoughts were, though. I wonder what they thought when they knew they'd walked long enough to get back to the cabin. Did they try to turn around? Which way was the way back? Which way was north? This was in the days before compasses, probably. In those days they had only the stars to navigate by. With the snow swirling all around them, and the darkness of the sky above, nothing to light their way, the candle in their tin lantern blown out by the howling wind, I just wonder what those pioneers thought.

When Tamar was giving birth in the truck tipped over in the ditch, did she know that one of her babies was going to die? Could she possibly have foreseen what was going to happen? Did she even know she was going to have twins?

"Ma! Did you know you were going to have twins?"

I yelled this to her back. Her loafers disappeared into the mounds of snow with every step. My boots had my snowpants pulled over them. My feet were protected against the blowing snow.

She didn't answer. She never does. She won't talk about it. She leaves me to wonder about it myself, to try to guess what happened. She keeps me in the dark.

It took us a couple of hours of blizzard walking to reach a house. After a while I put my head down and focused on Tamar's loafers. They were dark brown when she lifted them, with packed white around her feet. I kept my eyes focused on her feet. They became a visual blizzard chant: *don't let Tamar's feet freeze.* A rhythm set itself up in my head: *don't let Tamar's feet freeze*. One step for every emphasis. *Don't let Tamar's feet freeze*. The snow piled up on my neck. It sifted underneath my scarf, melted against my neck, and ran down my back. Then the process started all over again. Pile, sift, melt, run. Everything took on a rhythm in that blizzard. We walked and we walked. Walking became the only thing I could remember. I turned myself into the walking. There was nothing to think about because I was no longer a person. I was no longer a sentient being. I was no longer even a reader. My thoughts did not scroll across the bottom of my mind because I had no thoughts.

That's the one time in my life that I was not a human being. I was only a thing that walked.

Tamar's loafers that were dark brown and packed white around her socks changed direction. They turned. Because I was no longer a thinking being I did not know if they turned right or left. I followed because that was what the thing I had become did; it followed Tamar's loafers.

Tamar's loafers stopped. There was a tinkling sound outside the deafness of falling snow. Tamar's loafers were lifting up high in the whiteness and then disappearing. I stood there because they were gone. There was nothing left to follow.

Then she grabbed me. The second she touched me I went back to being a human being. Sentience returned. Words again started subtitling my brain: *don't let Tamar's feet freeze*.

"In," she shouted. "Get your butt inside. Climb right through that window. Now."

Then we were inside. It was somebody's house. Somebody who was not there. Where were they? South for the winter? Immediately the person who was not there became a Florida person to me. I could see her, lying on the sand in the sun with a small, thick paperback book facedown next to her. There was a thermostat on the wall and I saw Tamar go over to it. She angled her elbow toward it and gave it a jab, and then there was a sound of *heat*. Nothing is like the sound of a furnace leaping into action, lunging and thrumming somewhere way down in the basement, when you twirl a thermostat in the winter.

"Why'd you use your elbow?" I said.

My words sounded unusual. They came out thick, like slush, into the frozen air.

Tamar didn't answer. She was already gone. I heard water running. She was in the kitchen running water. Why weren't the pipes frozen? In an Adirondack winter, pipes are always frozen. I went into the kitchen of the Florida person's house.

"Why aren't the pipes frozen?" I said. Still slushy-sounding.

"Why *would* the pipes be frozen? Whoever owns this house is probably stuck in the blizzard, just like us."

My Florida person faded away. She turned into an Adirondacks lady sitting in Tam's Diner on Route 12, cupping her cold fingers around a mug of hot coffee, her car in the parking lot disappearing minute by minute under the snow.

"Oh," I said. "Why'd you use your elbow to turn on the heat?"

"Because my fingers are too cold to move," Tamar said.

She was sitting on a chair with her feet in the sink. She was running water on her feet that still had their loafers and socks on. It was hot water. I could see the steam.

Don't let Tamar's feet freeze.

I went over to the sink. I took my hands out from my armpits where I had been keeping them warm. Always put frozen hands in your armpits. That's something I learned from the pioneer books. I pulled at Tamar's loafers until they fell off. They clunked into the sink. They weighed a thousand pounds each. I pulled her white socks off. They weighed a hundred pounds each.

Her feet were white.

Not a good sign.

Dead white is a sign of frozen flesh. What is hoped for, when removing a pioneer's shoes and socks, is pink skin. Roaring red skin is even better. White is not what you want.

"Shut up, Clara," Tamar said before I even said a word. "I don't want to hear it. Keep your pioneers to yourself."

The hot water ran and ran. My cold feet in my moon boots were getting warm. My fingers were warm. The furnace thrummed and hummed. The person's house was getting warm.

"Go cover that broken window with a coat or something, would you Clara, please."

That was unlike Tamar. Please is a word not prevalent in Tamar's lexicon. I went and covered the window. Tamar ran warm water over her feet for a long time. I stood beside her and watched her feet. After a while she bent over and held her hands under the faucet too. Then she picked up the drainplug and plugged the drain.

"Dumb," she said. "Running all this hot water. Probably used up most of it."

Dumb is not a word used by Tamar. The hot water filled the kitchen sink and Tamar turned it off. Her fingers were bright red. That's a good sign. She submerged her feet in the sink.

"Dumb," she said again.

Tamar was crying. Tamar was crying and calling herself dumb.

"Ma?"

She shook her bright red hand at me. Drops of warm water spattered on my face. She turned her head away from me so that her brown hair hung down and I couldn't see her.

"Sorry, Clara."

Nor does Tamar say she's sorry.

"It's all right," I said.

It wasn't though. It was not all right. It has never been all right.

Winter is out there. It waits. It bides its time. Sometimes, when you're lulled into a false sense of security, it comes roaring out at you and tries to destroy you. It is ruthless. It has no mercy. Victims fall prey to it. The bodies of dead pioneers, found only after the spring thaw, are buried beneath the ground. Baby Girl died because of winter.

Tamar's shoulders shook with her crying.

"Did you try to save her?" I said.

That's a question that demands an answer.

But no answer was forthcoming.

We stayed in the kitchen for a long time. The furnace kept humming. There was no moment when the furnace heated the house as hot as we wanted it and then shut off because there was no more heating to do. That point was never reached. The furnace kept on going, and we kept on staying. We stayed in that person's house for three days, until the plow went through. It came through in darkest night. We were sleeping in the person's bed. I kept dreaming of her as a Florida person, lying on her Florida beach, drinking soda from a glass with a small pink umbrella on it. The house was eighty-eight degrees. That's the warmest Tamar has ever had a house. Usually she sets the thermostat at sixty-three.

"Put on a sweater," she says when I start to shiver.

That's one of her flat Tamar statements. But in that person's house she cranked the heat up as high as it could go.

"We'll fix the window," she said. "We'll pay their oil bill. They won't mind."

Tamar's feet hurt when they thawed.

"Damn it," she said, when they had been in the water a long time. "Damn it."

She gritted her teeth. I could hear them gritting.

"Is the feeling coming back?" I said.

That's a good sign. What you want is for your feet to hurt horribly, to be hideously painful. That means that the blood is returning to your extremities. Your feet will be saved. You won't have to chop them off. Gangrene will not set in and it's very possible that no toes will be lost.

She didn't answer. It's rare that Tamar feels the need to answer every question I ask her, despite the fact that most of the questions I ask her are ones that demand answers.

"Are they hurting?" I asked.

"They are hurting like hell," she said.

"Good. That's a good sign."

After a long time Tamar let the water drain out of the sink and she dried her feet. Her hands were still bright red and her fingers did not move swiftly. Her feet were also bright red except for a few small white patches on some of the toes.

"You see those small white patches?" I said. "They may very well be frostbite."

"Enough, Clara."

I did not mention frostbite again. But still, I could tell. I've read enough pioneer books to know that small white patches mean frostbite. When we got home Tamar went to the doctor at Slocum-Dickson in Utica, who confirmed my diagnosis. Her feet hurt her now when it gets cold. Her toes are especially painful. I can tell. She walks in a certain way. Tamar would never admit to it but still, I know. Once frozen, your flesh will never be completely unfrozen. The memory of cold becomes a part of you. You never forget.

My hermit grandfather would have known better than to venture out in the winter. My grandfather knew full well the power of a winter storm. He had watched it wreak devastation on his own family, for it was he who was behind the wheel of the truck when it went skidding into the ditch. Sometimes I strain my memory, trying to remember my grandfather's face. I must have seen it when I was born, even if only for a moment. I looked at Tamar, kneading her thawed feet, and it occurred to me that she might look like her father. She might be his spitting image. How would I know?

"Ma, do you think that a newborn is capable of remembering a face?" I said to Tamar.

"No."

"Not at all?"

"Not at all. A newborn doesn't even know what a face is. A newborn has never been outside the uterus; a newborn wouldn't know the difference between a human being and a goldfish."

Coming from Tamar, that was the answer I expected. Everything Tamar says must be taken with a grain of salt. You have to filter everything through the knowledge of what you know about Tamar.

"Do you believe in baby purgatory?" I asked Tamar.

"Enough, Clara."

"But do you?"

"I said, enough."

She wiggled her toes up and down. Her toes moved slowly, as if they had forgotten how to wiggle. I watched her right eye and saw it squint nearly shut while the left stayed wide open. Did my grandfather's eyes do that, too?

You can't blame my grandfather for becoming a hermit. He shunned society in favor of solitude. He had only his own thoughts for company. He depended on himself and only himself, except for his twice-yearly visits to town to trade his furs for cash to buy necessities. Maybe my hermit grandfather sang songs to himself at night, when he lay on his pallet. Maybe he went walking in the moonlight, only the stars and the silent moon and the watchful nocturnal animals as witness.

Maybe he thought about Tamar. He might have thought about her, his only daughter, and wondered what she was doing. He may have thought about me, the grandchild he had not seen since the day she was born. He might have thought about the other granddaughter, the ghost baby, the one he could not save.

Did he try?

Did he attempt everything he possibly could to try to save my baby sister's life?

"Tamar, did my grandfather have any paramedic training?"

"Why do you ask, Clara?"

"Just wondering."

"The answer is no. To my knowledge my father had no paramedical training."

"So he would not have been able to resuscitate a hypothetical dead newborn?"

"Enough, Clara," Tamar said. She held her hurting feet with both hands, twisting them to the right and back to the left. "Enough, enough, enough."

CHAPTER SEVEN

The old man was a hero for many reasons, not the least of which was that he once escaped from the solitary confinement to which he had been unfairly sentenced. Most often a solitary confinement is a hole in the ground, covered with a wooden door. Such was the case with the old man. When a prisoner is bad enough or, like the old man, unfairly sentenced for a fake offense—backtalk to a guard—they chain his legs and arms and drag him to a hole in the ground. They remove the chains and throw him in. They lock the wooden door in place and that's it. Once, possibly twice a day, the door is opened and a bucket of water and another bucket of slop are lowered into the hole. That's what the old man lived on. There was nowhere to go to the bathroom in the old man's solitary confinement except in the mud at the bottom of the hole.

I can picture the old man as a young man, crouched in the bottom of the muddy pit, curling himself into a fetal position on the filthy scrap of old horse blanket that the guards had thrown down on him. I can see that poor young man so clearly, reciting stories and poems from his childhood in an effort to keep from going insane.

If you can see it so clearly in your mind, it's real. Isn't it?

Few prisoners survive more than a few weeks in solitary confinement. If they are not allowed into the light of day within a fairly short time, they start to rot. Once you start to rot death comes quickly. People need light. They need sunshine in order to keep on living. They need sound, which is another thing that does not exist in solitary confinement.

How did the old man survive? He had a secret life. He knew from the very first day in the hole of solitary confinement that he would not be able to survive unless he had two things: a dream and an escape route. The very first night, he broke off a tree root that was growing into the side of the hole. For the next year, he used that root to dig silently at night. Using mental maps, he tunneled his way directly underneath the prison kitchen. Eventually, by tracking the vibrations of the ground above his head, he figured out where the prison kitchen root cellar was and tunneled up to it.

This took a total of eleven months. He kept track of the passing days in his head. Each night he made up legends and myths and stories. Georg Kominsky knew that unless he exercised his brain as well as his body, both would atrophy. What kept Georg going? What prevented him from giving in to despair?

His dream.

He dreamed of his metalworking tools.

Georg Kominsky had a vision and he did not allow himself to swerve from that vision. Despite the cockroaches that swarmed over his pallet at night and the pale worms that writhed in his nightly food bucket, he forced himself to eat and sleep and exercise and make up legends. He did not once allow the thought of death to enter his mind. Night after night, day after day, the old man kept on going.

It might seem that a dream of metalworking alone would not be enough. It might seem that someone would need more than the thought of tin snips, a solder iron, and a forge to stay alive.

Not if you were the old man. I know this because that's what he told me. Once, a few weeks after I told him about Baby Girl Winter and how I hated being without her, the old man looked at me and said, "You only need one thing, Clara."

"One what?"

"One thing to keep you going. One thing will do."

I looked at him. We were outside at his forge. He was working on a lantern, soldering decorative strips to the sides.

"Well, what's your one thing then?" I said.

He pulled his safety glasses over his eyes and touched the tip of the solder iron to the tin. Gray metal-melt trickled down the side.

"This. Making useful and beautiful objects of metal. This, and the memory of my mother in a dark room, singing to my younger brother."

"That's it?" I said.

"That's it."

"That's not one thing, that's two."

"Then I'm a lucky man," he said.

There came a night when the old man broke through into the root cellar. From then on he led a secret life. Solitary confinement by day, prison kitchen by night. In the early hours of each morning, this brave man made his way into the prison kitchen. Careful never to take more than would be noticed, he built up his strength with raw turnips, raw potatoes, and left-over bread. He used the prison sink to bathe in. He shaved with a kitchen knife and the light of the moon. He did calisthenics to keep his muscles strong. Every night he stretched and stretched to stay limber.

When he had completed his nightly foray, the old man covered his tunnel opening with a wooden crate full of potatoes and headed back to the hole.

He never gave up.

He did not allow himself to think beyond the moment. He did not allow himself to think of the day beyond the present day, the weeks stretching into months, into years, into a lifetime.

He never once thought: my youth has passed me by and I will die in this hole, an old, old man.

He thought instead of his tin snips, his forge, his solder iron, and his mother in a dark room, singing.

After ten years they opened the wooden cover to the hole and brought him up into the light of day. Blinking and squinting at the sunlight that he had not seen more than a glimpse of for a decade, Georg Kominsky regained his freedom. He lives on in the hearts and minds of his fellow prisoners, a symbol of the human spirit determined to survive at all odds.

"What would you like to do tonight?" the old man said one Wednesday night when I arrived. I looked out the window above the old man's sink. The choir members hadn't even turned the lights on in the Twin Churches. We had two hours.

"I would like to have some hot chocolate," I said.

I got out one of my hot chocolate packets from the cupboard. In the beginning, the old man bought me hot chocolate packets from Jewell's. But when I figured out that he was poor I insisted on bringing my own. I used to get hot chocolate packets free at the bank, at the little refreshment table in the corner where the armchairs are. There's a coffeemaker and a small wicker basket of tea bags, coffee bags, and hot chocolate packets. There are wooden stirrers and fake cream, which must be spelled creme or kreme. You cannot use the word *cream* if it's not real cream. That's the law.

They frown on nongrownups who avail themselves of the little refreshment table, but I used to take the packets anyway.

"It's for a good cause," I said once to the bank lady when I saw her giving me the once-over.

The old man was a good cause.

I don't go in the bank anymore.

I put hot water on the miniature stove and waited for it to boil. It's a fallacy that a watched pot never boils. I've proved it wrong many a time. While I was watching the pot and thinking about the young Georg Kominsky tunneling for ten years through dirt, the old man washed the supper dishes. The old man could stand in one place and reach the sink, the stove, the refrigerator, and the dish cupboard. He had just enough dishes. Two mugs. Three plates. Three bowls. Three forks. Three spoons. One table knife and one little sharp knife. He didn't need any more knives because the old man rarely ate anything that required cutting. You might think that having three plates and bowls is having one too many, but you would be wrong. What about the serving plate and the serving bowl? You've got to have an extra to serve from.

The old man had white plates with orange borders. Sad to say, orange is my least favorite color. The only way I like orange is as it occurs in nature, for example, orange poppies in gardens, orange tiger lilies by the side of the road, orange and black Monarch butterflies, orange Indian paintbrush in the field. When orange occurs elsewhere, as in borders on white plates, it is abhorrent. It is a crime against nature. That is my belief.

"Where did you get your white plates with the orange borders?" I asked the old man as he was drying them. He used to dry every dish separately. Forks, spoons, everything. He was fastidious about his dish drying.

"Scavenging night," he said.

The old man was a wonderful scavenger. I sometimes accompanied him on scavenging expeditions. He had a sixth sense.

"You've got to have the eye," he said.

I don't have the eye yet, but I'm trying. I'm training my eyes to be like the old man. It's difficult for two reasons: (a) I know how to read and he didn't, and (b) he saw possibility everywhere.

When you know how to read you can never get away from it. Your eye goes to words first and everything else second. The old man was not hampered by the knowledge of letters. His eye could roam free. He could take in the big picture, whereas I am bound to words first and foremost. Now that I know this I sometimes try to remember being a baby, before I was trapped by words. What was it like? I ask myself. I narrow my eyes and try not to see words and printing and letters. It's hopeless. I'm a reader.

While he dried the dishes I asked him my death row question again.

"I will ask you a variation of the question you never answered," I said. "Electric chair or life in solitary confinement with worms in your meal bucket every night and only a scrap of horse blanket to sleep on: which would you choose?"

He hung his dish towel over the oven door handle to dry. He always hung it in exactly the same way.

"Are they my only choices?"

"They are your only choices."

"I ask because there are many other ways to live and die."

"There are more ways to live and die, Horatio, than are dreamt of in your universe," I said. "But you are allowed only two. Which do you choose?"

"Which would *you* choose?"

He used to do that sometimes, turn the tables.

"I believe, sir, that you were the one asked the question," I said.

The old man finished washing and drying his dishes. No answer was forthcoming.

"It's scavenging night tonight," he said. "Do you want to go looking with me?"

"Sure," I said.

"Do you need anything special?"

Yes, I thought. I need a sister. I need my Baby Girl.

"How about cookie cutters?" I said. "Small metal objects that are useful as well as beautiful."

Tamar has a small cheesecloth bag of cookie cutters in our junk drawer at home. We don't use them. We don't make cookies. Tamar doesn't believe in sweet things. She has a streak of asceticism in her. She would not admit to it, but she does. If they do it the way it should be done, monks and nuns are ascetics. They live alone in cells. Absolutely bare. Stripped of everything worldly, which means anything colorful, anything frivolous, anything that is not essential to the sustainment of life. If they do it right, monks and nuns go to sleep on hard cots with one blanket in a cell that has one cross hanging on the wall, preferably at the head of their narrow single bed with its one, scratchy, thin, brown, wool blanket, similar to the kind of scrap of horse blanket that the young Georg Kominsky slept with in solitary confinement.

Our small cheesecloth bag of metal cookie cutters contains a bell, a heart, and a star. That's it. You can't get much more basic than that. To my knowledge, they have never been used. The most sugar the antisugar Tamar allows is a teaspoonful on her Cheerios. She's a thin woman, Tamar. Some might call her scrawny.

The old man saw possibility. The old man saw potential in things that I could not. Tinfoil, for instance. A person like the person I used to be would rip off just enough tinfoil to wrap the leftover with, wrap it, and stick it in the refrigerator. But the old man made tinfoil swans out of his leftovers.

"That's a waste of good tinfoil," Tamar said the one time I tried to make something pretty out of two leftover boiled potatoes at home.

I was not doing a good job of it. I tried for a swan first, but that didn't work. Then I tried for a heart shape, but it was lopsided, so I settled for a roll with twisted tinfoil tails.

"It's an abstract sculpture," I said.

"It's an abstract waste," she said.

If I had tried to argue with Tamar about the tinfoil abstract sculpture, I would have said that my abstract sculpture was useful because it protected the boiled potatoes. And that it was beautiful because it was an abstract sculpture. The waste of a few square inches of tinfoil is secondary to the beauty. That's what I would have said, had I tried to argue with Tamar. But the fact is, she's unarguable.

It is not common to find, for example, beautiful cookie cutters set out in the trash. Instead, the old man and I used to find pre–cookie cutters: strips of thin scrap metal behind the service station, for example, or old tin milk crates stacked up behind the Sterns Co-op. The old man had the eye. He could tell what had the potential to become a cookie cutter and what had a different destiny. I could see his eyes going from one trash pile to another. He looked and he kept on looking. Then he would pick something up and put it in the Jewell's bag.

"This has possibility," he said.

Or he said nothing.

There was an abundance of plastic bags that particular night. Thin, filmy plastic bags, the kind you put vegetables in at Jewell's. They were blowing around the trailer park. Patches of white on branches. One puffed up at me like a ghost.

"Why are there so many plastic bags blowing around here?" I asked.

The old man didn't answer. It wasn't a question that demanded an answer anyway. Some questions demand answers; others are rhetorical. I decided to ask a series of rhetorical questions.

"Rhetorical question number one: Why do people choose to let their plastic bags blow around in the wind? Two, would it kill them to put their vegetables all in one brown paper bag instead of a series of plastic bags, one vegetable species in each? Three, do these plastic bag people ever stop to think about the ten thousand years it takes a plastic bag to degrade?"

"Clara," the old man said.

That's all he said. What he meant was: quiet down, please.

I quieted down. We walked up Route 365 into the village of Sterns. Jewell's Grocery was closed, as was Crystal's Diner. The old man spotted a big olive oil can behind Crystal's. There was a picture of Italian hills and an olive tree on the front of the can. It had a big dent. I once remarked on the greenness of the oil I was observing Crystal mix with vinegar.

"That's because it's pure olive oil," Crystal said. "I use it because my grandmother was $\frac{1}{16}$ Greek. That's the only part of me that's not Polack, the $\frac{1}{64}$ of me that's Greek."

"That's one of Crystal's olive oil cans," I said. "Someone ran over it, looks like."

The old man nodded. He turned it around in his hands, looking at it from all angles. I could tell he was considering. He was mulling over the possibilities in his mind.

"I can see the wheels turning," I said. "Get it?"

"This has possibility," he said.

When he said that, I took the dented olive oil can and studied it myself, for the possibility. I'm training my eye. It's slow going.

The old man: *Dented olive oil can* $=$ *pre—cookie cutter.*

Me: *Dented olive oil can* $=$?

You have to look closely. You have to concentrate. You have to have the ability to see another destiny for something, a fate far removed from its original one. That's what the old man was good at.

"Okay," I said.

I never disagreed with the old man. You're not allowed to argue or disagree when you're an apprentice. You have to have the utmost faith that the master knows full well what he is doing. All things will be revealed to the apprentice in the fullness of time.

The old man held the dented olive oil can in one hand and we walked back to his trailer. The lady two trailers down looked out her window when we passed. She didn't wave. She never waved. Many was the time I considered giving up waving at her, but I kept on. You never know. There may come a time.

The old man washed the can with soap and water and got his tin snips. We sat down at the table and he snipped the can open down each side. He set the dented side apart and laid the others out before us. I watched everything he did. I used to observe every move the old man made when he worked on something. That's how apprentices learn. That's how Paul Revere became the silversmith he was, back in the colonial days. First he was an apprentice, then he was a journeyman, then he was a master.

"Tamar will be here in twenty minutes," I said.

"All right," he said.

The old man tilted his head and studied the pieces of tin. He studied tin, and I studied him. His tin snips lay on the table. That, and his solder iron, were the only two things he brought with him from his country that doesn't exist anymore. They were the only things that stayed with him to the end.

The old man also had a small forge. He kept the forge, along with a vise, in back of his trailer, on the patch of land that ran along Nine Mile Creek. That way the smoke didn't bother anyone. When the old man wanted to do some black-smithing, he used his forge. I used to sit on the bank of Nine Mile Creek and watch the smoke spiral up into the air.

The old man bought the forge and the vise at an auction in North Sterns. Mr. Jewell drove him up there. I know that because I once overheard Mr. Jewell ask the old man how the forge was holding up.

"Good," the old man said.

"The vise too?"

"The vise too."

Later I asked Mr. Jewell how he knew about the forge and the vise.

"Because, Miss Clara Winter, I drove him up to the auction where he bought them," Mr. Jewell said.

After the old man was gone, I found an old Sears Roebuck catalogue at the Back of the Barn Antiques on Route 12 north of Remsen. I went there with Tamar once, so she could visit her friend who works there. Tamar's friend owns a bird who sits on her shoulder all day long. The bird is silent. It is neither a talking nor a singing bird. For a while I thought it was a clip-on bird. That was before it blinked its eye at me and yawned.

In the catalogue there was a picture of a forge and a vise that looked like the old man's forge and vise. Here is the description of the forge from the Sears, Roebuck & Co., Cheapest Supply House on Earth, Chicago, Catalogue No. 111, page 613:

The Forge. We furnish a lever forge having hearth 18 inches in diameter.
It is furnished with 6-inch fan. The gear is the simplest, strongest and best

ever put on a forge. Only a slight movement of the lever produces the strongest blast.

The Vise. We furnish a wrought iron solid box and screw blacksmith vise, with steel jaws, weighing 35 pounds.

The vise and the forge came with a complete set of tools, and altogether the complete set cost $25. I asked Mr. Jewell how much the old man had paid for his forge and vise at the auction.

"I wouldn't know, Miss Clara," he said. "Why do you ask?"

The old man had been gone for months by then.

Why did I ask? I wouldn't know.

Next time I went to the old man's, on a Saturday afternoon, the tin-snipped pieces of olive oil can had disappeared from the table. The old man had screwed in large cup hooks all along the top of the far kitchen window frame. Hanging on the hooks were new cookie cutters. If you looked closely, and if you had personal knowledge of their previous life as a dented olive oil can, you might be able to tell that what were now cookie cutters had once been broken pieces of metal.

The olive oil can had been reincarnated as objects of light. One was in the shape of a decorative tin lantern, another was a candelier, another was a candlestick with a cutout of a burning candle in it.

"But soft!" I said. "What light from yonder window breaks? It is the east, and cookie cutters are the sun."

The old man smiled.

"Juliet," he said. "*Juliet* is the sun."

Did the old man listen to Shakespeare in his own language, back in his country that doesn't exist anymore? Is it possible that in his small village, there was a troupe of traveling actors who passed through the countryside every year, performing a different Shakespearean play each time? Is it possible that the old man loved the poetry of William Shakespeare and never missed a performance? Did he crouch as a small boy behind the cloth-curtained stage of the traveling troupe and absorb every word they spoke so that the language of Shakespeare became part of every fiber of his being?

I will never know.

I studied the former olive oil can carefully. This is something you must do when you're an apprentice. You must look at all finished objects with the knowledge that they came from something unfinished, something in an unbegun state. You need to consider all their states of being, all their transformations.

Each cutter had been created in the image of something that already existed: a lantern, a candelier, a candlestick. There was a theme to all three cookie cutters: they were all objects of light, they were all objects that had been most often used in a previous era, they were all objects most often constructed of tin.

The old man wanted me to learn how to find consistency. That was why he taught me by example. That is what it means to be an apprentice to the art of possibility.

A breeze gusted through the trailer and set the cookie cutters jostling and tinkling together. The noise that the cookie cutters made was like the noise of a thousand soda can tops strung together with string and shaken gently. Sunlight glinted off the metal. It was the same kind of beauty that you see in a sunshower, light broken to shards through rain.

Shards. How I love that word.

"There was a time," the old man said, "when most cookies were made with cutters."

The drop cookie is a modern invention, according to the old man. Cookies used to take time and care. They were not beaten together and immediately dropped onto a metal sheet and baked. They were not patted into a pan and called bar cookies. They were mixed, chilled, rolled, formed, cut, baked, dipped, powdered, sprinkled, iced, decorated. They were delicately sugared and a trifle brown around the edges. They were thin, not thick.

"Lemon peel," the old man said. "Always put lemon peel in your sugar cookies."

You wouldn't think that the old man would have known that much about baking. To look at his Jewell's shopping list you would never have guessed that the old man was a master cookie baker.

It's possible that the old man once baked sugar cookies with lemon peel for someone he loved, back when he lived in his country that doesn't exist anymore.

Did Tamar ever do anything like that?

I could come right out and ask Tamar some of my answer-demanding questions, such as, "Did you ever bake cookies for someone you once loved, such as my father? What is my father's name? Where did you meet him? Where is he now? Did he love you, and did you love him more than words can say?"

But I don't.

"How did you get pregnant?" is what I ask.

Tamar doesn't mind questions that sound scientific. She likes science, except when it runs amok as in the case of margarine.

"In the usual way," Tamar said.

Tamar knew what I was really asking. I was asking about my father. I was asking about love.

I should have asked the old man.

There's a chance that when the old man was seventeen and still living in his village that doesn't exist anymore, he fell in love. People grew up fast in the olden days. By ten you could be considered close to an adult. When the old man was a young man, fifteen or sixteen, did he meet a girl? Was she a girl that he had grown up with but had never noticed until she was a young woman with brown curls and he was a young man?

He saw her one day, walking down the road in the spring wearing a dress with yellow flowers printed on it, running upstairs to the stone house above the bakery where she lived with her family.

She was a graceful girl. She was singing, or humming, as she ran up the stairs. She was wearing brown leather sandals. The smell of yeast rising in the bakery below her home came to the young man's nose, and he breathed in and watched her run and listened to her humming.

Did the old man foreverafter associate the smell of baking bread with the image of a pretty, running girl?

When she got to the top of the stairs the young girl sensed something, and turned around, and saw the old-man-as-a-young-man. She met his brown eyes with her own. She looked right back at him. She knew his name.

She whispered it to herself: *Georg.*

She smoothed the skirt of her dress with the yellow flowers printed on it. She was just about to push open the door of her home—her mother had left it ajar for her—and her hand was suspended in the air while she gazed back at the young man. She stared for a moment, maybe two seconds, then laughed and pushed her hand at the air and opened the heavy wooden door and disappeared. The old man stared for a few minutes more and said her name to himself.

What was her name?

Was it Juliet?

Juliet, he might have thought. The sound of her name, unspoken, hung in the invisible air before him. *Juliet, Juliet, Juliet.*

Did the young Georg make cookie cutters for Juliet? Did he make her beautiful objects that were also useful? Did he bake sugar cookies for her and teach her the secret of adding lemon peel to the batter?

When I first met the old man I dreamed up a life for him, back in his country that doesn't exist anymore. His father, his mother, his younger brother Eli, all of them living together in their warm thatched hut, cornmeal mush or hot gruel for breakfast, a black iron pot of stew for dinner, the mother beating clothes white against the rocks, the father teaching his sons the art of the forge, how to turn heated metal into objects of use and beauty. I dreamed of the old man as a hero, rescuing tiny babies from floodwater, surviving ten years of unjustly sentenced solitary confinement.

Before he was gone I learned more about the old man's real life, but not all. You can't ever know all there is to know about a life. There will be gaps.

There may well have been a girl named Juliet. It's possible. She may have lived and breathed in the old man's village. The first time the old man ever saw that girl, she may have been running up the steps above the bakery, wearing a dress printed with tiny yellow flowers. Maybe the old man never forgot the sight. Maybe the old man thought of her every day of his life. He might have loved her more than words can say.

My only hope is that she loved him, too.

CHAPTER EIGHT

One day last fall Tiny pulled up to CJ's trailer just as CJ's white Camaro screeched off the road, up over the grass, and around the bus. The top was down. There was a man in a red flannel shirt behind the wheel. He gave Tiny the finger.

"Jesus H Christ," Tiny said.

I looked over at CJ. There was a look on his face.

"Who's that driving your car, CJ—your dad?" one of the North Sterns boys said.

"Yeah, is that the famous Chucky Luck?"

"No that ain't my dad," CJ said. "I told you about my dad. Does that guy out there look like a professional wrestler to you?"

The boys looked out the window.

"I guess not."

"Well there's your answer," CJ said.

"How about your mother? Is she a professional wrestler too?" one of the boys said.

Everyone was quiet. No one talks about CJ's mother. CJ Wilson's mother has never been seen that I know of. Were it not a law of nature, you might wonder if CJ even has a mother. CJ looked at the boy who asked the question. The boy looked right back at him.

"I'm asking about your mother, CJ."

CJ turned around and pointed to me.

"And I'm asking about Wipe's father. Wipe? Where's your father at?"

All the boys turned and looked at me. The boy who asked about CJ's mother laughed.

"Maybe he ran off with CJ's mother."

"Yeah. CJ's mother and Wipe's father!"

CJ looked at me while the boys laughed. Didn't say a word.

There must have been something CJ's mother loved about CJ's father. There must have been something Tamar saw in my father, something she loved, even though she won't talk about him. CJ may well wonder about his mother the way I wonder about my father and grandfather.

There was a time when I would have given anything to know about my grandfather, Tamar's father, that man living the life of a hermit in a patch of primeval forest near the Vermont border. I used to ask Tamar about him. One time I asked her when she was rubbing the once-frostbitten toes of her right foot with mineral oil.

"Is your foot hurting?" I said.

"No," she said. She wiggled it in my face, to prove how non-hurting her foot was.

"Do you think, Ma, that a hermit could survive on about fifty dollars a year?" I said.

"Absolutely not."

"How much then? How much do you think a hermit who does all his own trapping and food-gathering would need to survive with just the bare essentials?"

"At least five hundred," said Tamar.

She knows. She always has an idea.

"Why five hundred?"

"Food staples. Candles and waterproof matches. The occasional tool. One Greyhound bus ticket per year. Books."

Books. Would a hermit read books? Is that something a hermit would do?

"Are you sure about the books?" I said.

"All hermits read books."

"But he wouldn't have to spend money on them," I said. "He could hike into the nearest village and use the library."

"He could not use the library. To use a library, you must obtain a library card, and to obtain a library card you need a permanent address. A hermit does not have what would be considered a permanent address. Also, a hermit would not return to a village often enough to avoid huge overdue fines, which he could not afford to pay."

She made sense.

"A bus ticket?" I said.

"All hermits must leave their hermit dwellings once a year. It's an unwritten rule among hermits. It's part of the Hermit Bill of Rights. As a hermit expert, I would've thought you already knew that."

I took my roll of adding-machine paper and started out of the kitchen.

"Don't be mad," Tamar said.

"Then don't humor me. Good-bye."

"Where are you going?"

"To visit a friend."

"Which friend?"

"Georg Kominsky: American Immigrant," I said.

"That's seven miles, Clara."

"It's early in the day," I said. "I'm a good walker. I'll be there by lunchtime."

I put my roll of adding-machine paper in its tin holder and zipped it into my backpack.

"Be careful," Tamar said. "Watch for cars."

Do not ever walk seven miles in sandals without socks. I knew this before I was half a mile down Route 274 but I did not turn back. I refused to give Tamar the satisfaction. By the time I was at the intersection of Crill Road and 274 my feet were not in good shape. I took my sandals off and wound dandelion leaves around my toes so that they would stop rubbing up against each other. Every quarter mile or so the dandelion leaves would grind themselves into a pulp and I had to wipe them off and start over again. After a while blood from the blisters started mixing with the green dandelion leaf pulp. I wished desperately that it was fall, so that the milkweed pods along the road were ready to burst, and I could line my feet with the silky down inside them. For the last three miles I dreamed about the softness of milkweed in the fall.

The old man was working in his onion garden when I got there. By then I was barefoot, despite the possibility of rusty nails and broken glass on the road.

"Clara?" he said.

"It is I. Do you have a Band-Aid?"

"Yes."

He got up and went into his trailer. The minute he said "yes" tears started coming out of my eyes. I sat down on the floor in his miniature bathroom and he handed me a tin box of Band-Aids. The box had a hinged lid. It was unlike the flimsy paper box of Band-Aids that we have at our house.

"This is a very nice Band-Aid box," I said.

I picked out two large Band-Aids, two narrow small ones, and two round ones.

"This box is a metal object, and it is also useful," I said. "But is it beautiful?"

"Why aren't you in school?" the old man said.

"Why aren't I in *school*? It's summer vacation. Don't you know *anything*?"

I heard myself say those words. They came popping out. They hung in the air between us. They ran like subtitles in the bottom of my brain: don't you know *anything*? don't you know *anything*? don't you know *anything*?

The old man knelt down on the floor beside me. He unrolled some toilet paper and wadded it up and passed it to me. I did not say, *I'm sorry*. What would be the point? When words like that come out of your mouth they cannot be reclaimed. They already exist. They're in the world for the rest of your life and nothing you can ever say will take them away.

People are like that, too. Even if they die moments after they're born, they existed. They were alive. The memory of them can never be taken away.

I took the toilet paper and wiped my eyes. The old man pulled my sandals off.

"These are not good shoes for walking," the old man said.

I said nothing. I kept my silence. I forced myself not to say the words that were shouting themselves inside me: *don't you think I know that by now?*

The old man took another wad of toilet paper and wet it in his miniature sink. He dabbed some soap on it and washed my toes. The soap stung but I said nothing. When he was finished, he dried my feet with a white towel and put the Band-Aids on.

"You walked the whole way?"

"The whole way."

I did not put my sandals back on. I looked inside them and saw the reddish stains from my blood on the toetips. We went back outside to the onion garden. The old man grew nothing but onions and onionlike plants such as chives. He used to eat an onion a day. For good health, he said. That's something they did in his village that doesn't exist anymore. Everyone ate the equivalent of one raw or cooked onion every day. Everything they cooked was cooked with onion. Onions have special properties that protect your health. That is what the old man believed to be true.

His breath didn't smell like onion either. You'd think it would, but it didn't. That's because the old man developed an immunity against onion breath. He ate so many onions in his life that they didn't affect his breath. He had an affinity for onions.

In his onion garden there were some onions that came up every year. The chives were the first things up in the spring. You could see them poking their narrow green stalks up before the snow melted, like miniature quills from the olden days. Chives thrive in the cold. They are not intimidated by lingering snow and ice. They are indomitable.

Now that the old man is gone, and his trailer has been crushed into a slab of scrap metal, I wonder if the chives are still there. Do they still live beneath the ground? Will they push themselves up through the last of the snow and ice when spring comes again?

That day, the old man and I sat by his onion garden next to the bank of Nine Mile Creek, near the forge that he bought at the auction in North Sterns, as he wet a rag and wiped the dried blood off my sandals.

"You fought with your mother?"

I said nothing. Awful words chased themselves around the bottom of my mind but I did not let them out.

"Here," the old man said. "Divide this clump of chives."

He gave me a trowel. I used to call a trowel a spade until the old man corrected me. "A spade is a long, shovel-like tool," he said. "You are talking about a trowel."

"Plunge the trowel straight into the center of the chives," he said. "Then work it back and forth until you can lift out half the clump in one trowelful."

I did not hesitate. If I had been on my own I would have, but because I was with the old man I plunged without hesitation. He was the master. I believed in what he said. The chives came out easily.

"That clump is for you," the old man said. "Plant them at home."

"Tamar is keeping my grandfather from me," I said.

The old man took the clump of divided chives from me. He packed some dirt around the roots, wrapped the whole thing in wet newspaper and then put it in a plastic Jewell's bag.

"I have a grandfather out there and Tamar won't tell me anything about him," I said.

"Where is he?"

"He lives in a primeval forest. He's a hermit."

"What is a hermit?"

Sometimes that happened. I forgot that he was an immigrant. I forgot that English was not his first language. I forgot that he couldn't read. He had no idea how to sound a word out, how to go to the dictionary and look it up. The old man couldn't absorb the meaning of a word from the writing around it, the way I do when I read a book. He had to hear it in conversation. Probably several times he had to hear it, before he could even register it as a word he didn't know. Then and only then could the old man start to grasp the possible meaning of a word like hermit.

"A hermit lives in a cave in the woods," I said. "He spends most of his time foraging for basic necessities. The rest of the time he sits and smokes a pipe and thinks."

The old man pulled a large bunch of his scallions. Four or five scallions to the old man were the equivalent of one raw yellow onion. Two walla-walla onions counted as one raw yellow onion. Chives did not really count as part of a raw onion. Chives are ornamentation and flavoring more than anything else, according to the old man.

"So your grandfather is a hermit who lives in a primeval forest," he said.

The old man pulled the large drooping green outer layer of scallion off each of the scallions and tossed them back into the onion garden. The old man wasted nothing. What some people might think of as garbage—the outer layer of a scallion—he viewed as fertilizer for future scallions.

"He might be," I said. "He very well may be. But Tamar won't tell me anything about him."

"So you do not really know where your grandfather is?"

"That is correct. But I think he's a hermit up near Vermont."

"You think."

"I'm *conjecturing*," I said. "It's a definite possibility."

He said nothing. He took his garden hose and uncoiled it, then turned on the water so a thin stream trickled out. The old man did not believe in a hose gushing water. The old man believed in a trickle of water over time, as opposed to a burst of water in seconds. He lay the hose down next to the middle row of walla-wallas. At first the water soaked straight into the ground. Then the ground directly underneath became saturated and the water started trickling down the middle row and spreading into the rows on either side. That was the old man's plan. That's how he used to water his entire onion garden.

"This is a real possibility?" the old man said.

"Of course it's a *real possibility*," I said. "Why do you talk that way anyway?"

The old man wrapped the scallions in more wet newspapers.

"I'm sorry!" I said. "Forgive me!"

Exclamation marks kept stabbing out into the air after the words that I didn't want to let out. Stab and stab and stab, words and more hurtful words pushing against each other inside me, dying to get out.

"Clara."

Then I could stop. The sound of the old man's voice saying *Clara* started running through my mind instead. *Clara clara clara clara clara clara clara*, chiming like a bell.

"Come here," he said.

Clara come here, Clara come here, Clara come here.

I followed him. He went into the trailer and lifted a cookie cutter in the shape of a star down from its hook and put it in his shirt pocket. He carried the wrapped scallions in one hand and he held out his other hand to me. I did not allow myself to think that there might be some kids from my class at Sterns Elementary in town, buying candy at the drugstore or a cone at the Woodside. I did not allow myself to imagine what those kids from my class might think and what they might say if they saw me walking with bare bloody feet into town at age eleven, which is how old I was last summer, holding the hand of an elderly American immigrant who was carrying a bunch of scallions in his other hand.

I took his hand. I walked with him. We went into town.

"Are you hungry?" the old man said.

"I am hungry."

The old man opened the door of Crystal's Diner for me and held it while I went in. I go to Crystal's quite a bit. In addition to food out of cans and jars, Tamar will also readily eat a hamburger and a milkshake. Tamar prefers strawberry-chocolate milkshakes. It's an unusual combination.

Crystal lives in North Sterns, farther out than us, with her nephew Johnny. Johnny's special ed. The old man would call him retarded. Johnny has his own booth at the diner. It's only out-of-towners who ever sit in Johnny's booth. Even they learn fast, because Johnny comes walking up sideways, which is the way he walks, and just looks at them with a sad look. After a while they realize that they're in his booth. They get up and go to a different booth. They take their forks and spoons and knives, their plates and their coffee mugs, their jackets and their purses. They wipe up any water-condensation puddles with their napkins and they take their wet napkins with them, too. They leave the booth perfect for Johnny, as if no one but Johnny had the right to sit there. That's the effect Johnny has on people. One look at him and even out-of-towners want to take care of him. Nobody wants to hurt Johnny. Everybody wants the sad where-is-my-booth look to go away from his face.

Crystal's never had to say a word.

Crystal and Johnny live in a two-person family. I live in a three-person family—Tamar, me, and Baby Girl—although Tamar would disagree.

Tamar would say, "It's you and me, kiddo. Get it through your head."

Johnny Zielinski was in his booth coloring in a coloring book. You might think that because he's fifteen, Johnny's too old for a coloring book. You would be wrong. Coloring helps to improve Johnny's coordination, which is not good. He falls quite a bit. He has a hard time with a pen or a pencil, so Crystal keeps a mug filled with giant crayons in his booth. Johnny will color for an hour or more at a time. Many's the time I've watched him.

"Hello, Mr. Kominsky," Crystal said. "Hello, Ms. Winter."

"It's not *Winter*," I said. "It's *winter*. Lowercase w."

Crystal gave me a look.

"And how do you know I was saying it with an upper-case w?" she said.

"I can tell."

"You're right. I did say it with a big W."

"I know you did."

Crystal said nothing about my bare feet, which were covered with Band-Aids but still oozing blood.

"Mr. Kominsky?" Crystal said. "Do you prefer your name spelled with a lowercase k?"

"He doesn't care," I said. "Big K is fine."

"I was asking him," Crystal said.

"Big K is fine," the old man said.

How would he have known? How would the old man have had any idea whether a big K was fine? He couldn't see the words scrolling by in the bottom of his head the way I can. He had no idea what the difference between a big K and a little k is. All he could do was listen for the difference, and the listening difference without the seeing difference is so tiny as to be naught.

We sat down in the booth next to Johnny's booth. He was coloring with a giant red crayon held in his left hand. The old man took the star cookie cutter out of his shirt pocket and put it on the table in Johnny's booth. The sun shone in the window and sparked off the shiny metal. Johnny put down the red crayon and picked up the cookie cutter. He swung it from the tip of his finger. He laughed in his own particular way, which if you didn't know better you'd think was crying.

Crystal brought over two hamburgers and two milkshakes. She set down a bottle of ketchup and a bottle of mustard. The old man gave her the bunch of scallions wrapped in wet newspaper.

"Thank you, Mr. Kominsky," she said. "I will put these to use in the tuna salad."

Was Crystal Zielinski the old man's friend? Did she know he couldn't read? Did the old man love Johnny Zielinski? These are the things I wonder about now that the old man is gone. I remember that day and I wonder.

"Do you love Johnny Zielinski even though he can't read?" I said.

It was a day when I could not stop myself. The words kept flying out of my mouth and there was nothing I could do to stop them. Words that would ordinarily just meander through my mind gathered speed, took wing, and flew into the air.

The old man took off the top of his hamburger bun and squeezed a ring of ketchup around the border of the hamburger. Then he took the mustard and squeezed two drops for eyes and a curved line for a mouth. Then he put the top of the bun back on and mushed the whole thing.

"Do you love me?" I said.

Crystal brought over two glasses filled with ice and water. Johnny clinked his star cookie cutter on the window to see the sun sparkle off it. The old man looked at me.

"Tamar's keeping me from my grandfather," I said. "He's my only family. He's all I have."

The old man gave me his napkin so I could wipe my eyes again.

"Tamar won't tell me about my baby sister," I said. "She will not allow me ever to mention my father. She has no idea how much I need to know."

"Why did your grandfather become a hermit?" the old man said.

That was the old man. That was something he used to do, take what you said and not question it. He just kept on going with what you had told him, as if it were the truth.

"The guilt," I said. "He couldn't take the guilt."

The old man nodded.

"He had to live with the guilt," I said. "Day in and day out, there it was. Wake up in the morning, there it was staring him in the face again."

"And what was it that was staring him in the face?"

"Guilt, because he killed his grandchild."

"I thought it was winter that killed his grandchild."

"Winter played a role," I said. "I do not deny that winter played a role. But who do you think was behind the wheel of that truck? Who do you think was driving when it slid into the ditch? Who was it who decided to go Glass Factory Road instead of Route 12?"

The old man stirred his water with his straw. All the straws at Crystal's Diner are red. Red is Johnny Zielinski's favorite color.

"Everyone knows what Glass Factory Road is like in the middle of a snowstorm," I said. "You don't go Glass Factory. You take Route 12. Route 12 stands at least a chance of being plowed. Route 12 is the only logical route if you're trying to get to a hospital in a snowstorm. If you take Glass Factory you're doomed."

"And so he became a hermit."

"And so he became a hermit," I said. "Can we go find him?"

"I don't think so."

"Why not?"

There was a mean sound in my voice. I could hear it. The words kept going around in my head: *why not, why not, why not.* Stop, I thought. I said my question again. I took the meanness out of my voice.

"Because you don't know where he is," the old man said.

"He's a hermit near the Vermont border!"

The old man said nothing. I listened to my voice again, going on in my head. *He's a hermit near the Vermont border.* But that was only a story.

Again I had made up a story.

My grandfather was a hermit who lived in a patch of primeval forest near the Vermont border. In the summer he gathered berries and dried them in the sun. He traded pelts for the bare essentials. He wore deerskin clothes that he tanned himself. Over the long winter nights, sitting beside the small fire in his tipi, he chewed the deerskin to make it soft and supple. He cut it with his sharp knife and stitched his clothes together with rawhide threaded through a needle made of bone. His moccasins were reinforced with double rows of stitches.

My grandfather was alive up there. He was living that life right now. I could feel the life he was living. I could feel the silence of his life in the tipi, how he wanted his granddaughter, his only surviving grandchild, to come and show him how to make useful and beautiful metal objects. My hermit grandfather was longing for me. I looked at the old man.

"He's up there," I said. "He's in his tipi."

The old man nodded.

"He could very well be waiting for me," I said. "Tamar isn't always right. No one in the world can be completely accurate one hundred percent of the time. It's a law of nature."

He kept nodding.

"Do you know your grandfather's name?"

"Of course I do."

Knowing names is a point of pride with me. I know not only the first names of people, but I know their last names and any middle names they might have. I know all the names of every kid at Sterns Middle School. It's not hard to learn their middle names. You need only look at the teacher's list. One look is all I need. Once there, never gone. That's reading for you.

"Clifford Winter," I said. "That's his name."

It took many a year for me to glean that from Tamar. It took me years of sneaking in a question here and a question there, years of plotting to ask questions when Tamar would least expect it, such as:

"Ma, what was Grampa's name?"

That stopped her. Tamar didn't even hear the question, she was so stunned by me saying the word *Grampa*. I saw that I had made a mistake. There was a look on her face.

"*Grampa?* Did I just hear you say *Grampa?*"

"Yes. What was his name?"

She was still stuck on the word *Grampa*. She started shaking her head and muttering. I had my notebook ready, but I saw that it was a useless proposition. When Tamar starts to mutter, there's no hope.

"*Grampa?*"

Is it really that strange? When I was born in that truck in the ditch in the middle of the blizzard, wasn't I his grandchild? But Tamar was muttering and shaking her head and I closed my notebook and left the kitchen. When I came back an hour later she was forking bread and butter pickles out of the jar and eating them, one slice at a time.

Many moons later I tried again.

"Ma, what's your father's name?"

"Clifford."

No questions, no looks, no muttering. That one just slipped right out of her.

"What do you want to know for?"

"School. Do they call him Cliff or Clifford? Or Ford, maybe. Would Ford be a possibility?"

"What do they want to know in school for?" she said.

"A genealogy project."

She looked at me.

"Family tree. That kind of thing," I said. "Charts. Diagrams. Ancestors. *Et al.*"

Her eyes narrowed. I kept on talking.

"Cliff? Clifford? Ford?"

Suddenly she looked tired. She gave up. I could tell. I can always tell when she decides to stop pursuing something. A tired look comes over her all at once. It invades every cell of her being, and around her the air slumps, too.

"Cliff."

"Thanks Ma. By the way, I also need the name of my father."

I tried. You have to give me credit for trying. I know it's in there somewhere. The name of my father is in Tamar's brain and there is a way to get it out. I have not found it, but there must be a way. A way must exist.

"You don't have a father."

"Everyone has a father. It's a law of nature," I said for the hundredth time, and then we were back to square one. That was all she wrote.

The old man and I sat in our booth and watched Johnny Zielinski play with the star cookie cutter. He could play with something shiny for hours.

"So that's my grandfather's name," I told the old man. "Clifford Winter."

Crystal poured more coffee into the old man's coffee cup. "Cream?"

"Thank you," he said. "Do you have a telephone book?"

She brought it over. The old man slid it across the table to me.

"What's this for?"

"Look in it," he said. "Look in it for Clifford Winter."

I couldn't breathe right. I kept trying to take a deep breath but the air wouldn't go all the way in.

"He's a hermit," I said.

The old man said nothing. I opened up the phone book to Utica, to a page with Clifford Winter on it.

Winter, Clifford   1431 Genesee Street   732-7953.

"You can call him," the old man said.

I kept looking at his name in the phone book. Had it been there the whole time? My grandfather, who chewed deer hide to make it soft enough to slip his bone needle through, who traded pelts for salt and sugar and coffee, who collected only dead wood for his campfires, lived at 1431 Genesee Street and had a phone?

"It's not the same person," I said.

The old man carried our dishes to the counter and passed them to Crystal. When he came back, he had a tinfoil gum wrapper in his hand. He started to fold it into a tiny animal, for Johnny.

"My grandfather is a hermit," I said. "It's possible. My grandfather could just as easily be a hermit as you could be an immigrant who lives in a trailer in Sterns and doesn't have any family."

Words, words, terrible words. They kept tumbling out of my mouth. My chest hurt. There was a feeling of despair in my rib cage. Nothing of the person I wanted to be was coming out in my words. The wrong words kept bubbling and churning inside me, that whole long day. My hermit grandfather started slipping away from me, fading north into the Vermont woods. In my mind I reached for him, but he shook his head.

Meanwhile the image of a man I didn't know, sitting hunched at a table in the kitchen of a Utica apartment I'd never seen, started taking shape. Terrible words that hurt the old man kept spilling from my mouth, and Johnny Zielinski was laughing but it sounded like crying.

CHAPTER NINE

There is much I still wonder about the old man. Questions I have that I did not have the chance to ask. What did he eat on the ship to America, for example? Was there food on board or did they have to bring their own? Did they eat hardtack and drink water from big wooden barrels belowdecks? Did the ship have a rough crossing? Did it hit a small iceberg and almost plunge beneath the surface of the waves, like the *Titanic?* Where did the young Georg Kominsky go when they finally let him through at Ellis Island? Did he sleep on the street? Was there anyone in New York City who could speak his language? Was anyone nice to him?

They never found out. His parents must never have known what happened to their sons. There were no other children. I know because the old man told me when I was doing his oral history.

"My parents. Myself. My brother, Eli."

That was it, the four of them. Georg, seventeen, and Eli, eleven. They probably told the old man to take care of Eli on the journey. To watch over him. Keep him safe. If they were religious, they probably said prayers every night: God, keep our children safe. But they never knew. *What happened,* they asked themselves. On their deathbeds they were probably still wondering. *What happened?*

Georg's family may have written to the authorities in America.

Dear America, We have not heard from our beloved sons Georg and Eli. Have you heard of them? Are they alive? Georg's identifying characteristics are these: he is seventeen years old, he has a slight limp in his left leg from a fever he had at age nine, he works well with tin and other forms of sheet metal, especially making decorative lanterns, and he writes in the air with his nose. Eli is eleven. A child. Please help us. They are our children and we are missing them terribly.

I asked the old man about it once.

"Did your parents write to you after you came to America?" I asked.

"No."

"Why not? Didn't they miss their children?"

"No."

"Then why not?"

"They were dead," the old man said. "They died before I came to America."

He got up and took one of his extralong fireplace matches out of its extralong box and went to the furnace and lit it. He blew the match out and looked at me.

"Don't worry, Clara," he said. "It's all right. They died long ago."

My dreams of the old man's mother and father—the mother in her apron, the father bent at his forge—shimmered in front of me and faded away.

"It was T.B.," the old man said. "Many people died of it then."

I knew about T.B. Consumption. When you're near the end, your eyes sparkle and shine and your cheeks burn red. To the unschooled, a person near death from consumption might look like the picture of health.

"It was soon before we left for America," the old man said. "With both of them gone we decided to leave."

The old man stacked the dishes in his sink and ran hot water over them. He squirted in a little dish soap. Miniature bubbles rose from the steam and then popped.

"My mother used to sit in the bedroom with Eli," he said. "I remember her as a young woman, with Eli a baby. She sat in the dark, singing him to sleep. That's how I like to remember my mother: the sound of her voice in a dark room, singing."

The old man taught me to seek consistency. "Consistency is a part of the art of possibility," he said. "Everything is related to everything else." That's what he was training me in. I wasn't far along in my apprenticeship when suddenly he was no longer there. I was only a beginner. It takes years, many years, to become a master. That's why I'm starting to think that the old man was a child prodigy. He may well have been a prodigy in his hometown. He may well have been the first child in the world to master the art of metalworking at such a tender age, the age of thirteen or fourteen.

It's possible. Think of all the Dalai Lamas, discovered at the age of three or four or, at most, five. There are certain signs you look for. There are rituals and secrets that only this child, the future Dalai Lama, can divine. He can't be taught how to be the Dalai Lama. He can only be born into it. It is his destiny.

I started looking for relationships that would explain my destiny, and the destiny of Baby Girl. That's what the old man taught me:

"Everything is related to everything else. Consistency is a part of the art of possibility."

There's got to be an explanation somewhere. It's hard to know what to look for, though. How do you figure out destiny?

Every week the old man and I baked a different kind of cookie. The rules were few but always consistent; our cookies were (a) rolled, (b) thin and crisp, (c) fully baked. Sugar cookies, gingersnaps, lemon cookies, and the like. We tried out all the cookie cutters. All worked perfectly. All were beautiful. All were constructed from cast-off materials. These were the consistencies among the cookie cutters, and their relationship one to another.

"I'm studying the art of possibility," I said to the old man. "I'm looking for consistency."

"Good," he said.

"Consistencies among cookie cutters, snow, twins, and babies dying in winter."

The old man looked at me.

"Are you sure you understand what consistency means?"

"Consistency," I said. "The agreement of parts or features to one another or a whole."

I do that sometimes. I look things up and get the exact definition. You'd be surprised how many definitions there are for a single word. Take an ordinary word. Snow, for example. Or winter. You would think there would be one, possibly two meanings at most for either of those words. You would be wrong.

"Actually there are several definitions for consistency," I said. "But that's the one I like the best."

"Why?" the old man said.

"Because it means that things fit together," I said. "Things that don't ordinarily go together *can* go together and then the whole will be consistent. It means that there's a reason why things happen the way they do."

"Take a baby," I said. "And take a truck in the ditch. Those are two things that don't ordinarily go together. But if you're looking for consistency you can find it. It can be done."

"How?"

"Well, that's what I'm in the process of finding out. I'm looking for consistency. I'm training my eye to see possibility. Someday the two will mesh."

"And then you'll have your answer."

"In the fullness of time I will have my answer," I said. "That is what I believe to be true."

If I knew for sure that it was Baby Girl's destiny to die, my mind might be eased. If only I had the unshakable belief that she was never meant to take breath in this world. That would be something for me to believe. I could look people in the eye and say, "It was her destiny to be stillborn." That simple statement of fact would answer all my questions. Facts are not arguable. Facts preclude argumentation. I asked Tamar once about this issue.

"Ma, do you believe in predestination?" I said.

"No," she said.

Immediate. Simple. Clear. She didn't have to mull it over for a second. That's Tamar. Tamar is not a muller, nor is she a hemmer or a hawer.

"So what do you believe in then?"

"Luck," she said. "Hard work. Marinated artichoke hearts."

That's Tamar also. Once in a while she comes out with a *non sequitur*. She likes to amuse herself that way. It's a rare occasion that Tamar laughs. A laughing Tamar is an occasion to make the most of.

Later I asked her a follow-up question. That's something that reporters often do. They ask a question, it leads them down another path of thought, and they ask a follow-up question. Sometimes I treat Tamar as if she were the subject and I were a reporter. I used to take notes on my roll of green adding-machine paper, neatly inserted into the paper holder that the old man made for me, but my green adding-machine paper no longer exists. It is no longer part of this world.

Tamar had a strong dislike of my roll of adding-machine paper anyway.

"I hate that thing," she used to say. "I hate its narrowness and its green color. I hate the fact that it's one endless roll. Be like the vast majority of the population, Clara. Use a normal sheet of paper."

I humor her and use my legal pad in her presence. Most legal pads are yellow. Mine is orange. It came from the reject bin at Jewell's. I hate the color orange, but I feel an obligation to the reject bin.

"So, if I understand you correctly," I said, "you believe that luck and hard work, not predestination, determines a person's chances in this world."

"Correct."

"Does destiny play a role in life at all, then, according to you, Ms. winter?"

"Very little if any."

"What about a baby who seemed normal in every regard but who died at birth? Did luck or hard work play a role in this instance?"

Tamar stood up. She headed outside.

And that was it. Sometimes reporters keep on asking their questions and they keep on asking and they keep on, and once in a while their subject screams out the truth, just to shut them up. I hoped that Tamar would do that, too. But she didn't. She never does. On the subject of Baby Girl, Tamar's a closed book.

My baby sister was born with perfect fingers. I know because once I asked Tamar and she answered without thinking. I sprang the question on her. If there were anyone else to ask, I would ask anyone else, but who is there? My grandfather is a sore subject. I know that because that's how Tamar refers to him.

"Sore subject," she said to me when I inquired about him. "Moving right along."

That's another one of Tamar's famous flat statements: *moving right along.*

"Just tell me one thing," I said. "Did she have all her fingers and toes?"

"Who?"

Tamar knows who I'm talking about. Still she pretends ignorance.

"My baby sister. Did she have ten fingers and ten toes?"

"Yes," Tamar said. "She had all her fingers and all her toes. But she wasn't your sister. Your sister is someone who lives with you and grows up with you. That's not what she was."

I didn't answer. I didn't touch that remark. Not with a ten-foot pole. Tamar has all her answers ready. The not-being-a-sister, the what-makes-a-sister and what doesn't. How would she know? Did she ever have a sister?

"Do you consider yourself an authority on sororal relations?" I said.

"Where do you get these words, Clara?"

"Sororal relations is not a word, it's a phrase."

"Where do you get these *phrases*, Clara?"

I gave her a look. I can do it, too, give looks, although I rarely choose to do so. The truth is that I attract unusual words and phrases. They come drifting toward me out of thin air, invisible, and then they sense my presence and quickly attach themselves to me. That's because I'm a word-person. My first-grade teacher told me that.

"Clara Winter," he said. "You are a word-person and don't ever forget it."

He was right. He knew. He could tell. It's something that can be sensed. There's a difference between word-people and non–word-people. The old man, he was a non–word-person. Was the old man's mother a word-person? His father?

Who knows?

It all comes back to the truth, and what the truth might be. Still, it's easier to make up a story than to tell the truth. I don't even know what the truth is. Tamar will not answer my questions. She does not even allow me to *ask* my questions. It's a force she exudes. It's an aura that surrounds her. I want to know everything about my baby sister, and everything is what I don't know. There is so much left unasked, so much that can't be answered.

"Was I a premature baby?" I asked Tamar.

Notice how I did not say "were *we* premature babies." Tamar would not have responded if I had used "we." She does not respond to me when I refer to myself and my baby sister as "we." Tamar answers only to "I." I have to phrase everything in the singular, as if it was ever only me, me myself and I, no baby sister twirling and somersaulting beside me.

"A little."

I've done a lot of research. There's a great deal I know about conception and pregnancy and birth, things that Tamar may not even know despite the fact that she has experienced all three and I am but a callow youth.

Can a girl be callow? Or is it a boys-only word?

Tamar is a straightforward person. She believes that knowledge is power. More than once she's told me, *Knowledge is power, Clara. If knowledge is power, then why won't you tell me about my sister?* is my silent response. You can't say that to Tamar though. She's not that kind of person.

Baby Girl may have had undeveloped lungs. She may have been unable to take a breath of frigid Adirondack air even if she had wanted a breath of it.

A baby's heart beats extremely fast. Not as fast as a hummingbird, but far faster than a grown human being's. If you're trying to get a baby's heart going, you have to keep jabbing and jabbing at a baby's chest. I doubt if that's something Tamar knew how to do. This was quite a while ago. This was eleven years ago. They may not have known much back then, about how very fast a baby's heart beats, and about how hard you have to work to keep it going.

Was Baby Girl an old soul? Was she not supposed to be born? Was she accidentally trapped inside my mother's body, a terrible mistake? Do babies have a choice? Do they have the ability to choose to live or die?

My roll of green adding-machine paper used to sit snugly in the holder the old man made for me. I can still see it, even though it no longer exists. When last I saw my roll of adding-machine paper, many notes had been taken about the old man. Most of them I took down when first I met him, when he was my immigrant oral history project. Some of them were about his little brother, Eli.

The day I asked him about Eli, the old man was wrapping tinfoil in the shape of a butterfly around a sweet potato. The old man loved sweet potatoes. He often ate one for lunch.

"Okay," I said. "Why didn't Eli come to America with you? That was the plan, wasn't it?"

The old man pinched the tinfoil butterfly until it had antennae, then he carried it over to the fridge and put it inside next to his quart of Dairylea milk. The old man only bought a quart at a time. It would last him a week unless I put too much in my hot chocolate. Then he ran out and had none left for his coffee. He never said anything though. He just drank it black. I wonder now if the old man hated drinking black coffee, those times when I drank up his milk.

"Wasn't Eli supposed to come with you?"

"It was snowing," he said. "There was a lot of snow."

He got up and went over to the sink and ran some water onto the dishes.

"Snow that was blowing straight into my face. I couldn't see."

I unspooled some more of my green adding-machine paper and wrote on it. *Snow . . . straight . . . couldn't see.* I know about snow like that. The old man drank the rest of his coffee. It had to have been extremely cold by then, but he never wasted anything.

"Was Eli wearing boots?"

I pictured boots, heavy lace-up boots such as they must have made long ago in the old man's country that doesn't exist anymore.

"Yes."

"Did he follow in your footsteps? That's what I did when I was nine and Tamar and I were stuck in the blizzard."

"No."

"Did you carry him then?"

"I left Eli with the lantern," he said.

I held the thickly spread bite of toast under the table, then I put it into my mouth. I tried to swallow it without biting, the way Catholics do with the wafer.

"It was too cold," the old man said. "There was too much snow. It was the dead of winter. I couldn't carry him."

The old man couldn't carry him.

There was too much snow.

It was too cold. Too much snow. That was all I needed to hear: *There are many ways to die,* I remembered the old man saying to me, long ago.

I wrote it all down. Then I wound the spool of green adding-machine paper back up. Around and around I went. It took a long time. Then I put it in my backpack. The old man finished wiping the dishes dry, plucked up his damp yellow dish towel, and hung it over the oven door handle. He hung it exactly the same way he always hung it, smoothing out the damp wrinkles.

Too cold. Too much snow. I couldn't carry him.

The old man's little brother, Eli, died in the snow. I watched the old man smoothing out the wrinkles in his yellow dish towel. Even if I closed my eyes so that the sight of the old man smoothing his dish towel disappeared, I knew I would still see him. Nothing would ever be the same as it had been minutes earlier. Now everything was different. Now he was an old man who had lost his brother.

The church lights were on across Nine Mile Creek, but they wouldn't be on for much longer. Choir practice was almost over. Tamar would soon be driving up to the entrance of the Nine Mile Trailer Park. The windshield wipers would be on because of the almost-freezing rain, and the broken one on the right would be squeaking. I looked out the window at the church across the creek, trying to see the lights through the rain, but all I could see was a young boy—eleven years old—lying still in the snow, wearing a pair of heavy lace-up boots.

Inside my chest, my heart hurt. It came to me that my whole life long, I would carry with me the memory of the old man standing by his stove, smoothing his dish towel. Up and down, up and down, yellow stripes appearing and disappearing under his hand. Across Nine Mile Creek, the lights blinked out. The old man sat across from me at the formica table that he found on scavenging night, lost in his dark lantern world, unspeakably sad.

Six minutes ticked by, and it was time to go. I folded my jacket over my arm and took two sugar cookies wrapped up in a paper towel, one for me and one for Tamar, for the ride home. I wiped my eyes on my jacket sleeve. It was dark. Tamar wouldn't notice.

She noticed.

"What's wrong?"

"Nothing."

Tamar kept one arm on the steering wheel and one eye on the road. She kept looking over at me. She knew to be quiet. When we drove into the driveway, she leaned across me and unbuckled my seatbelt. She stretched her arm way out and opened up the car door for me. She used to do that when I was a child.

It was cold in the house. It's always cold in the house. I turned up the thermostat to 72 degrees and sat on top of the register in my room. Warm air came blowing up underneath me. It made my hair fly up in the air. It came seeping through the layers of socks and pants and underpants. I curled up with my knees to my chest and lay right on top of the register. Two floors below me, the furnace hummed. I love that hum. Warm air blew around me and through me. I warmed. My muscles started to unclench.

There were footsteps in my room. I kept my eyes closed. I stayed curled up. The footsteps came over to where I lay on the register. Something clinked onto the floor next to my head.

Footsteps receded.

I opened my eyes. Steam curled out of the mug on the floor next to me. I breathed in sharply through my nose, to try to draw the steam over to my nose so I could smell what was in the cup. Tea? Hot chocolate? The steam would not cooperate and drift itself over to where I lay breathing in quickly. I started to hyperventilate from trying so hard to drag it over.

Coffee? Hot mulled cider, which I had once read about in a book?

None of the above.

A mug of hot water, with slices of lemon floating in it. I took a sip. It tasted sweet. Could there be sugar in it? Could Tamar have spooned in some white poison, which is what she's been known to call sugar? I lay back down on the register. Tamar had not turned the thermostat down, she had not said anything to me about wasting energy, she had not told me to put a sweater on if I was cold. Tamar, my mother, had brought me something sweet and hot to drink.

I closed my eyes and tried to let the young Georg drift through my mind, standing on the pier at Ellis Island, drawing stars and stripes in the air with his nose, his dark olden-days coat hanging down on his shoulders.

But he wouldn't stay. He disappeared.

What came to me instead was the old man at his forge, the one he rescued from the auction in North Sterns. The old man stringing aluminum soda can tops together. The old man searching for possibility on scavenging night. The old man making me a lantern that was not a match for my missing lantern earring.

Warm air kept blowing up through the register. I sipped at the hot lemon water until it was all gone.

There's many a time I've missed Baby Girl, missed her terribly. She would have walked beside me in the halls at school. Her locker would have been next to mine, in the last row of lockers where the U-V-W-X-Y and Z lockers are. There're only a few of us at the end of the alphabet. There's not all that many students at Sterns Middle School to begin with.

She would have understood without explanation why I changed the W in Winter to w. That's what twins do. They don't have to explain things to each other. Or maybe the W would have remained uppercase after all. If my baby sister were alive, winter would not have won. Tamar and my grandfather would not have been defeated by a blizzard.

They would have triumphed in the face of adversity.

They would have laughed in the face of death.

My baby sister would have been born, taken her first breath of icy Adirondack air, and screamed. My grandfather would have had no reason to flee to a patch of primeval forest near the Vermont border and become a hermit. There would be only one topic to avoid with Tamar, and my sister and I, together, would have insisted that she tell us about our father. Helpless against the mysterious power that twins together exert, she would have agreed.

Perhaps Tamar would choose to eat foods not necessarily jarred or canned. She might like not only marinated artichoke hearts but fresh artichokes steamed and eaten with lemon mayonnaise, such as I once read about in a magazine. Tamar might have allowed more sugar in the house. The three of us—Tamar and her twin daughters—might have baked sugar cookies together.

Everything might be different, if my baby sister had lived.

CJ Wilson might never have looked at me with those eyes. He might never have flipped up my skirt, the first day of school last fall. My chickens might not have turned out mean. There would have been someone to feed them with me, to research chicken violence with. There would have been someone else to love the words I love. Peter Winchell, who has a locker next to mine, would be the person who was supposed to have a locker next to mine, instead of being a boy taking away a locker belonging to someone else, someone he's never met, someone the school never heard of, someone no one besides me has ever known and no one besides me has ever dreamed about, a ghost girl: my sister.

CHAPTER TEN

It was the old man's idea that I go to Utica and seek out my grandfather. We were at Crystal's Diner. It was a Wednesday afternoon, and instead of going home after school I had walked to the old man's trailer. I used to do that sometimes. I was taking notes on my roll of adding-machine paper, which I started keeping at the old man's trailer when it continued to irritate Tamar.

"The very sight of that damn green thing annoys me, Clara," Tamar had said, one time too many.

The old man was stirring cream into his coffee and watching Johnny Zielinski play in his booth. Crystal brought Johnny a plate of french fries and a little bowl of ketchup— red, his favorite color—to dip them into.

"Now, how close was your father's forge to your house?" I asked the old man.

I was asking a series of questions for *Georg Kominsky: American Immigrant* and I wanted to get the details right. Take a fake book report for example. You have to get the details right, otherwise who would ever want to read the fake book?

The old man looked at me.

"My father's forge?" he said.

Then I remembered. I had made the whole story up. It was all a figment of my imagination. It's hard to get away from things once they're written down. Written down, things become real. I had a memory of the old man as a child, little Georg, living with his father and mother and his baby brother, Eli, in a hut next to a forge, in their town that doesn't exist anymore. Georg and his father, every morning eating their cornmeal mush and heading out the door for a day's work. Georg the apprentice, his father the master.

None of it existed.

None of it was true.

"My father's forge?" the old man said again. "What are you talking about, Clara?"

"Nothing," I said.

He watched me tear away the part of my roll of adding-machine paper that had the made-up story notes on it. I rolled it into a tight tube and then I folded the tube over onto itself. Then I put it into my mouth and chewed.

"Clara?"

I shook my head at the old man. The paper wouldn't chew. It just got soggy in my mouth. There was a taste of paper throughout my entire nose and mouth. How do spies do it?

"Clara."

The old man couldn't read anyway, so I took the paper out of my mouth and threw it into the trash behind the grill. Crystal watched but she didn't say anything. I pictured the old man the night I first saw him, hanging lanterns in Nine Mile Woods.

"What will happen when you're gone?" I said to the old man.

It was happening again. Words, tumbling out of my mouth without heed.

"Like if you move away or something?" I said.

Too late. The old man already knew whereof I spoke. He already knew I was looking ahead to the day when he wouldn't be there, to the day when he would be gone.

"Clara."

Clara clara clara.

"It happens," I said.

He said nothing.

"Everyone will be gone," I said.

"You have your mother."

"I want my grandfather. I want my sister."

The old man regarded me. That's the term for a certain kind of look.

"It's true that I will be gone someday," he said. "So will Tamar."

"I know," I said. "I know. That's what I'm talking about."

"But by then you will have found something, Clara," the old man said. "You will have found the one thing that will change everything, the thing that will make sense of your life and keep you going."

I asked Tamar about my father once, point-blank. *Is my father dead?* I asked her. *For all intents and purposes,* she said, which is a typical Tamar response. *Where does he live if he's dead only for intents and purposes?* I asked. *As far as I'm concerned he doesn't live anywhere,* she said, which puts him in the same category as my hermit grandfather, who may or may not be living in a patch of primeval forest near the Vermont border. I kept on, though, and finally Tamar caved in just to make me stop talking.

"Your father was someone I met one night at a party," she said. "The next morning he drove to Virginia and I never saw him again."

She made her eyes huge and stared back at me.

"There," she said. "Does that answer your question?"

"Yes and no. What was his name?"

"He didn't have one."

"Everyone has a name."

"I have no idea what it might have been."

"Is he still alive?"

"No idea."

"Did he know about me and my sister?"

"You mean did he know about *you*," Tamar said. "You don't have a sister."

"Did he know about me?"

"What do you think?"

She stared at me and didn't blink. That's another of her skills. Tamar can go a long time without blinking. It's very difficult to go without blinking. Try it. I didn't answer her question. Answering questions gives the question-asker the upper hand. That's what I wanted to avoid. So I just repeated my own question.

"Did he know about me?"

That's the kind of thing I've learned to do just from observing Tamar.

She shook her head. "Your *biological father* does not know about you. He has no idea about you. I doubt he even remembers meeting me, and therefore it is as if he does not exist."

She stabbed an artichoke heart with her fork.

"Got it?" she said.

She stuck the fork in her mouth.

"Got it," I said.

Then I cleared my plate and scraped it into the wastebasket and put it in the sink. I threw my napkin into the wastebasket. I put my glass of milk into the fridge for breakfast tomorrow morning.

"Good night," I said.

Then I left the kitchen. I went outside and started down the dirt road. The daisies were nodding on their long stems. The Queen Anne's lace was standing tall, with the tiny black dots in the center of each that always make me think of bugs. Queen Anne's lace is not native to North America. It came from another country. It's an immigrant plant.

"And that's all she wrote," I said to the old man. "So as far as I know, my father is alive and living somewhere in this world."

"Then there's still a connection. You have a connection to your father."

If you are ever close to someone in the world, then there exists an invisible connection between you and that person, a connection beyond the ken of ordinary people. I read that in a book about reincarnation and near-death experiences. It's a true book. I didn't make it up. I told this to the old man once and he nodded. He believed it, too.

Tamar? Not a chance.

"Ma? What do you believe happens when you die?"

"You're dead, that's what happens."

"But at the exact point of death, what happens? Where does your spirit go?"

"In the ground, along with the rest of you."

That's Tamar. I knew I could count on an answer like that, and that's the answer I got. Still, I persisted. It's my nature to persist.

"What about the white light?" I said.

"What white light?"

"The tunnel of white light that envelops your spirit. The people you loved who come back to help you from this world into the next."

"Oh, that white light," Tamar said. "That's just the last neurons popping off in your brain. Pop, pop, pop. It's like a camera flash."

"Then how do you explain the many documented cases of eerily similar near-death experiences?"

"I don't," she said.

That's another thing about Tamar. She feels no need to explain or excuse. That's why you can't argue with her. You run into a brick wall. Any time she senses the presence of Baby Girl, for example, the wall appears.

"Ask your mother about your grandfather," the old man had told me.

"You don't know Tamar," I said. "She is unaskable."

"Ask anyway," he said. "You have nothing to lose."

I could feel the truth in what he was saying. I had nothing to lose. The other half of that sentence is *and everything to gain.* My third-grade teacher was fond of that saying. "Children, you have nothing to lose and everything to gain." She made that saying fit a variety of situations, situations that you wouldn't ordinarily think it would fit, such as putting plastic bread bags over your shoes before you put your shoe-boots on.

A few days later I tried to ask Tamar about my grandfather. She was eating her dinner, which was the dinner I had made. If I make dinner, she'll eat whatever I make. Even if it goes against her personal rule of cans and jars, she'll eat it: green beans, chicken surprise, and corn pudding. I read how to make corn pudding in a recipe book in the library. In my corn pudding recipe, there is a consistent relationship among all the ingredients.

One can of creamed corn, *one* can of regular corn. *One* cup of sour cream, *one* stick of butter. *One* package of cornbread mix. I like that kind of recipe—all the ingredients in a ratio of *one* to *one*—because it means I never have to write it down.

Did the pioneers write down their recipes? They did not.

"So," I said.

I could see Tamar's face get a look on it. She could tell that something was coming, just from the way I said "So."

"So," I said again.

I thought of the old man. *Ask her about your grandfather anyway,* the old man had said. But I couldn't.

CJ Wilson may sometimes ask his father, Chuck Wilson Senior, about his mother, or CJ's mother may be a forbidden topic in the Wilson trailer. Still, there must be times when CJ thinks about his mother, wonders where she is and if she is still living somewhere in this world. CJ might dream about his mother, at night when he's asleep on the pullout couch in the living room of his trailer, which is where I imagine him sleeping.

"Clara, would you clear the table, please?" Tamar said on a Tuesday night the week after the old man told me I should ask her about my grandfather. "It's court night. Chuck Wilson's done it this time."

That was uncharacteristic of Tamar. She does not discuss the dealings of the court with me.

"Second DWI with a suspended, doing 70 in a 25 zone, totaled his Camaro. Plus a resisting arrest and attempted battery of a police officer. State trooper," she corrected herself. "Which is worse."

"What does that mean?"

"Six-month minimum. And the state'll get his kid, I guess. Do you know this boy, Charles Junior Wilson?"

"No," I said. "Never heard of him."

I did know CJ Wilson the chicken, though. I knew that chicken inside and out. I could sense the soul of CJ Wilson, the chicken, emanating from the broken-down barn. Sometimes at night, last year, when the old man was still in his trailer in Sterns and my chickens were still scratching and pecking in the broken-down barn, I lay awake at night and thought about them. I told no one, though. Those chickens were my secret. I said nothing about CJ Wilson the boy, either. Never once in our time together did I ever mention CJ Wilson to the old man.

Tamar was annoyed by the lack of eggs from my chickens. There were still only a few eggs, the ones that I could reach in and grab from outside the pen.

"Clara! When are we going to see some more eggs out of those girls?" Tamar had started to ask.

"Pretty soon, I guess," I said.

I did not tell Tamar that the barn had started to stink, nor did I tell her that the chickens had gone insane. Even on a twenty-below day, I could smell the barn coming from way across the field. Through the snow I trudged, bearing my heavy buckets of feed and water, just as Laura Ingalls Wilder, Pioneer Girl, would have done.

On court night I watched out my bedroom window for Chuck Wilson. A big man driving a pickup with gigantic tires dropped him off and then backed fast out of the driveway. Chuck Wilson's short hair was flattened down on his head. I could still see comb marks. His red flannel shirt strained at the bottom of his belly.

Next day, the day after court, CJ reached out and gave me a shove. A sound that could be a laugh or could be a phlegmy cough came out of Tiny. He reached in his half-pounder M&M bag on the dashboard and selected three red ones. There's a story that he keeps dirty pictures underneath his candy bag. It's possible.

I said nothing. I sat tight on a green vinyl seat next to Bonita Rae Farwell, a North Sterns girl. The North Sterns girls are quiet most of the time but loud when they have to be. They know how to talk mean. They know how to handle the boys; some of the boys are their brothers.

Those girls would not worry about being murdered by a flock of insane chickens. This is what I believe to be true.

From the back I noticed that CJ's head was shaped like a bullet. His dusty dark hair was shaved close to his scalp, with a few dried lines of blood where he got nicked. I once heard him tell the other boys that he and his father took turns shaving each other's heads. In a little while he came swinging down the aisle.

"Wipe," he said. *"Wipe."*

The night before, I had stayed in my room while Chuck

Wilson Senior was in court in the kitchen with Tamar. I did not listen through the furnace duct. I turned on the radio and read *The Long Winter,* by Laura Ingalls Wilder. Thus was I able to ignore CJ on the bus. What you don't know can't hurt you. That's how the saying goes.

Crystal Zielinski heard the old man talking about Clifford Winter who lived on Genesee Street in Utica.

"Utica?" she said. "Do the both of you need to get to Utica, Mr. Kominsky and Ms. winter?"

Crystal stood there with her red dishrag and Johnny's plate of half-eaten french fries. Ketchup smeared like blood.

"Because if you need to get to Utica you can use my truck," Crystal said.

"That would be good," the old man said. "Thank you."

"You're welcome." Crystal took some keys out of her apron pocket. "Be my guest. I just filled it and I won't need it until I close at ten."

Johnny Zielinski loves red so much that even Crystal's truck is red, redder than a fire truck.

"You're a good driver," I said to the old man when we had driven halfway to Utica. He knew how to drive, even though he didn't have a driver's license. Why didn't he? Reading, that's why.

I will keep the old man's secret forever. Nothing will drag it out of me. Even if I'm strapped in a folding chair in the basement of a building with a bare lightbulb shining in my eyes and deprived of food and water and sleep for days on end, I will not give away the old man's secret.

Before I went in to Clifford Hazzard Winter's apartment building at 1431 Genesee Street, the old man asked if I wanted him to come with me.

"No."

"Are you sure?"

"Did the pioneers head westward?"

"Yes," the old man said.

"And that's your answer," I said.

But there was nothing I wanted more than the old man walking next to me down the hallway with the dirty floor and the dark brown paint chipping onto it, and into the elevator that wouldn't go up even when I pressed 6 seven times in a row, then kept my finger on it for a count of fifteen, and then pushed open the stairs door and walked up and around the five flights of stairs to 6.

The old man waited for me outside Clifford Winter's apartment building. He let the motor idle. Only motors and people can idle. It's very rare that you see that word used with anything other than motors and people. If you're a person, you can idle your time away. If you're a motor, you can idle while someone sits behind the steering wheel, drumming his fingers in a rhythm that you can't hear.

If the old man had been with me, I might not have noticed the broken light halfway down the hall. I might not have counted as high as I counted. If you're extremely nervous, you can count. That's a trick that my fourth-grade teacher taught me.

"Class, if you ever find yourself extremely nervous," she said, "try counting. Count as high as you possibly can. If you want, insert 'one thousand' between each number."

That's how I got to be so good at counting exact seconds. It was on the advice of my fourth-grade teacher.

The buzzer next to the door was broken. The cover was hanging half-on and half-off. There was a ripped piece of yellow paper with *C. Winter* written on it stuck on a piece of chewed gum above the buzzer. How do I know that the adhesive was used chewing gum? Because. I looked. I looked around that hall for quite a while. The floor was marble. There was a large cobweb high up in one corner of the hall. It was next to the ceiling, where even the tallest broom could not have reached.

I looked at the door across the hall from C. Winter's.

M. Trivieri.

Down the hall: S. Klusk.

Does no one in Utica go by a full first name? Does everyone use initials only? Is this an unwritten rule? I was pondering these questions and lining my feet up perfectly evenly on the dark brown crack between two marble tiles when C. Winter's door swung open.

"What do you want?"

I knew it was C. Winter speaking to me. I turned around and gazed upon him. He looked right back at me.

"What do you want?"

He did not sound impatient, nor did he sound suspicious. He sounded as if he would ask what it was I wanted as many times as it took, until he had an answer. He sounded like Tamar.

"I'm Clara winter," I said.

The air around him became still. If you train yourself, you can learn to sense the quality of the air around someone, how it moves, whether it shimmers, when it freezes. The air around C. Winter had been ordinary air, invisible, bored even, until I told him who I was.

"And you are C. Winter, are you not?"

He nodded. Then one of his eyes started to move. It moved just a little bit. The air around him shook itself, broke apart and started moving again, fast and furious even though he said nary a word.

"May I come in?"

I stood there, waiting. His one moving eye moved a little bit more. Then I was inside his apartment and standing in C. Winter's hallway. I closed my eyes for one brief second and thought of the old man waiting for me outside, down five flights of stairs, the motor idling in Crystal's bright red truck. I stood in the dark hallway of C. Winter's apartment and pictured the beautiful, unearthly red of Crystal's truck.

C. Winter—my biological grandfather—was not a hermit, nor was he a pioneer. He was so unlike what I expected that I became confused in his apartment and had to get out my roll of adding-machine paper so that I could look up the questions I wanted to ask him.

"What's that?" he said.

That was one of the first things that C. Winter said to me.

"Notes," I said.

After he asked about my paper roll I could no longer unroll it. C. Winter's eyes were upon my spool of green paper and I couldn't let him see it. You know when there're things you can't do. It's an instinct. Instinct told me not to unroll my adding-machine paper in front of him.

I cleared my throat. I picked up my pen and balanced it between my thumb and my forefinger. If you do that, and then wiggle the pen slowly and curvily, the pen looks as if it's made of rubber. This trick also works with a pencil.

C. Winter sat in his chair. His eyes didn't rest on me the way a hermit or pioneer grandfather's eyes rest on their beloved granddaughter. C. Winter's eyes roamed. I saw them roaming around his living room: the blue chair, the TV that sat on top of a wooden crate, the mattress on the floor. His living room was nearly his whole apartment. Off behind one corner was a small kitchen, called a galley kitchen. Galley kitchens are ship kitchens, small, in which you can stand in one place and reach everything you need. Everything in a galley kitchen is within arm's reach. I learned about this in a book I read on boat-building. It was a real book.

"I admire your galley kitchen," I said. "It must be very convenient."

When I said that to C. Winter, I didn't mean it. I didn't like his galley kitchen, even though it was clean and neat and didn't smell. I didn't like C. Winter's galley kitchen because it was not the old man's kitchen, and all I could think about was the old man's galley kitchen in Nine Mile Trailer Park, with its yellow-striped dish towel hanging over the stove door handle.

C. Winter's eyes kept moving around the room. There are people with eye diseases whose eyes never stop moving. They jiggle back and forth in unison, or one eye roves. It's possible that one eye can remain stationary and the other can rove free within the eye socket. I read that in the medical encyclopedia.

"Isn't it?" I said. "I mean, you can reach everything without having to take a step."

C. Winter's foot started jiggling. Some people have a disease in which their entire body trembles. Every muscle, every bone, all the time. I forget what it's called. The trembling cannot be controlled. Twenty-four hours a day, the victims of this disease live with the trembling.

"Do you ever have to take a step?" I said. "Just a tiny one, I mean?"

"I don't cook."

His voice was a surprise. You don't know that you have voice expectations until the actual voice is there, the sound waves coming at you and entering into your skull, and then you realize that you had expected something entirely different. C. Winter did not sound like what I believe a pioneer or a hermit would sound like.

"Nor do we, except on rare occasions," I said. "Tamar believes that food tastes best when eaten directly from a jar or can."

"Why do you call her Tamar?" he said.

I couldn't answer him. I was already into my train of thought. Words had piled themselves up in my brain and they could not be stopped. They had to emerge in the order I had already given them.

"Tamar, for example, will not eat margarine because she says it's science run amok."

He smiled.

"She always used to say stuff like that."

"She still does," I said.

He was still smiling.

"She still does," I said again. "Tamar says stuff like that all the time. Margarine is science run amok, food should be eaten out of cans and jars, the most ingenious invention on God's green earth is the Swiss army knife."

"That sounds like her," he said. "That does indeed sound like her."

"Don't call her 'her,'" I said. "Her name is Tamar. Everyone's got a name."

He shook his head. His eyes roamed. His knee jiggled up and down.

"Everything on God's green earth has a name," I said. "Or *should* have."

I saw Crystal's bright red pickup the minute I came out of the apartment building where C. Winter, my biological grandfather, lived. I kept my eyes trained on the drumming fingers of the old man the entire time I was walking down through the green-plastic-awning roof over the little slanting tunnel that leads out of the apartment building—in case it rains?—and walking across the parking lot where a few rusty cars and a few rusty trucks were parked. I watched the drumming fingers of the old man sitting behind the steering wheel of the idling truck until I was at the truck itself. Then the old man stopped drumming and let me in.

"Well?" the old man said.

I shook my head. I climbed in next to him and strapped the seatbelt over my shoulder, across my chest, and buckled it. It was too loose. I pulled it as tight as it would go. If I had had access to my emergency seatbelt system I would have hooked it up, but the only place in the world where my seatbelt system exists is in Tamar's car, at home.

Dark gray air hung above us, a winter sky. Across the street there was an A&P store with three shopping carts left in the parking lot.

"Look at that," I said to the old man. "Is it that hard to take a shopping cart back to the store?"

He didn't say anything.

"To the entrance, even? I mean, is it that hard?"

At Jewell's Grocery, no one leaves shopping carts in the parking lot. That's because there is no parking lot. There's only the road, right in front of the store. The old man put his hand on my seatbelt buckle and tugged at it. He untwisted the shoulder belt where it was spiraled behind my neck and smoothed it down. Then he pushed my hair off my cheek.

"Well?" he said.

"Well," I said.

He pulled the lever so it pointed to "D" and put the blinker on. Down Genesee Street he drove, past the Boston Store, past Bremer & Bullock Liquor, past Munson Williams Proctor Museum of Art, and on to the overpass that leads to Route 12 north. I counted three hundred seconds, the way my teacher had taught me, and looked back. Utica lay behind us, with a rim of snowy hills and dark sky above it. We were climbing out of the Mohawk Valley, heading into the foothills.

"Tell me about your grandfather," the old man said.

"That wasn't my grandfather. That was C. Winter."

The old man looked at me.

"They don't use first names in Utica," I said. "They go only by their initials. Did you know that?"

I forgot that the old man couldn't read. He wouldn't have known an initial from a surname. I turned away and looked out the window at Utica in the distance.

I wanted to keep my grandfather, my real hermit grandfather, where he belonged. I wanted him in his patch of primeval Adirondack forest near the Vermont border, living in his tipi, selling his pelts or trading them for sugar and coffee. The bare essentials. I wanted him to be there, alive and well and full of the answers to my questions. Even as I sat in

Clifford Winter's Utica apartment, my true hermit grandfather, the one I had based my fake book report *Tales of an Adirondack Hermit* on, was working quietly in his tipi near the Vermont border. He was even then chewing rawhide, making it soft so that he could cut it and stitch it into moccasins for me, his granddaughter. I asked him a question in my mind, in italics, and sent it winging through the sky toward him.

Why did you take Glass Factory instead of Route 12?

My hermit grandfather couldn't hear me. He was too intent on working the deerskin for my moccasins, softening the stiff leather so that the moccasins he was making as a gift for me would fit my feet like flesh and never, never hurt me.

CHAPTER ELEVEN

The night of the fire, it snowed. It was the kind of snow that falls straight down, each flake thick and furry. Silent snow that silences everything it touches. Snow that makes the entire world quiet.

The old man and I were going to make gingersnaps that night. We were moving on, past sugar cookies and into gingersnaps. A true gingersnap is thin and crisp, a dry, light cookie. The opposite of the kind of snow that was falling that night.

"A gingersnap should break cleanly," the old man said. "It should snap."

Hence the name. A name reflecting the purpose, the very sound of the cookie when broken. When Tamar dropped me off at the entrance to Nine Mile Trailer Park, I stood by the sign for a minute and tried to catch snowflakes on my tongue. It's not easy to do. You would think, in a snow falling so thick and straight and heavy, that you would be able to have a mouthful of snow in just a minute or two. Just lean your head back, open your mouth, and let the cold whiteness enter.

It doesn't work that way. I stood with my head back and my tongue out until I saw the lights go on in the church across Nine Mile Creek. Stained glass, throwing stained shadows on the white ground. You could barely see them, through the falling snow.

Across the creek Tamar was practicing with the choir she's never sung in, and in his trailer I imagined the old man laying out the measuring cup, the measuring spoons, the flour and salt and sugar and ginger, everything necessary for making gingersnaps. Former olive oil cans were hanging by the window, waiting for their destiny to be fulfilled.

I can still see them in my mind. I can see the way they swung in the breeze in the summer, when the old man opened all the windows. I can hear the sound the cookie cutters made then, like ice when it freezes on Deeper Lake up in the Adirondacks, pushing against the shore with a sound like broken glass tinkling. I can still see myself on that night, standing at the entrance to Nine Mile Trailer Park, halfway between my mother across the creek and the old man in his kitchen.

When I stopped trying to catch snowflakes on my tongue, I walked up the lane to the old man's trailer. At first I didn't understand the light in his window. It was an odd light, orange. An irregular light. The light from a lamp is not irregular. Then I saw the lady two trailers down fling open her door. A sound in the air around me grew high and loud. Then I knew that the orange dancing light was a fire in the old man's trailer, and the sound all around me was me, screaming.

"Did you see him come out?" I screamed to the lady two

trailers down. She leaned out her door. She had socks on her feet and she kept stepping on one foot, then the other. Her feet will freeze, I heard myself thinking at the same time as I was yelling at her.

"Did you see him come out?"

My voice kept screaming out of my throat. I could hear my throat getting raw just in the sound of my words. The lady hopped to her other foot.

"Did you see him come out?"

She frowned. I could see her trying to figure out what I was saying. Then she figured it out and shook her head. Back and forth. She mouthed some words at me. *No. No. I didn't see him.*

She hopped onto her other foot, then she went back inside her trailer. The door was still open. I stood in the old man's yard. I listened for sirens: none.

"Call the fire department!" I screamed.

I wanted to hear those sirens. I wanted the Floyd Volunteer Fire Department to be on their way. I looked across Nine Mile Creek. The church windows were lit up. They were still singing. Did no one see the flames? Did none of them stop their singing and look out the window and see that the old man's trailer was on fire?

My feet were numb. My sneakers were no good in the snow. What I had intended was to get out of the car and walk only on the trailer park road, and then only on the path that the old man shoveled to his steps. That's what I had intended to do.

"Put your boots on," Tamar had said before we got in the car.

"They're wet."

She gave me a look.

"Soaked," I said. "I would catch my death of pneumonia, should someone force me to wear those boots."

I could see her thoughts chase themselves around on her face. *And why are they soaked?* she wanted to ask. *Can this be my daughter, Miss Prepared For All Snow Emergencies, refusing to wear winter boots on a cold winter night?*

And whose fault is that? she would've said, if I had told her why my boots were wet. There was no good reason. It was a reasonless situation. I got off the bus, and I saw the drift, and for once my feet just wanted to jump into it.

The church windows were still lit. You could hardly see them because the flames from the old man's trailer had grown so much brighter. The lady came back out on her trailer steps. She had put her boots on and she was carrying a broom. She ran through the snow to where I was standing.

"Did you see him come out?"

She shook her head again. She looked angry.

Then she started beating at tiny flames with the broom, the tiny flames floating from the window. Black and white wisps with a glow of orange coal, drifting down to the snow.

What good would that do?

Then I remembered my roll of green adding-machine paper. I could picture it, lying in its special drawer on the curved wall at the end of the old man's kitchen that was burning up.

Black dots were crawling through the snow when I looked over to the church again. The windows were still bright through the woods, but black dots were crawling in the snow. The biggest dot, the one in front, ran right through the creek and up the bank toward me. It got bigger and bigger. It turned into Tamar, running so fast that she looked like someone I didn't know.

"Did you see him come out?" I screamed at her. "Did you see him come out?"

She came running up to me and grabbed me. She had no jacket or boots. No gloves or hat.

"Did you? Did you?"

Tamar couldn't talk. She was breathing too hard. She bent over in the middle and sucked in air. I hit her on the back. "Did you see him come out?"

How could she? She was practicing with the choir in the church with the lit windows. No one but me knew about the secret patch of clear glass in the stained window in the churchhouse, that if you stood on a chair you could peek through it and see the Nine Mile Trailer Park through the woods. All Tamar could've heard was the sound of singing. She couldn't have heard the snow drifting down. She couldn't have heard the scrape of a match, whatever match it was that lit the fire that was burning down the old man's trailer.

There was fire coming out of the bedroom window now. No one in all the people standing around us now would've known that was the bedroom window except for me. I was the only one who knew the trailer from the inside. I was the only one who knew that behind that window was where the old man slept. I was the only one who knew that my spool of adding-machine paper, which held the old man's life in its curls of words, was trapped in its tin paper holder in the special curved kitchen drawer.

I cupped my mittens full of snow and shoved them against my mouth. Then I jerked away from Tamar and ran into the trailer. My head was down when I ran in, and the snow was white-cold against my mouth and cheeks. Then there was a peculiar feeling on my head. I had never felt that feeling before. I smelled a certain smell and I knew that the feeling was the smell, and that it meant that my hair was on fire. Where was the old man? Where was the special kitchen drawer? Where was Clara winter? I sucked in air through my ball of snow, but there was no more snow. The snow was gone, and fire had taken its place.

PART TWO

—*Ductility*, the ability to undergo deformation (change of shape) without breaking.
—*Elasticity*, the ability to return to the original shape after deformation.
—*Fatigue Resistance*, the ability to resist repeated small stresses.

From *Metalworking*

CHAPTER TWELVE

I asked the old man a question once, on how he would choose to die, and no answer was forthcoming. I repeated my question several times, in several different ways, but the old man never answered. Instead, he posed a question to me.

"Am I guilty?" he said.

"That's not the question," I said.

"But am I?"

"You're on death row!" I said. "You have to choose: lethal injection or electric chair. It doesn't matter if you're guilty or not."

"But am I?"

I gave up. I took the advice given to me by Tamar when asked about Baby Girl Winter: "Give up." No answer to my death row question was to be forthcoming from the old man. He was fixated instead on the question of guilt. Now that the old man is gone, I think about that. I wonder how my question sounded to the old man. I wonder if he thought I was asking him about guilt.

My death row question was the kind of question that

I used to ask during lunch in the Sterns Middle School cafeteria. It was a Clara winter type of question. I once posed a dying question to the entire lunch table, after I found out about the old man leaving his brother, Eli, in the snow. The old man was still alive then.

"Here's a question," I said. "How would you rather die? Burning to death in a fire, or freezing to death in a snowbank?"

They stopped eating to consider.

"That is such a Clara Winter type of question," Jackie Phillips said.

"Burning," one of the other girls said. "It's quicker. Or wait. Maybe freezing."

"Freezing," another one said. "Burning's too painful."

"Yeah," somebody else said. "Definitely freezing. I heard that if you freeze to death it's painless after the first few minutes."

"You just fall asleep. You stop shivering, and you fall asleep."

"First your toes go, then your fingers, then your lower legs, then your forearms, then your thighs, then your upper arms, then your crotch, your stomach, your chest, and finally your head."

"Your head's the last thing to go."

"That's because all the blood goes to your brain, because that's the most important thing."

I betrayed the old man when I asked that question. There's more than one way to betray someone. You can tell a secret about someone. You can let loose something that you know about an old man, something that happened to him, something that the old man did, without ever mentioning him by name, and then that secret is alive in the world, living and growing and being talked about. At the lunch table five girls sat talking calmly about what happens when you freeze to death, without ever knowing that in our town, in a trailer only half a mile from the school cafeteria, there was an immigrant whose little brother had frozen to death. The girls at the lunch table were talking about how Eli had died, and they didn't even know it.

But I did. That's one way you can betray someone.

"Stop talking about freezing to death," I said.

They looked at me.

"Why?" Jackie Phillips said. "You're the one who asked the question in the first place, Miss Clara."

"You haven't even talked about burning to death," I said. "Isn't there anyone who would choose burning to death? That's the martyr's way to die."

They made faces.

"Too painful."

"Yeah. It's a horrible way to die."

"Think of Joan of Arc," I said. "Think of those poor women in Salem. Think of widows in India committing suttee."

They looked at each other. Had they ever heard of Indian widows committing suttee? No. They may have heard of the Salem witch hunts, but they would not have known that the Salem women died by drowning or stoning. Maybe one non-witch was killed by burning to death. But that's something most people don't know. Mention "Salem witch hunt," to most people, and all they think of is being tied to a stake and burned to death.

"It's a fine way to die," I said. "It's a martyr's death. It's the death of someone who sacrifices her or his life for the sake of principle."

"Objection," Jackie Phillips said. "Irrelevant. Freezing's the way to go."

They all agreed. End of subject. On to sloppy joes.

When I asked the girls at the lunch table that question—*if you had to, would you rather die by freezing or burning?*—the old man was still alive. It was an idle question then, but I think about that day now. Now that the old man is dead by fire, I think about it. Every one of the girls chose freezing to death. There was no question. No debate. Burning was rejected out of hand.

But burning is how the old man died. The old man died in a way that was categorically rejected by everyone at the table.

When I was still in the hospital, reading the dictionary with the tissue-paper pages that Tamar bought for me, I looked up *martyr*. It's one of my favorite words because of the way it has four consonants, including one consonant that occasionally doubles as a vowel, in a row which begin and end with the same letter: r, t, y, r. It's unusual to see a word with that particular four-consonant pattern. Try to think of as many as you can. You'll soon see.

Martyr. 1. one who voluntarily suffers death as the penalty of witnessing to and refusing to renounce his religion. 2. one who sacrifices his life or something of great value for the sake of principle. 3. Victim, esp: a great or constant sufferer < a ~ to asthma all his life>.

Martyr is a tragic word, but these days it's become a word of scorn. People use the word *martyr* indiscriminately, but it's a word that should be used with great care. People tell other people that they're being martyrs to make them stop acting put-upon. That is a misuse of the word *martyr*. It hurts me to hear people use such a word in that way. What I want to say when I hear someone call another person a martyr is this: Martyrs are *dead*.

The whole time I was in the hospital I measured time by four-hour segments. That was the number of hours I had to wait until the nurse brought the small paper cup with the pill in it. The pill was for the pain of the burns and the burned lungs. Toward the end of the third hour and throughout the fourth hour, my mind would sharpen. I could feel the edges honing, the blurriness dissolving. It was during that sharpening time that I concentrated on not thinking about the old man.

When they let me go home the nurse with the brown hair that's shorter on one side than the other gave me a balloon.

"Here you go, sweetie-pie," she said.

I said thank you and took the balloon. It was orange. Tamar was waiting by the nurse's station. She was finishing some forms that they had given her.

"Ready?" she said.

I nodded. I was being chary with my words. *Chary* is a word I learned in the hospital, from the dictionary that Tamar brought in for me after I'd been in the hospital a couple of days. It's the kind of dictionary that in the olden days would have rested on a tall wooden stand in a library, the kind of dictionary that pioneers would've consulted in the New England cities they lived in before they headed west. Laura Ingalls Wilder would have loved such a dictionary. It's possible that she would have consulted such a dictionary to write one of her famous school compositions, which were never fake.

"Thank you, Ma," I wrote on my small memo pad. When Tamar gave it to me, I still couldn't talk too well because of sucking in all the burning air. Quickly I got into the habit of writing short notes if I needed to say something. When writing notes is your only means of communication, you learn to conserve language. You become chary with words.

At night in the hospital, after Tamar went home, I read the dictionary.

> *Chary. [ME, sorrowful, dear, fr. OE cearig sorrowful, fr. caru sorrow]*
> *1. archaic: dear, treasured. 2. discreetly cautious: as a: hesitant and vigilant*
> *about dangers and risks. b: slow to grant, accept, or expend <a man very*
> *~ of compliments> syn see cautious.*

Do you see what kind of a word chary is? It means something and its opposite at the same time. You can be slow to accept a compliment and slow to expend one, and the word *chary* will fit either side of your personality. You can be discreetly cautious about danger and risk, and at the same time treasure something dear to you. All these meanings are related.

The old man would have been able to see that immediately. The old man was an expert at seeing the relations between things.

They left it to Tamar to tell me. She waited until we were in the car.

"Buckle up," she said.

I buckled up. Then she reached around me and pulled out my safety system. She strapped on the bungee cords and wrapped the other belt around me.

"Ma?" I said. My throat still hurt and my words were whispery. But one word isn't worth writing down. She could tell that I was asking her why she was strapping me into my safety system.

"Ma?"

Tamar started the car. While I was in the hospital she'd fixed the nonopening passenger door. I noticed right away. There was an indentation in it, as if she'd kicked it or taken a hammer with a towel wrapped around it to my door. She's taken towel-wrapped hammers to things before. So the finish doesn't scratch, is what she said. But the door worked now. I pointed to it.

"Thanks Ma."

Her hand moved to the steering wheel as if she were going to push the lever to "D," but she didn't.

"Clara," she said.

I raised my eyebrows. Raised eyebrows give you a look of inquiry. That's something I've noticed. When you're being chary with your words, but you want to indicate interest in what someone is saying to you, if you want to let them know that you want them to keep on talking, then all you need do is raise your eyebrows. It worked.

"Clara," Tamar said, "the old man died in the fire."

No mincing words with Tamar. She is a woman who is naturally chary with her words. I watched her words go scrolling by the bottom of my mind, then I fell. You can fall in a car. It's possible. What happens is that you sag, and if there's not a complicated system of safety belts and bungee cords to hold you up, you fall right onto the floor of the car. Right into the pit.

The old man died in the fire, the old man died in the fire.

It sounded like a nursery rhyme.

"Are you sure?" I said. I had to whisper.

She nodded. Her hand was in front of my safety system, helping to hold me up. Then her arm came around the back of my head and neck and clamped onto my shoulder. She kept nodding. Ahead of us the parking lot of the hospital was scattered with cars. They shone in the sun. It was a shining winter day, three weeks after they brought me to the hospital with burned lungs. Tamar's hand came up and tried to touch my hair, but my hair was gone. Burnt off.

There had been some of it left in the back of my head, but when I looked in the hospital bathroom mirror I knew that I should cut it off. I cut it myself, with nail scissors that the nurse with curly brown hair gave me when I told her my toenails were getting too long. I did not lie to the nurse. My toenails were in fact getting too long, but that doesn't necessarily mean that you'll be using the toenail scissors that the brown-haired nurse gives you to cut only your toenails. You could also use them to cut hair. Why not? Both hair and toenails need to be cut. The relationship is consistent.

I stood in front of the bathroom and gathered as much of my leftover hair as I could and then chopped it with the scissors. Nail scissors are not the best kind of scissors to cut hair with. They don't have long enough blades. You have to keep sawing until finally all the leftover hair is chopped off.

If you're missing your eyelashes and eyebrows, if for example they've been singed off in a fire in a trailer belonging to an old man, then you're better off with no hair on your head either. This is what I believe to be true. Tamar's hand didn't know what to do when it touched the wisps of hair in back of my head, so she put it back on my shoulder. She was still nodding.

"He's dead?"

"Yes."

"Did they bury him?"

She nodded. If someone's buried, they're dead. They're truly dead. It came to me that I had never asked the old man if he wanted to be buried or cremated.

"Did he want to be buried?" I asked Tamar. But it was a useless question. It was a question without an answer. How could Tamar possibly know if the old man had wanted to be buried?

"I don't know," she said.

That's Tamar. She does not lie.

"Where did you bury him?"

"In the Sterns Village Cemetery."

"Does he have a headstone?"

"Not yet but he will. The Twin Churches are raising money to get one for him."

Her hand was still on my shoulder. I felt myself rocking in my seat. You can rock in the front passenger seat of a station wagon. It's possible. But you might not know you're rocking unless your mother has hooked up your safety system and all the bungee cords are holding you in tightly. When you push yourself forward you can feel them pressing against you. That's how you know you're rocking. I kept whispering despite my throat.

"What will his headstone say on it?"

Tamar shook her head. "George Kominsky, I guess."

"*Georg,*" I said. "It's not *George.* It's *Georg.*"

She nodded. She was either shaking her head or nodding, nodding or shaking her head.

"You're just like everyone else," I said. "Aren't you? You don't even know his real name."

She looked at me.

"You don't even know how to pronounce his *name.* For all you care, the old man could have been named Clifford."

Still looking.

"Everyone has a name," I said. "Everyone deserves to have his name pronounced the way it should be pronounced. But people don't know. People don't care."

Her fingers pressed into my shoulder bone and then let go. Pressed and released. Over and over.

"They do, not, care," I said. "And that's the whole problem."

She pressed and released. Her arm made no movement to put the lever into the "D" for drive slot. I know a lot about driving. When it comes time for me to get my permit, I will be a quick study. That's what my fourth-grade teacher used to call me, a quick study.

Tamar wasn't going anywhere. I could tell she was going to sit in the car, with the motor on and me strapped into my safety system, as long as it took. My throat was raw and my words were whispers. Still, she wasn't going anywhere. So I asked my question.

"Did he die because of me?"

There. It was out there. It was a question out in the world now, hanging in the air between us. The words were out of me. They existed on their own.

"He died trying to get you out," Tamar said.

"I killed him, then."

"He died trying to save you," Tamar said.

Then she took her hand away and put the lever into the "D" position. She took her foot off the brake and moved it onto the gas. The cars in the parking lot winked and blinked in the sunshine. It was winter sunshine, too bright. Painful on the eyes.

"We're going home," said Tamar. Then she put on her blinker and we started up Route 12, out of Utica, heading into the foothills.

When I was very young, when I had first thought of my death row question, I had asked it of Tamar.

"Ma, you're on death row. How would you rather die? By electric chair or lethal injection?"

"Neither," Tamar said.

"But if you *had* to pick."

"I don't have to pick," Tamar said. "Therefore I shall not pick."

She never answered my question. I myself have never answered it either. The day I asked it of the old man, I had my answer ready: lethal injection. That used to be my response to my own question. Injection wins out over electric chair any day. It wasn't even a real choice, it seemed to me. But that's what I know now, and that's why I can never ask that question again. It isn't a choice. You don't get to choose.

Did the old man get to choose? That's what I wonder about. When he came up to the trailer, and saw Tamar screaming, and saw the people all holding her by her feet and arms and legs so that she wouldn't go running into the fire after me, did he choose?

The choir director told me that the old man had a plastic Jewell's Grocery bag in each hand. They spilled when he dropped them.

"What was in them?" I asked her.

She gave me a look, but she answered anyway.

"I don't remember everything, but there was a bag of sugar and a can of ginger. A quart of milk, which spilled when the carton broke."

"Dairylea milk?"

"Yes, Dairylea milk," the choir director said. "I remember the orange flower."

Tamar was screaming like a crazed person. She *was* a crazed person. That's what the choir director told me.

"I have never seen your mother like that," she said. "She was literally out of her mind. There was a look on her face that I hope never to see again in my life."

Tamar wasn't around when the choir director told me that. The choir director also brought me a green rubber frog.

"Something to keep you company," she said.

An orange balloon, a green rubber frog. The world of my childhood is behind me, and I have put away childish things, but you can't tell people that.

"We were all trying to hold your mother back," the choir director said. "There were at least six of us holding her down. The next thing we knew George was past us and running up the steps of the trailer."

Not George. *Georg.* But they don't know. They never knew.

How could the old man have been running? His feet hurt him from the frostbite that he got when he was seventeen. If you didn't know the story, you couldn't tell that his feet hurt him. But when you knew the story, and you knew that when he was seventeen he was caught in a blizzard that killed his little brother, and that he had to walk for two days to find his way out of the woods, then you could tell how much his feet hurt him. All his life, his feet hurt him. But no one who didn't know the story would know that about the old man.

The choir director squeezed the green rubber frog. It squeaked.

"Oh, I didn't know it squeaked," she said. "How cute. And then the next thing we knew the window in the middle of the trailer was open, and you came sliding out of it. He must have found you and opened that window and heaved you out."

That window was the bedroom window. The window in the middle of the trailer was the window above the old man's built-in bed with the built-in drawers below. The old man used to lie in his bed and look out the window at the night sky. I know this because three times, Tamar and I drove past Nine Mile Trailer Park before dawn on our way to the State Fair in Syracuse. Each time we passed the trailer park, I looked out just at the right time to see the old man's trailer. Each time, his window was open and the curtains were pushed aside. It was still nighttime. The old man was still asleep. That's how I know that he went to sleep looking out an open window at the dark night sky. It would have been filled with stars some nights. It would have been streaked with lightning sometimes, or invisible through rain. There is a chance that once in a while, the old man would have climbed onto his built-in bed, looked out the window, and seen the heavens pulsing with the Northern Lights.

"And the next thing we knew, there you were. Lying in a snowbank," the choir director said. "We let go. Tamar got to you first."

And the next thing we knew, and the next thing we knew, and the next thing we knew. The choir director kept saying that, as if every one of her memories was a surprise to her.

The old man must have crawled through the trailer on his hands and knees until he bumped into me. He would have known it was me by my foot hitting him on his lowered head, or the feel of my hand under his crawling hand, or maybe the smell of burnt hair. That's a smell you can't not know. He must have picked me up, stood up, and pushed me out of the window.

Did he try to crawl out after me? Did he make it up onto his bed and then be overcome with smoke? Or did he just crumple back onto the floor once I was out the window?

The choir director had her arms out like she was directing the choir. While her eyes were still shut I took the green rubber frog and threw it under the bed.

Did the old man hear Tamar screaming my name? Did he know that I was still alive, and that they would revive me? Did he know that even then the Floyd Volunteer Fire Department was nearly there, and that the men would jump out and put the oxygen mask on me and take my pulse and make sure I wasn't dead, and that then the ambulance would come and take me to Utica Memorial, and that Tamar would stay in a chair next to my bed the whole first three days?

That's what the nurse with the brown hair that was shorter on one side than the other said.

"Your mother sat right in that chair for three whole days and nights," the nurse said. "She wouldn't even hardly leave the room to pee."

What I want to know is when they got the old man out. Did the firefighters go in there and try to save him? Did anyone think of the old man?

Mr. Jewell came to see me a few days after I was home.

"I was walking home," he told me. "George's place was on the way so we walked back together. He waited for me to close up, that's why he was a little later than usual. You must've thought he was inside, because we both saw you run on in there."

Mr. Jewell put a paper bag that said "Jewell's Groceries" on the bed next to me. I opened it. A can of ginger, a can of tuna, a bag of egg noodles, a small spiral notebook.

"When George saw you run in there, he started running too," Mr. Jewell said. "He dropped his bag and they all spilled out."

A spiral notebook? I took it out and turned it over. Red, flimsy, flip-top. Fifty miniature lined pages.

"I wanted to give them to you," Mr. Jewell said. "I know he was your friend."

"Thank you," I said.

After he left I picked up the little spiral notebook again. Why did the old man buy it? What did he plan to do with it?

I will never know.

I thought of things that weren't going to happen anymore because the old man was gone, such as biscuit baking. I had told the old man my pioneer recipe for biscuits. Pioneers carried their recipes in their heads. I know this because I once wrote a report on pioneer cooking. It was a true report, I researched pioneer recipes in the Utica Library. It's hard to find pioneer recipes; they were passed down mother to daughter. Daughters learned by observing and practicing. They were apprentices to the art of cooking.

Take some flour and cornmeal and rising and some good fresh lard if you have it. Rub it between your fingers till it's crumbly. Add some salt. Cut into rounds. Bake, covered.

"'Rising'?" the old man said. "Baking powder, that must be."

"Must be," I said.

"And lard. We used to use that. That was all we used to use. That, and butter."

He sifted even though I told him not to.

"Did the pioneers sift?" I said. "They did not. They had to pare down to bare essentials before they headed out west. Was there room in a covered wagon for a sifter?"

He said nothing.

"There was not," I said. "A sifter is not a bare essential. You shouldn't be using one."

The old man got a stick of butter from his miniature refrigerator.

"Halt!" I said. "Did the pioneers have butter?"

The old man started cutting butter with two knives.

"Nay sir, I think not!" I said. "Where's the good fresh lard?"

He smiled at me. That was rare from the old man. Smiles were not his forte. The old man finished rolling out the dough, then he took one of his three water glasses and pressed it into the dough. Each round he placed on a pan that he had already greased. They didn't take long to bake. They would have been much harder to bake over an outdoor fire. You wouldn't be able to regulate the temperature. You'd have to use a regular frying pan with the lid on it. They'd be burned on the bottom and maybe underdone on the top. That would be an authentic pioneer biscuit, I thought. Not a perfect round biscuit.

Still, the pioneers would love their biscuits. After a day in the open air, walking behind the wagon in the tracks left by the wheels, or riding one of the ponies off to the side, or leading the cow by its halter, those biscuits would have been delicious. Nothing would taste better than an authentic pioneer biscuit, baked in a frying pan over an open fire. There would have been no leftover biscuits in a true pioneer camp.

The old man was the master and I was his apprentice. That's the way they did things in the olden days, and that's the way the old man and I did them. These are my terms, not his. I don't know if the old man knew the words *master, journeyman,* and *apprentice*. I don't know if his English was good enough to know those sorts of words.

I observed him. I used to watch his every move.

Under cover of darkness, the old man and I used to go out. We escaped from Nine Mile Trailer Park and headed out for scavenging night. Possibility was there, waiting for me. An old colander with only one of its three little curved metal legs was there. You would think that someone had known I was coming, and left it there, bagless, unboxed, so that I would be sure to see it. It was the kind of colander that they still make, that they have been making for all eternity—a round metal bowl with holes in the shape of stars punched all through it, propped on three little curved metal legs that are screwed into the bottom.

Two of the legs were missing, and the colander was tilted. It was a lame and punch-drunk colander.

I held it up to my face and pushed my nose up against the bottom of the bowl. My face was encased in colander. It smelled cold and clean, like clean metal. Someone must have washed it before they put it out for the trash. Maybe they debated before they put it into the trash. Maybe they thought, there's got to be more use in this colander. Maybe they tried to make little legs for it to stand on, so that they could continue to use the star-shaped-hole colander. It might have been a going-away gift from the owner's mother, or a wedding gift from fifty years before. But because the owner of this colander did not understand the art of metalworking, they were unable to fix the colander.

"A new colander is only a few bucks at the hardware store," you can imagine someone saying to them. "Get rid of this old thing."

I looked at the old man. He nodded. That's how I knew I was learning, learning to see with the old man's eyes.

The colander owner did not have the old man's eyes. The colander owner could not see the art of possibility, the possibility of beauty. They did not have the hands and the tools to repair the snapped-off legs of the colander and make it whole again, make it new again, so that it would stand upright and fulfill its potential.

Sometimes we stopped at Crystal's Diner. I had a milkshake. He had a cup of coffee.

He left things at the diner. The money for the milkshake and coffee, plus a quarter. Always that. But he left other things too, things that he made, things that we made together. Sugar cookies wrapped in a tinfoil swan for Crystal. Once a bracelet made of curled-up soda pop tops strung on a piece of red string. The kind of thing that Crystal's nephew Johnny is crazy for. Shinies, and small red things, that's what Johnny loves.

On our way out once, as we passed Johnny's booth, I saw the old man's hand go into his pocket and come out again. The candelier cookie cutter lay shining up from Johnny's table. Johnny wasn't there, but it waited for him. Next week when we went back to the diner, there was Johnny, waving the candelier in the air under the light, so that it threw sparkles onto the chrome sugar shaker.

The old man knew things about people.

On our first trip under cover of darkness, with me as his apprentice, we walked by Mrs. J'Alexander's house. Her son was sitting in the window. He can't talk. He can't walk. That happened in the Vietnam War.

"Her son almost died," I told him. "His name's Joe. His legs were blown off in the war."

Everyone knows that. It's common knowledge.

"He's deaf dumb and blind," I said.

"He is not," the old man said.

"It's common knowledge," I said.

"Knowledge is not common."

"He can't hear, he can't talk, and he can't see," I said. "That makes you deaf dumb and blind."

"He can see and he can hear."

I looked in the window, lit up by a lamp. Joe was sitting in his wheelchair.

"What can he see? What can he hear?"

"Everything you can."

If that's true, how did the old man know it?

"Are you psychic?" I said.

He shook his head. It could be that the old man didn't know that word, or it could be that he was truly not psychic. Then I remembered that I was an apprentice and I stopped talking. I made a vow to continue to observe the old man and learn his ways.

I didn't know then that our time was almost up.

I am still the old man's apprentice in all things. Paul Revere started that way. Back in those days there was a system for apprentices and journeymen and masters. You followed in their footsteps. That's how Paul Revere learned to mold silver and create useful objects of great beauty. I've seen the Revere-ware factory in Rome. It's only fifteen miles away. I've been past it at night, when the red neon horse gallops against the dark sky. I think about that horse sometimes. I think about the young Paul Revere, apprentice to a master craftsman.

CHAPTER THIRTEEN

Once, when I was still eleven and the old man was still alive although I had not yet met him, I asked Tamar a sraightforward, answer-demanding question.

"Ma, did you want kids?"

Tamar looked at me. I looked back at her. I raised my eyebrows and held them up there.

"Yes."

That was it. That was her answer. No quibbling, no equivocating, no hemming or hawing. It took me by surprise.

"You did?"

"Yes. I did."

That gave me something to chew on. As my hermit grandfather chewed on deerskin through the long winter to make it soft and pliable and ready for the needle, so did I chew on Tamar's answer. She was busy with her lumberjacket. How she loves her lumberjacket. Her mother bought it at the store in Speculator. I used to think eighteen was old enough so that your mother could die, but now I'm not sure.

Tamar was working the new zipper on her lumberjacket, trying to get the teeth to fit together smoothly and not snaggle halfway up. She had replaced the zipper herself when it gave out. Tamar is not a seamstress, however. Neither a needler nor a threader shall she be. Already the zipper had come apart at the bottom. Tamar was using duct tape to keep it together. When the duct tape made its appearance, I asked another answer-demanding question.

"Did you fall in love with him?" I said to Tamar.

She didn't look up. She was wrapping the duct tape around the bottom of the broken zipper.

"Were you in love with my father?" I said. "Even for just that one time?"

Duct tape doesn't tear. You have to cut it. She cut it with the kitchen shears, as opposed to the tiny sharp scissors on her Swiss army knife, which would have gummed up had she tried to use them on duct tape. Tamar can't stand her Swiss army scissors to be gummed.

"Even for a few minutes? I'm just trying to understand."

"No," Tamar said. "I did not love your father."

"At all?"

"At all."

"Then why did you do that with him?"

"Well, that will have to remain a mystery," Tamar said.

She finished wrapping the zipper and smoothed down the duct tape seam. Then she slipped her feet into her worn-out moccasins and wiggled her toes. I watched her face for a silent wince. That happens sometimes, when her toes are remembering being frozen. There was nothing.

"Why?"

"Because."

"Things don't have to remain mysteries."

"This one does," Tamar said. "There are some things you are too young to understand."

That was a rare thing for Tamar to say. Usually she stops after, "This one does," and that would be the end of it. Tamar is not a qualifier of words. Things are, things are not. That's the sort of person she is.

"I'm not a child," I said.

But that was it. She was finished. She stretched her arms in her old lumberjacket carefully, so that the worn-out seams wouldn't rip any farther, and tested the zipper for snags.

"There's going to come a point at which you will be forced to buy a new lumberjacket," I said. "There will come a day when you will get in the car and drive to Speculator, walk into the lumberjacket store, and buy a new one."

But even now, that day has not yet come. That day in Speculator remains in the future. There's no way to predict when it will come, no way to know when Tamar will wake, put on the lumberjacket her mother gave her, look down at it and realize that it is no more, that the seams are destroyed and it will not zip. That the cold cannot be kept out. The lumberjacket as it once was will have disappeared. Tamar's lumberjacket from her mother will have entered a new, nonjacket life, and in her gut Tamar will know it.

When you lose your hair in a fire, you might not recognize it when it grows back in. It doesn't look like the same hair that grew on your head your whole life long. New hair is soft, and patchy. When new hair grows in over a patch of scalp that was burned in a fire, it grows in tentatively, unsure it should be there. You look at your hair in the mirror and you wonder whose hair it is, and if it's always been this way and you just never noticed it before.

Think about it. You walk around with dead hair hanging off your head. The only thing about hair that's alive is its roots. The roots push up new hair, but that new hair is already dead. In a way, having your hair burned off in a fire is not a tragedy at all; that hair was not alive.

They hauled the old man's trailer away. One day it was there, with bent metal strips hanging out of the black windows, with black cement steps leading up to the door that was burned away, with the curved kitchen end burnt into a lump, and then the next day it wasn't.

"Where's Georg's trailer?" I asked Tamar.

I've started calling him *Georg*, so that anyone who's listening will know the way his name was pronounced.

"They hauled it away."

"To where?"

"I'm not sure."

"Who hauled it?"

"I don't know."

"Then how do you know it was hauled?"

"That's what they do with trailers that are too old, or burnt up, or are otherwise unusable."

Did anyone go through the old man's trailer before they hauled it away? Did anyone search through the rubble to see if there was anything worthwhile preserving in the ruins? Were there people with masks and white suits and boots, moving slowly from miniature room to miniature room, sifting through the ashes, looking for remnants of the old man's life?

"Did they take the forge, too?" I asked Tamar.

"What forge?"

"His forge," I said. "Don't you even know about his *forge*?"

"No."

"He was a metalworker," I said. "Have you ever heard of a metalworker without a forge?"

"No," Tamar said. "I guess I haven't."

"Have you ever heard of a metalworker without tin snips? Jewelry pliers? A soldering iron? A torch? Pre—cookie cutters?"

"Pre—cookie cutters," Tamar said. "Pre, cookie, cutters."

"That's right," I said. "Pre—cookie cutters. Don't ask me to explain. Don't ask me to show you the relationship between things. Don't ask me about consistencies, and objects that are beautiful as well as useful."

Tamar looked at me. Words kept spilling out of me, secret words, words and phrases that were the old man's and mine. I ran out of the room to stop those precious words from wasting themselves in the blank air between Tamar and me.

I asked Mr. Jewell if he knew what had happened to the forge.

"I don't know, Miss Clara," he said. "One day the trailer was there, and the next it wasn't, and I don't know what happened to the forge."

No one knew. I wondered about the forge. Did someone under cover of darkness steal into the ruins and take it while I was in the hospital with burned lungs? Is someone in North Sterns now working with fire at a backyard forge? Or did it tumble into Nine Mile Creek when the fire trucks were putting out the fire? Is it possible that the forge is even now rusting in the dark water of Nine Mile Creek? In the fullness of time the destiny of the old man's forge may be revealed to me. But I doubt it.

The old man had no family. He had no friends, except silent friends. His silent friends were friends like Crystal Zielinski at Crystal's Diner, who took the onions that the old man brought her and chopped them into tuna salad. Friends like Harold Jewell, who sometimes used to give the old man a Persian doughnut for free.

"He has the money to pay for that Persian," I said to Mr. Jewell once.

I wanted Mr. Jewell to know that the old man was not a bag person. He had a home and an onion garden. He had a visitor every Wednesday night. He had enough money to pay for a Persian doughnut without it being given to him for free.

"You don't have to feel sorry for the old man," I said to Mr. Jewell.

He gave me a look.

"I don't feel sorry for Mr. Kominsky, Clara," Mr. Jewell said. "I give him a Persian doughnut because I consider him my friend."

I am the last of my line, the old man had said to me in the beginning of my oral history project. That was one of the first things the old man ever said to me, despite the fact that he was chary with his words.

"Did the fire start because the old man used a can of flammable stuff in the wrong way?" I said. "Is that how it started?"

Tamar looked at me.

"What are you really asking?" she said.

If it had been common knowledge in Sterns that the old man didn't know how to read, then Tamar would have immediately known what I was trying to ask. What I was trying to ask was: if the old man had known how to read, would the fire not have started? Would the old man still be alive? Would

I still be going down on Wednesday nights while Tamar was at choir practice, eating toast thickly spread with margarine and drinking hot chocolate with extra milk?

"Did he use something flammable in the wrong way? Did he not pay attention to the directions?"

She was still looking at me.

"Are you what-iffing?" she said. "Are you retracing? Are you saying if that hadn't happened then that wouldn't have happened and that wouldn't have happened and the old man would still be alive?"

I looked back at her.

"Is that what you're doing?" she said.

"What I'm doing," I said, "is asking if the old man neglected to read the fine print."

"What does it matter, Clara?" Tamar said. "What does it matter now?"

Tamar forgot about my chickens when I was in the hospital. For three weeks in March, a flock of insane chickens were without food or water. Insane chickens paced and pecked the cracked concrete floor of the broken-down barn, while Tamar slept on a cot by the side of my bed at Utica Memorial. The day I got home I put on my boots and headed down there. Tamar was busy patching her moccasins with duct tape.

I walked into the broken-down barn, breathing through my mouth because of the stink of the chicken manure. It was quiet. No peeps, no clucks. No pecking and scratching around in the dirt. I put my sneakers one in front of the other like an Indian guide. I glided up to the pen, stuck my head over the side.

All their necks were broken. I could tell by the weird angles of their heads. My chickens had died not by starvation but by murder. Over in the corner the dollhouse lay tipped on its side, with a chicken lying half-in and half-out of the living room, its wing sticking through the window. Over in the other corner there was a hole burrowed through the broken-down barn siding. Weasel, I thought. I knew about weasels from my research. They kill for fun, just to be mean. They might suck a little blood, but that's it.

Tamar put on her boots right away when I told her the chickens were all dead.

"Oh Jesus," she said. "I completely forgot about them."

"They died not from starvation but from murder," I said. "A weasel got them while I was in the hospital."

She wasn't listening. "I can't believe it," she said. "They never once crossed my mind. Clara, I am so sorry."

But halfway across the pasture Tamar stopped and got a look on her face.

"Clara, what is that smell?"

I tried to pretend I didn't know what she was talking about. "Smell?" I said. "What smell?"

Then I saw the way Tamar was looking at me.

"Oh, that smell," I said. "I guess I do smell it after all. Dead chickens."

"That isn't dead chickens I'm smelling, Clara."

She started walking fast toward the broken-down door to the broken-down barn.

"Ma," I called.

The back of her ripped lumberjacket was getting away from me.

"What," she called back without turning around.

"Ma! I forgot to tell you that those chickens were not normal. They were abnormal chickens. They were . . . *psychotic* chickens."

She turned around.

"Yes," I said. "Psychotic chickens. The rooster tried to kill me."

I scrabbled around on my scalp where there was still hair, searching for old scabs to show her. Too late, though. She was already into the barn.

"My God," she said.

I came up behind her. Afraid to touch her plaid shoulder. I looked around the barn with her eyes. Fermenting feed in heaps in the pen, where the water I tossed had landed on the feed I spilled. Piles of chicken manure smeared on the pitted cement floor. Massacred chickens strewn like garbage. A searing smell of sulphur and manure and death. Tamar's eyes turned on me were full of a look I had never seen from her before.

"You smell that sulphur smell, Clara? On top of the manure smell?"

"Yes."

"Well, there's a pile of eggs somewhere in this pen. Those hens were laying all this time."

Tamar opened up the gate and walked on in. She waded through the smeary manure piles, kicked a dead hen out of the way. She went over to the pile of hay in the corner and swiped off the top wisps.

"Here they are."

There they were. A million brown eggs, a mountain of brown eggs. Some crushed against each other, some whole and perfect. I stared at that pile of eggs. There was a little heave from the heap of dark feathers in the dollhouse. Another little heave. It was the CJ Wilson chicken. I crouched down in front of him. His beady eye stared back. He kicked a yellow claw. I could tell he was not going to live. I didn't know how he had managed to live as long as he had.

I started to sing to him. "Oh Susannah, oh don't you cry for me . . . For I've come from Alabama, with my banjo on my knee."

I couldn't remember the rest of the words.

"Clara," Tamar said.

She came up and knelt by me and the CJ Wilson chicken. She put her arms around me.

"Why didn't you tell me?" she said.

"Tell you what?"

"Tell me about these chickens."

"What about them?"

Tamar squeezed my arms and rocked. "Everything about them," she said.

"There's not much to tell," I said. "They're not normal chickens. They never were. They're psychotic chickens, especially that CJ Wilson one."

Tamar's arms around me were too tight.

"Could you stop?" I said. "I can't breathe."

All around us the smell rose, thick and heavy. I felt as if I were choking to death in a broken-down barn full of dead insane chickens. All the months, the months and months I had kept the secret of my vicious chickens came crowding down on me and I couldn't stand it. Days and weeks and months of not telling anyone about the chickens, their meanness and cruelty, the way they kept after me, pecking and hissing and clawing, came crawling up out of the heaps of dead dark feathers,

snaking around me, invisible and strangling. I started to cry
and I couldn't stop.

"You should have told me," Tamar said. "You should have
told me about these chickens."

"Why?" I said.

"I could have helped."

"You wouldn't have helped. You've never helped."

Words, crawling out of me, me not stopping them. Tamar's
arms falling away and a choking sound coming from her. The
smell of death rising around us like the locusts that once ate
up all of Laura Ingalls Wilder's summer fields, and the CJ
Wilson chicken convulsing where he lay. Tamar leaned away
from me.

"You never told me about my grandfather, or my father, or
Baby Girl," I said. "No matter how many times I asked, you
never told me. That's the only thing I have ever asked you for
help with, and you never helped."

Tamar reached out to the CJ Wilson chicken but didn't
touch it. She took a deep breath of the rotten air around us.

"You listen to me," she said. "Listen to me, Clara Winter."

I held my breath against the stench of the broken-down
barn and listened.

"There is nothing I could tell you that would help," Tamar
said.

I kept holding my breath.

"Nothing would help, and everything would hurt," Tamar
said.

I stared at CJ, lying there, heaving up now and then, its
black eye dull. You must kill this chicken, I told myself. I said
it out loud to give myself strength. *You must put him out of his
misery.*

"Don't worry," I said to the chicken. I bent down close to where its ear must be. "Don't you worry. It won't hurt."

Quick and clean, I thought. Make it quick and clean.

I picked up a chunk of broken-off cement and I brought it down on CJ Wilson's head.

CHAPTER FOURTEEN

Tamar was at the kitchen sink brushing her teeth when C. Winter came to the door. I recognized him immediately. He was the same man who had sat in his apartment on Genesee Street in Utica, unable to meet my gaze. He came up the steps to the kitchen door. Tamar was behind me. One of her many oddities is that she prefers to brush her teeth at the kitchen sink, in front of the window. She likes the morning light, she says. At night, when it's dark, she brushes in the bathroom.

"Hey," he said.

What do you say to your grandfather, when you don't know him?

"Hi."

Behind me the sound of brushing stopped. I felt Tamar walking across the kitchen. The air she displaced moved before her. She held her toothbrush like a gun.

"Tamar?" my biological grandfather said.

She said nothing. She stood there with toothpaste foaming out of her mouth. When Tamar brushes her teeth she brushes for a long time. She leans against the sink and stares out the window while she brushes. I timed her once: five minutes, thirty-three seconds.

"Tamar," he said again.

He took his hat off. It was a Yankees baseball cap, one with the intertwined N and Y. That's what they used to do in the olden days. A gentlemen, in the presence of a lady, would take his hat off. It was a social given. It would have been an extreme insult not to take your hat off in the presence of a lady. There were other places you had to take your hat off, too. Church, indoors, dinner. That was the social *more* of the time.

Tamar said nothing. She stood there with her toothbrush. She looked at him.

"Hi," I said again to C. Winter.

"Hi," he said.

C. Winter still couldn't look at me. His eyes kept moving around. He stood there with his baseball cap in his hands. The time for hesitation was past. She who hesitates is lost, and much had already been lost. I looked up at C. Winter and asked him a question.

"Why did you take Glass Factory instead of Route 12?"

He twirled the cap in his hands. His eyes darted. He said nothing.

"Route 12 would've been plowed," I said. "What was your reasoning?"

He shrugged.

"Please," I said. "Tell me."

He looked up at me. Tamar stood still beside me. The toothpaste on her brush was drying. I could see it turning hard and white. My biological grandfather cleared his throat.

"Tamar—" he said.

"Please," I said. "Please."

"Because I made a mistake," C. Winter said.

I felt around for my roll of note-taking adding-machine paper in its useful and beautiful paper holder, but it was gone. It was lost to flames, and unlike the famous Rocky Mountain lodgepole pine it would never regenerate. I resorted to air-writing. *Because I made a mistake*, I wrote in the air with my nose. Clifford Winter gave me a look but I kept on.

"You made a lot of mistakes," Tamar said. The white foam at the sides of her mouth was dry, too. It moved along with her jaw when she talked.

"Tamar—"

"Dad."

"I did," C. Winter said.

"Grampa?" I said.

They both turned to me. *Grampa* was a surprise word, an ambush word, startling them both, hanging in the air like a bubble.

"What was my father's name?" I said.

He might come out with it. My father's name might be waiting on the tip of C. Winter's tongue, and topple off, and then I could write it in the air with my nose. I could write it and keep it forever. For the rest of my days, my father's name would be mine, to have and to hold. C. Winter said nothing.

"My father's name," I said. "What was it?"

Nothing.

"Her father's name," Tamar said. "What was it?"

He shook his head.

"Surprise surprise," Tamar said. "I don't know it either."

"I'm talking to my grandfather," I said.

"So am I," she said.

"But you can't *remember* his name," I said.

"I never *knew* his name. There's a difference."

C. Winter reached over and put his cap onto the stack of wood in the woodbin. He placed it carefully on the top row of wood, which I myself had stacked. I take pleasure in stacking wood. Even in a woodbin, which is meant to hold chunks of wood any which way, I will stack. I like neat and orderly stacks of wood.

"You did so know his name," I said. "You just forgot it, is what you said."

"I never knew it," Tamar said.

C. Winter rocked back and forth on the balls of his feet. Tamar threw her toothbrush, with its stiffened bristles, at his cap. It hit the intertwined NY and didn't leave a mark. I wrote Tamar's words in the air: *never knew his name.*

"So neither of you know my father's name," I said. "And you made a mistake in taking Glass Factory."

"Yes," my grandfather said.

"Did you have any knowledge of infant CPR?"

He looked up at me.

"What's that?"

"Infant cardiopulmonary resuscitation. Did you have any knowledge of it?"

He shook his head. Still rocking.

"Did you try to save my sister?" I said.

Rocking.

"Was there any attempt made on the part of either of you to save my baby sister?"

I looked at Tamar, who was looking at C. Winter, who was looking at the porch floor.

"My father's name is unknown," I said. "You by mistake took Glass Factory Road. Neither of you knew infant CPR, nor did you try to save my baby sister. Is that right?"

No answer.

"Is that right?"

No answer.

"And what about winter?" I said. "What about the ice and the snow? What about trucks in ditches?"

"They didn't have infant CPR back then," Tamar said.

"It was eleven years ago," I said. "Of course they did."

"Eleven years ago is a lifetime to you," Tamar said. "But all it is is a snap of the fingers."

She snapped her fingers, something she's very good at. There was a crack on the porch like a whip; that's how good she is at snapping.

"They didn't think about things like that back then," Tamar said.

"You tried, though."

That was C. Winter. He was still rocking. His head was still shaking. Back and forth it swung.

"You tried, Tamar."

I looked at him.

"Your mother tried to save your sister," he said.

I fell. You can fall while sitting down, strapped into a bungee cord safety system in your car, and you can fall from a standing position. I fell on the porch and then I wrapped my arms around my knees. His words went scrolling along the bottom of my mind: *your sister, your sister, your sister.*

"So I had one," I said. "I had a sister."

"Yes, you had a sister."

"No," Tamar said. "Sisters are alive. Sisters are living. Clara never had a sister."

"She did," my grandfather said. "She had a sister."

I closed my eyes and watched the words in my head: *sister, sister, sister.* I had had a baby sister. We had swum together, drunk the same salty water, heard the same sounds. From far away Tamar's voice had come to us over months. We had known the sound of her voice, and the way she moved. We had known the rhythm and feel of our mother's heartbeat as she lay sleeping in darkness that for us remained dark. My sister might have held my hand. She might have touched my face. If babies can love before they're in this world, my sister might have loved me.

"What was her name?" I said.

"Her name was Daphne," my grandfather said.

Her name was Daphne. My grandfather moved across the porch. He stretched out his hand to Tamar.

"Tamar."

Tamar was crying.

"She had no name," she said.

"You gave her a name," my grandfather said. "Her name was Daphne. Daphne Winter."

"She never had a chance."

"No, she didn't," my grandfather said.

Then his arm went around Tamar. She didn't hug him. She didn't lean her head on his shoulder. She just stood there, crying. She didn't wipe the tears off her cheeks, or blow her dripping nose. She just stood there.

"I'm sorry," my grandfather said.

"Sorry's not good enough," she said.

He rocked on his heels and kept on rocking and finally Tamar turned around and went inside. I was alone on the porch with C. Winter.

"What are you sorry about?" I asked.

"You name it, I'm sorry about it."

"Are you sorry that you took Glass Factory?"

"Yes."

"Are you sorry about Daphne?"

"Yes."

"Are you sorry about Clara winter?"

He looked at me. I didn't know I was going to say that until I heard it coming out of my mouth. *Are you sorry about Clara winter?* I could hear the words hanging between us.

"Yes," he said. "I'm sorry about Clara winter."

He said it with a lowercase w. I could hear it. I could hear it in his voice, and the way the word formed itself on his tongue: *winter.*

"Would you say your own name for the record?"

"Cliff Winter."

"Clifford Winter," I said.

"That's right."

He said his own name with an ordinary W. But that wasn't what I was thinking. I was thinking how, if I had known my nonhermit grandfather from the time I was a baby, I would know that he was known as Cliff. I wouldn't have to ask him, for the record, what his full name was.

"What else are you sorry about, Mr. Winter?"

He was still on the porch, rocking. He could rock from the balls of his feet to his heels and then roll back up again in a smooth movement. His hands were in his pockets. His baseball cap was still lying on the top row of stacked wood. He nodded over at the wood.

"I'm sorry I didn't see you stack that wood," he said. "That would have been a pretty sight, I'm sure."

"How did you know it was me who stacked it?" I said. "It could have been Tamar."

"No," he said. "Tamar is not a stacker. She's a thrower. When it comes to wood, Tamar's careless."

It was true. Tamar doesn't care about stacking wood. She feels that it's just as good to toss it up on the porch in a jumble and then pluck a piece from the jumble on an as-needed basis. Tamar cares not for neatness in firewood. Were it not for me, we would have a porch strewn with chunks of wood. No rhyme, no reason.

"That's something I'm very sorry to have missed," he said. "Having a granddaughter who's a stacker. Who taught you to stack like that?"

"I taught myself," I said. "I looked through the catalogs and saw how they stacked the firewood in the pictures."

He nodded. "Mmhm," he said. "Just as I suspected."

I laughed. I couldn't help it. Then he started laughing. We both laughed, him rocking, me holding onto the post by the steps.

"But I'll tell you what I'm most sorry about," he said when we were finished laughing. "Clara winter. That's what I'm most sorry about."

The old man as a young man might have stood across the street and stared at a young girl named Juliet, and loved her.

Someday, maybe, I will be walking into Jewell's Grocery, or standing on a folding chair in the Twin Churches church-house, and a boy will look at me and love me. It's possible. It could happen.

It doesn't always happen that way though.

Take Tamar. She did not love my father, nor did he love her. She does not know his name, and it's doubtful if he ever knew hers. She wasn't lying. She was telling the truth.

The music was extremely loud, is what Tamar told me. The music was so loud that no one could hear her.

"He turned up the music," she said.

For a while that's all she said. She put her hands over her ears as if she was hearing the loud music. Tamar hates loud music. She will not allow loud music in the house. When Tamar listens to music she listens to the radio at a volume so low that I can barely hear it. She does not wake up to music, nor does she like to listen to it at a volume above a whisper. When I set my clock radio, I do not set it to music. I set it to WIBX's morning radio show, which is conversation, and I set it at a whisper. This I do in respect for Tamar.

I didn't know what Tamar was telling me.

"He turned up the music?"

She nodded. "Way up. No one could hear me."

"No one heard you."

That's something you can do if you're not sure of what to say to someone else. You can repeat what they say, with a little twist. You can turn a statement into a question, such as "he turned up the music?" or you can twist the statement and repeat it, as in "no one heard you," instead of "no one could hear you."

"No one," she said.

She put her hands over her ears again. She rocked back and forth, like her father had done on the porch when he said he was sorry.

"How old were you?" I said.

"Eighteen."

I thought about that for a while. Eighteen is how old Tamar was when her mother died. I used to think that eighteen was not a young age. It was almost twenty, and twenty used to seem quite old.

"My mother had just died," Tamar said as if she could read my thoughts. "It took a long time for her to die. I ran away. I couldn't stand it, stuck in the house with my father and that incessant sadness."

Incessant is not a word I would have associated with Tamar. Even as she spoke and I listened, the word *incessant* went scrolling across the bottom of my mind.

"All I could see ahead of me was days and nights and weeks and years of sadness and quiet and darkness and stale air in a shut-up house," Tamar said. "I was too young. I couldn't see that a day would come when it would get better."

"Where did you want to go?" I said.

"Florida."

"Why Florida?"

"Sun. Beach. No more winter."

"But you love winter," I said. "You're Tamar, lover of snow and cold and ice."

She shook her head. "It was a long time ago," she said. "A long, long time ago."

"Not so long ago," I said. "Twelve years, is all."

"Twelve years and a lifetime."

"So what happened?" I said.

"What happened is what I told you. I packed my bag. I left. I went to a party at Roy Cover's house because his house was in Utica and the Greyhound station was three blocks away and the bus left at 2:00 A.M. And when it was time to go I went upstairs to get my sweatshirt—you don't need a winter jacket in Florida—and he followed me and shut the door and locked the door and turned the music up."

"Roy Cover?"

"No. Not Roy Cover. Him. The guy."

The guy.

"My father?"

Tamar barked. That's what you call that kind of a laugh. "You don't have a father," she said.

"Did my grandfather know what happened at the party?" I said to Tamar.

"Yes. Your grandfather knew."

"So what happened then?"

"What happened was that your grandfather told me it was my own fault, and that he would not help me raise the child. You're on your own, Tamar, is what he said."

You're on your own, Tamar. That's all she wrote. End of story. No ifs ands or buts. Sore subject. Moving right along.

The next time C. Winter came to the house on a secret Wednesday night visit I asked him about it. Usually he sat on the porch and talked to me while Tamar was at choir practice.

"Did you know what happened to Tamar at that party in Utica?" I asked him.

"Yes."

"Did you tell her it was her fault?"

"Yes."

We sat there for a while. It was cold.

"On my next birthday I'll be thirteen," I said.

"I know."

"Why didn't you ever come out here before?"

"I did, once, a few months after it happened."

"And?"

"And I saw Tamar out by the barn splitting wood. You were in the house bawling. I saw that I hadn't split enough wood for half a winter's worth, and she was out there chopping away, and you were screaming, and I thought of what happened to Daphne, and I turned around and left."

"And that's when you went up north to live in the primeval forest?"

He looked at me. "What?"

"Tamar told me you lived in a tipi in a small primeval forest up near the Vermont border."

"She did?"

Then I remembered that Tamar hadn't told me that. I had made that up. It was a figment of my imagination.

"No, she didn't," I said. "I made it up. It all started with *Tales from the Cave: Story of an Adirondacks Hermit.*"

"I have no idea what you are talking about," C. Winter said. "Anyway. I went back to Utica. I left Tamar chopping and you screaming. And now I'm back and Tamar's at choir practice and you're twelve. And that's the end of the story."

The old man taught me how to see the possibility of beauty. He taught me how to make objects that are useful as well as beautiful. I keep my eyes open. At any moment something may shine out at me. There may be something sparkling in the ditch. It may be half-buried beneath fallen maple leaves. Last fall I went walking down Williams Road, the colors of autumn flaming in the trees. Someone was burning leaves even though it's not allowed anymore.

I smelled those burning leaves and thought, I will never leave. I will never leave the Sterns Valley in the foothills of the Adirondack Mountains, where burning leaves smell this way in the fall.

I lay down in the middle of Williams Road, which is a dirt road where almost no cars ever come, and looked up at the sky. *A September blue sky,* is what Tamar would have said. Her words scroll across the bottom of my mind like all words scroll. I'll never not be able to read. I'll be a prisoner of letters the rest of my life. Every time I sign my name I'll remember the way the old man signed his name, the way he made a slash instead of a dot above the "i," the way he underlined his last name as if someone might not take it the way he intended.

The morning after the CJ Wilson chicken died I woke up and I knew that Georg Kominsky, American Immigrant, was truly gone. I could picture him, sitting on his chair at the cigarette-burned kitchen table where we used to drink our coffee and our hot chocolate. But the table was gone and the kitchen was gone and the forge was gone and the trailer was gone and the old man was gone and so was my roll of green adding-machine paper.

That roll of adding-machine paper contained all my notes for my future true book about Georg Kominsky, American Immigrant. There were words on that spool of paper that were the first words I ever heard the old man speak, and there were words on there that were among his last. Bits of the old man were caught on that paper. I had planned to keep it for the rest of my life, so that I could take it out and unroll it whenever I wanted, and remember the old man.

Will there be more spools of paper in the reject bin at Jewell's? There are no guarantees. It's a reject bin. It's a bin filled with items that others don't want, that don't sell, that have flaws, that are in some way peculiar.

"It takes a certain kind of person to want a roll of green adding-machine paper," Mr. Jewell said when I bought it. "And you, Clara Winter, are that sort of person."

Just before it was lost in the fire, I came to the end of the roll. The notes for *Georg Kominsky: American Immigrant* were finished. All the raw material, the heart and soul of the old man, was there. It's amazing to reach the end of an entire spool of adding-machine paper. When I first bought it, when I had just chosen it from its peers in the bin at Jewell's Grocery, I thought it would last forever. It was a pristine spool of paper. Untouched by human hands. When I wrote my first word on the first inch of narrow, curling green paper, I never stopped to think that one day the spool would be filled. But words turn into sentences turn into paragraphs turn into curl after curl of writing, bouncing on the floor.

The old man as a boy of seventeen must have tried to find help, someone, anyone, a cottage in the woods, to help him carry his young brother Eli to safety. Why couldn't there have been a cottage in the woods, smoke coming out of the chimney, paned windows with firelight glowing behind the glass, visible even in the middle of a blizzard? Inside a family sits around a table covered with a red-checked cloth. A gun hangs over the fireplace mantel. The man of the family is a hunter, wise to the ways of the woods. He comes immediately when Georg pounds on the door. They retrace Georg's steps, fast disappearing in the whiteout conditions, and make their way back to Eli, lying helpless in the snow. Together they make a seat with interlocked hands, the way they taught us to do in gym class at Sterns Elementary, and carry Eli to safety. The wife of the family makes hot broth and spoons it into Eli's mouth. They wrap him in feather quilts and stoke the fire. Winter rages outside the door, winds howl, but inside all is safe and warm. In a few days Eli has recovered enough to start out on the journey again. The snow has stopped and all is peaceful and calm, a winter wonderland of quiet whiteness.

"Bon voyage," the hunter says.

His wife presses a basket of bread and cheese and dried berries into their hands. They wish them well on their journey to America.

"Remember us," the wife says.

I almost wrote that whole story down on my adding-machine roll of paper. Everything was good. Everything worked out. Eli recovered. He did not lose any fingers or toes. Together Eli and Georg made their way to the dock, together they endured the hard Atlantic crossing. They ate hardtack belowdecks and drank musty barreled water from the same tin ladle. Together they entered America through Ellis Island. They lived together forever, as close as only brothers can be.

I almost asked the old man about that cottage once.

"What about the cottage in the woods?" I almost said. "What about the hunter, and the roaring fire, and the featherbed?"

CHAPTER FIFTEEN

The story of my birth is an astounding one. I was born during a February blizzard in a truck tipped sideways into a ditch on Glass Factory Road. My grandfather was trying to get Tamar to Utica Memorial in time for the delivery, but there was no such luck. The most amazing part of the story of my birth is that my mother, Tamar, delivered me herself. There was no one there to help her, including my grandfather, who was trying to slog through a blizzard to reach a house and get help. My mother, Tamar, had to push. She knew that once you have to push there's no going back.

Tamar closed her eyes and prayed to God that the urge to push would stop. She felt darkness closing in on her, and the winds of the blizzard howling around her, and she was afraid. Please God, keep my baby safe, she prayed. She did not know that there were two babies.

Outside, in the depths of the blizzard, my grandfather kept on. Sheer luck kept him from losing his way in the darkness of the night and the whiteness of the snow. He found a house. The people who lived there called the police. But there was nothing that could be done. The blizzard was that bad. Even had it been on Route 12, the police said, there was no way an emergency vehicle could get through in that kind of weather. My grandfather headed back to the truck. He tried to retrace his steps but his steps were gone. By the grace of God he found the truck but it was hours later and hours too late. Tamar was unconscious and Daphne was dead. I was alive, lying on Tamar's bare stomach, covered with her parka.

"And that's the story," Tamar said.

"That's the whole story," my grandfather said.

"That's not the story I made up," I said. "My story had a midwife in it, named Angelica Rose Beaudoin."

Tamar and my grandfather said nothing. We were sitting on the porch. Piles of wood left over from the winter, neatly stacked, stood silent around us. It was a cloudless night in the Adirondacks. High in the firmament, stars glittered. The air was still and cold and smelled not of spring but of winter, tired old winter whose time was past.

The day after the judge sentenced CJ's father was warm and sunny. I could sense the presence of spring. Underneath the last of the snow, bulbs were beginning to push their way toward light.

"Wipe," CJ said when I got on the bus. His eyes were filled with his hatred for me.

"Guess what," CJ said to the boys. "Me and my dad, we're leaving here. Getting out of this dump. My dad's going back on the road again. Going on a Chucky Luck comeback tour and taking me with him."

CJ was telling the boys about the hotels he was going to stay at and the cars he was going to drive when Tiny pulled up at CJ's trailer.

"Hey CJ!" one of the boys said. "What happened to your famous car? You decide to start a junkyard instead?"

The white Camaro was bashed in on the driver's side. CJ gave the boys the finger. I saw him look over at me.

"Some drunk smashed it up," said CJ. "Some drunk totaled it."

"Some drunk, huh?" said one of the boys. "Go tell that to Chucky Luck."

CJ's ears turned red below his buzzcut. "I *said* a drunk smashed it up."

"Uh huh," said the same boy. "Uh huh."

She who hesitates is lost. I put my hand in my pocket. I was wearing old white Carter's that had a rip at the side seam. I felt for the rip through the thin cotton. Then I leaned out of my seat.

"CJ's right," I said. "He's right. I heard my mother talking about it after court last night. This drunk guy, he just drove right over the yellow line on Glass Factory Road and smashed up CJ's Camaro."

CJ didn't look at me.

"See? I told you," he said to the boys. "That Camaro was rusted-out anyway. It was a mess. I hated it. My dad, he's going to get me a new one instead. A brand-new one, when he starts making money on the tour."

I slid back in my seat and looked out the window at the mountains coming closer. I kept my hand in my pocket, covering up the rip in my Carter's. That was before the state took CJ away and Tiny stopped pulling up at his trailer.

• • •

The old man was a highly prized tinsmith in his former village. Once I asked him about it. You had to space questions few and far between with the old man. He was like Tamar in that way.

"If you were only seventeen when you left your village," I asked the old man, "how could you be such a good tinsmith?"

He didn't answer right away. I didn't have a sense of unanswering, though. I waited.

"It was a different time," the old man said. "It was a different country. People grew up faster. I had been a metalworker for a long time by the time I was seventeen."

That was all he said. There was much that he left out, much I never found out. How had he come to learn the art of metalworking so early? How had he never learned to read? Did his father say: *You must go to work, Georg, there are too many mouths to feed and I cannot earn enough myself.*

Maybe his mother put him to work helping her in her work as a laundrywoman. She may have been a charwoman. It's possible. She may have had a large wicker basket that she took from cottage to cottage in the old man's village that no longer exists, gathering the weekly wash from each family and taking it down to the river, where she washed it in the cold clear water with brown softsoap she made herself. She may have pounded the clothes on the rocks to get out the stubborn stains, like cabbage-roll-with-tomato stains, ox-plow-dirt stains, muddy-boot stains, dried-sweat stains. She then may have draped the wet clothes over lingonberry bushes by the banks of the river to dry in the sun, while she sat and rested after her work. Her hands may have been large-knuckled and reddened from all the washing and pounding and folding. Georg would have helped her. He would have rinsed the soapy clothes.

Careful, Georg, she may have said. *Get every bit of soap out. If you leave the soap in the clothes will be scratchy. If the clothes are scratchy we will lose our laundry business and then how will we eat? Your father does not earn enough from farming to feed us. The land is poor and the potatoes do not grow as they should. Take good care, Georg, and rinse the clothes till the water runs clear.*

That's what she may well have said to her son Georg, the little laundry helper. When baby Eli came along six years later she may have laid him in a basket with a cloth draped over it to keep the sun out, letting him sleep by the bank of the river as she and Georg worked. When Georg's father was done in the potato fields he may have come down to the river to wash himself, to dive into the clear cold water and rinse the grime of the fields from his sweaty skin. Then the whole family— mother, father, Georg, and little Eli—would have walked home, Georg's father helping his mother with the heavy wicker basket full of freshly washed and folded laundry, Georg singing songs to baby Eli. They would have had boiled potatoes and cabbage soup for dinner. They would have bowed their heads and given thanks for their humble fare—

The old man's life still tumbles through my heart and soul. A story starts itself and I watch it unfold. The old man is gone. Who am I to say what may or may not have happened, what the old man's life as a child may or may not have been like?

Next time Tamar went to choir practice I rode into Sterns with her. She dropped me at Crystal's Diner so I could wait there while she practiced. Crystal brought me a vanilla milk-shake. She knows they're my favorite. Johnny was coloring in his booth.

"Can I sit with Johnny?" I said to Crystal.

"Why not?" she said.

Johnny seemed happy to see me. He had a coloring book and an eight-pack of crayons that were all red. How did that happen? Did Crystal buy eight packs of assorted crayons and then pick out the reds from each one?

"Here," Crystal said. She set a tunafish sandwich down in front of me. It came with a pickle and chips.

"Do you still use real olive oil in your salad dressing?" I said.

"Indeed I do."

Johnny held one of his red crayons up to the lamp and laughed the way he laughs.

"My grandfather's name is C. Winter," I said. "Most people call him Cliff."

"I know," Crystal said. "I remember your grandfather from when Tamar and I were growing up."

"Did his eyes jiggle around back then?" I said.

"I don't remember his eyes doing that."

"Did he rock back and forth?"

"I don't remember him doing that either."

"Do you know if he told Tamar that certain things were her fault that actually were not her fault?" I said.

"No, I do not," Crystal said.

"Do you remember if C. Winter loved Tamar?"

"He must have."

"It's not a law of nature," I said. "It's not written in stone."

"Her mother loved her. Of that I'm sure."

"Her mother died," I said. "So did Georg Kominsky, American Immigrant."

"Yes, he did."

"I don't know C. Winter, and Tamar didn't know Georg Kominsky," I said.

"She knew more about Mr. Kominsky than you might think," Crystal said. "She went to see him. She wrote him a letter about you."

"She did not."

"Yes she did. Before you ever met him. When you told her you were going to do your, what was it, oral history project on him."

A customer came in and sat down on the one of the red stools that twirl around at the counter. Crystal went over to him and took his order. She did not write it down. Crystal has the ability to remember any order given to her, no matter how many people in the group, and she never fails to remember who ordered what. It's one of her talents. After she brought the man his grilled cheese she started wiping down the other end of the counter. I slid out of the booth and went over to where she was scrubbing at a dried chocolate fudge stain with her red rag. All Crystal's rags are red, because of Johnny and his craving for it.

"Why?" I said.

Crystal rinsed the rag and resoaped it and started in on the stool tops. It's not everyone who will scrub the top of every single diner stool every single day.

"Why do you think?" Crystal said. "She was making sure he was all right. She was making sure he was a good person who wouldn't hurt her daughter. She was being a mother."

"She didn't tell me."

"No, she didn't. She thought you wouldn't have wanted her to. Was she right?"

I considered.

"Yes," I said. "Yes, she was right."

Crystal didn't know the old man couldn't read, just as Tamar didn't know. The old man would have taken the letter and nodded his head. I could see him nodding his head, the way he used to do. He might have laid the letter on his kitchen table and let it sit there a while. Then he may well have put the letter into one of his kitchen drawers, ne'er to be touched by human hands, ne'er to be seen by human eyes.

Tamar picked me up at the diner after choir practice. I was helping Johnny write his name. I put my fingers over his and guided his hand around the piece of newspaper we were practicing on. J, o, h, n, n, y. It's not easy to guide someone else's hand in writing. Johnny loved it though. He loved seeing the red crayon letters of his name appear. He laughed and laughed. Tamar ruffled his hair on the way out of the diner.

"Bye, Johnny," she said.

On the way home I pressed my nose against the cold car window. By cupping my hands around my eyes I blocked out the light from the car and stared out at the dark night sky.

"'Tis a clear night," I said to Tamar. "And the stars glitter thickly in the firmament."

"My thoughts exactly," Tamar said. "You took the words right out of my mouth. 'And the stars glitter thickly in the firmament' was right on the tip of my tongue."

"What did you say to the old man when you went to see him before my oral history project?" I said.

An ambush sentence, hanging in the air between us. She didn't miss a beat.

"I told him that you were my daughter, a child of eleven, and that I would kill anyone who harmed you," Tamar said. "I told him I would be watching him."

No hemming or hawing, no mumbling, no prevaricating. That's Tamar.

"And what did he say?"

"He listened. He nodded. He looked at me and I looked at him. We shook hands. I left."

"And what did you say in the letter you wrote to him?"

"I told him about you."

"What about me?"

"I told him that you were a strange child, that he should expect the unexpected when dealing with you. I told him that you were obsessed with the memory of a baby. I told him about your love of books, your book reports, and your stories."

"Stories? What about stories?"

"I told him that stories are the way you look at the world. That stories are your salvation."

Stories are your salvation.

"And?" I said.

"And what?"

And what, I thought. And what about Daphne Winter? What about a fake Adirondack hermit living in a primeval patch of forest? And what about the old man? What about his trailer, and his forge in the backyard, his dark-green sink in the bathroom? What about his refrigerator that held one quart of milk per week, no more no less, and his cupboard with its three orange-rimmed plates? What about his kitchen drawer that contained letters he couldn't read, the wall lined with hooks that held our cookie cutters? What about the tin paper holder he made for me, and the adding-machine paper that contained his heart and soul?

"What about his heart and soul?" I said to Tamar.

"His heart and soul," she said. "His heart and soul are up to you, Clara. They're your department."

My mother, Tamar, holds contradictions within herself. They coexist, battling each other inside her. She craves and hates her father, C. Winter. She longs for and tries to forget her mother, that slow-dying mysterious woman. There may be no one she loves more than me, but every time she looks at me she sees my sister, Daphne. Warring ghosts fight each other inside my mother's heart, and the battles have made her stern and strong.

CHAPTER SIXTEEN

They never sifted through the ashes of the old man's trailer. I asked the Floyd Volunteer Fire Marshal.

"Did anyone sift through the ashes?" I said. "Did anyone comb through the rubble, looking for anything salvageable from the old man's belongings?"

He shook his head.

"There was nothing left to look through," he said. "It burned to the ground."

"No half-burnt belongings, even?"

"Nothing," he said. "I'm sorry, Clara. I know he was a friend of yours."

If someone had looked, they might have found salvageable objects from the old man's trailer. Things that were scorched, bent from the heat, but still usable. There might have been things that to the untrained eye looked like junk, burnt beyond any conceivable use, but that to the someone in the know would have been useful. The trained eye can see the possibility of beauty and usefulness. The old man, had he not died in the fire at his trailer, had he come across the burnt ruins of another trailer in another time and place, would have sifted through the rubble. The old man would have come away from the ruins of that fire with his hands full of possibility. After a time, the old man would have changed something that was only a possibility into something that existed, something whole, something with a place in the world.

I think about his hands sometimes. The hands of a metalworker are hands that work with fire. Most people may have looked at the old man's hands and seen nothing but fingers, tendon, bone, and the skin that covers them all. They would not have known about the knowledge in the old man's hands, what he knew how to do with his fingers, how he could take something that was a possibility and make it into something real.

If we had had more time, I might have asked him many questions, questions that I did not have time to think of. There are questions waiting in the future, questions that I will come to, and some will be questions that I want to ask the old man, and the old man will not be there to ask.

Some people may have thought of the old man as ugly or evil. The possibility exists that in Sterns, there are people who thought of him in that way. I used to think that the lady two trailers down from the old man thought of him as evil. There was something in the way she used to lean out her window and watch. She never said anything. Sometimes she came out of her door, onto her front step, and watched. If I had to pick, I would have picked that lady as someone who thought of the old man as evil.

But I would have been wrong.

That lady thought highly of the old man. She told me so. When I went back, after I got out of the hospital, and stood by the entrance to where the old man used to live, she came out of her trailer and walked down to where I was standing.

"They hauled it away," she said. "The other day. Put some chains around it, pulled it up onto a flatbed, and then it was gone."

"Where?"

"I don't know," she said.

We stood and looked at where the trailer had been for a while. Then I wanted to go. I had looked enough. There was no rubble to pick through. That had been cleaned up. With what, I don't know.

"Well, bye," I said.

"He was a good man," she said. "He shoveled my steps every snowfall."

"He did?"

"He did. Every snowfall, even an inch or two. An inch or two would've been easy enough to sweep off with my broom, but he was there first."

I turned and started down the dirt road that leads to the entrance. She went back to her trailer.

"I thought very highly of George," she called after me. "He used to bring me onions from his garden."

The possibility of beauty exists in an enameled pot rusted through at the bottom, lying in the woods just off Sterns Valley Road. There's a curved handle on the rusted pot, attached to either side. I lifted it up by the handle and swung it back and forth. It squeaked a little, and the handle was rusty, but the possibility was there.

The old man would have seen it, too.

I have the old man's eyes. He trained me to see the possibility of beauty, and that is what I see. I can see it everywhere, in a dented olive oil can, in an old pioneer pot on the Sterns Valley Road.

Fragments of rusted metal flaked off the worn-out bottom of the pot, and the sides of the pot gave when I pushed on them. It crumpled in my hands, all except for the handle. This pot's been through a fire, I thought. It could have been left over in the ruins of a long-ago blaze on Sterns Valley Road.

This pot may have been a pioneer pot, suspended over the glowing coals of a pioneer fire.

It may have belonged to a pioneer mother on her way west. Every night she used this pot to cook stew for her pioneer husband and children. Every evening her oldest child scrubbed it out with sand by the creek, and every morning the pioneer mother cooked cornmeal mush in it for breakfast. You have to be extremely careful when cooking cornmeal mush. You have to sift the cornmeal into the boiling water in a fine stream between your fingers, stirring constantly all the while, or else the cornmeal mush will be an inedible mess of lumps.

That's a true fact. I read it in a pioneer book.

One morning, as the pioneer family packed up their belongings from camping overnight on what is now the Sterns Valley Road but back then was a nameless trail winding through tall meadow grass, the pioneer mother placed the pot on a pile of quilts near the back of the covered wagon. The quilts were folded neatly after keeping the pioneer family warm through the long cool spring night. The pot rested on top of the patchwork quilts, and the pioneer mother thought it was secure.

"Ready," she called to her pioneer husband, who was up front sitting on the wagon seat with the oldest pioneer child.

"All right then," he called back.

He may not have said "all right then." He may have said something else that meant "all right then." It was a long time ago. It's hard to know exactly.

With a sudden lurch, the covered wagon started moving. The pioneer mother was busy tending to her youngest child, who was a baby still in nappies. That's what they called diapers back then. She did not notice when the cooking pot slipped from its perch atop the patchwork quilts and fell to the ground behind the moving wagon. She did not hear the tiny thump it made as it landed.

That night, the pioneer mother searched frantically for the cookpot. She did not find it. Fifteen miles back, the cookpot lay in the tall grasses. Already, leaves had started to sift over it. A curious primeval woodchuck or skunk sniffed at it, then lost interest and waddled away.

It was their only cookpot. The family went hungry that night and had naught to cook their cornmeal mush in the next morning. The baby, still in nappies, wrapped in a yellow blanket, cried piteously. He wailed mournfully through the night.

What happened to them?

A freak snow fell in Sterns, and the ground was newly white in September. You might think that a September snow in the foothills of the Adirondack Mountains is an impossibility. You would be wrong. On the night of that snowfall, I got out all my false stories. All my books waiting to be written. Waiting for their endings. Waiting to find out what happened.

I stalled for a while. There were more fake book reports than I had thought. They were stacked in a wooden crate that I bought at a garage sale in North Sterns. You wouldn't have thought I'd have had that many ideas for books. If asked I would have said ten, maybe twelve. But there were many more than that. Many, many more, all stacked up. I did not allow myself to go through any of them.

Tamar watched me carry the box out the door. She was eating a jar of marinated artichoke hearts. She likes to eat them with a miniature fork that she says is actually meant for pulling lobster meat out of lobster shells.

Tamar raised her eyebrows.

"Burn barrel," I said. "Cleaning my room. Trash."

It hurt me to say that. It hurt me to call the works of my own imagination trash. I thought of the old man, standing in line on Ellis Island, writing in the air with his nose. I thought of him seeing the official people watching him, talking about him, whispering. I thought of him standing straight and willing them to let him in, him alone, no brother Eli who was supposed to be there, too.

"Trash?" Tamar said. "Are you sure?"

"I'm sure."

"Because they look like book reports to me," Tamar said. "Grade-A book reports, if I'm not mistaken."

"That is correct."

"Read me one," Tamar said.

Read me one. That was something I had never before heard from Tamar, eater of artichoke hearts.

"*Read* you one?"

"Read me one."

I closed my eyes and dug my hand into the box.

"*The Winter Without End*, by Lathrop E. Douglas," I said. "New York: Crabtree Publishers, Inc. 1958."

"Sounds good," Tamar said. "Carry on."

I carried on.

It was the longest winter that Sarah Martin had ever known. Growing up on the Great Plains, she had known many a stark December, many an endless January, and the bitter winds of February were not unfamiliar to her. She was a child of winter. But that winter—the winter of 1879—Sarah knew true cold.

The potatoes had long since run out, as had the cabbages and carrots buried in sand in the root cellar. The meager fire was kept alive with twists of hay. When the first blizzard came, followed every few days by another, Sarah's parents had been trapped in town. It was up to Sarah Martin to keep her baby brother alive and warm until the spring thaw, when her parents could return to the homestead.

The true test of Sarah Martin's character comes when her baby brother wanders into the cold in the dead of night. Sarah blames herself for this; she was too busy twisting hay sticks in a corner of the cabin to notice that he had slipped from his pallet next to the fire and squeezed his way outside. "He's only two years old," thinks Sarah. "How long can a tiny child survive outside in this bitter cold?"

Will Sarah Martin be able to find her little brother in time? Will she be able to rescue him from a fate so horrible that she cannot bear to think about it?

Did Sarah Martin have the foresight to dig a snow tunnel from the house to the pole barn where Bessie and Snowball are stabled? Or is there nothing beyond the cabin door for her beloved brother but blowing snow, bitter wind, and a winter without end?

Will Sarah have to face the responsibility of her brother's death?

Will her baby brother be forgotten by everyone but her?

Will she miss him her whole life long?
Read the book and find out.

Tamar ate the last artichoke heart.

"Well?" she said. "How does it turn out?"

"Read the book and find out."

"It's hard to read a nonexistent book," Tamar said. "You run out of words fast."

How Tamaresque, to have known all along that Clara winter was the author of dozens of nonexistent books. How like Tamar never to have said a word.

"So you tell me," she said. "*Does* Sarah Martin bear the responsibility for her baby brother's death? *Does* everyone forget Sarah Martin's baby brother? *Does* Sarah Martin miss him her whole life long?"

"Yes, yes, and yes," I said. "Yes, she bears the responsibility. Yes, everyone else forgets him. And yes, she misses him her whole life long."

"You're wrong," Tamar said.

I watched her pick up her miniature artichoke-eating fork and wipe its tiny tines with her napkin.

"You're wrong on all three counts," Tamar said. "One, it wasn't Sarah Martin's responsibility that her brother died. It just happened. Two, Sarah Martin's mother will not ever forget her child. Every minute of every day of her life, she will be remembering the baby she lost."

Tamar pressed the tines of the miniature fork into the back of her hand and studied the marks they left.

"And that's not all," she said. "Sarah Martin's mother will have to watch Sarah Martin be sad. She will not know how to help her child. Worse yet, Sarah Martin's mother will be unable ever to talk about what happened, and that will only make Sarah Martin feel more alone."

Tamar took the empty jar of marinated artichoke hearts to the sink and rinsed it. She came back to the table.

"And you're wrong about something else, too," she said. "Sarah Martin will miss her brother her whole life long, but Sarah Martin will also be happy. She will grow up strong. She will be an amazing adult."

"How?" I said.

"How takes care of itself."

"I'm going to burn these up," I said.

"You'll write more."

"I won't."

"You will," she said. "You can't not."

Winter Without End fell back into the box. Tamar got up from the table, went over to the kitchen drawer, and brought back a clean dishcloth. She wiped my face.

I carried the crate out to the burn barrel.

They went quietly to their deaths. They puffed into the air, black words curling into gray ash, spiraling away into the sky. I did not allow myself to think of all that I had imagined, all the families I had put together or torn apart, all the children I had sent on perilous journeys, all the people who never found out what happened.

The old man would have gone north with me, through the Adirondacks, up near the border of Vermont. He would have made the trip with me. I was going to ask him to do that with me, and his reply would have been yes. The old man would have known that I wanted to find a small patch of primeval forest, near the Vermont border. He would have known that all I wanted to do was sit there for one day, sit in the patch of primeval forest. The sun would have shone down on us and slowly made its way across the sky. The old man would have sat with me on the soft moss. He would not have talked unless I asked him an answer-demanding question. He would have sat perfectly still with me, hardly breathing, so that eventually the primeval animals would have thought we were part of the landscape. They would have come forth from the woods, dipping and raising their heads, and gazed upon us with their soft eyes. They would have been curious about these new animals that sat as still as dawn.

Primeval animals have never seen human beings. They don't know yet that humans are to be feared, that they carry guns and traps, that the soft fur of animals is something to be sought and taken.

My hermit grandfather would have scared these animals away. Animals living within a few miles' radius of my hermit grandfather would have known fear, and they would have learned that fear from my hermit grandfather. They would have learned distrust of humans, how to step around their traps, how to melt into the underbrush in the fall and barely breathe as the hermit hunter-trapper glided past, his gun at the ready.

Those primeval animals would have passed that distrust and fear on to their young, and their young would not have been primeval animals. They would have been a new breed of animal, one with human added to their list of enemies.

After the old man died in the fire, my hermit grandfather disappeared. My hermit grandfather, who lived in that patch of primeval forest and traded pelts in the village for bare essentials on his twice-yearly trading trips, no longer lives there. No one knows where he went. He took his tipi, his stored pelts, and his flint with him. His gun and his traps he loaded onto the travois and dragged it away behind him. He found a new life.

After he was gone, the primeval patch of forest grew over the spot where he had lived for those years. Moss crept back over the circle of flattened earth where his tipi had been pitched. Birds eventually grew bold and built their nests in the tops of the towering pines that had shaded his summer camp. Once-primeval animals who still knew the fear of a human being watched and waited until the day came when they knew that my hermit grandfather would not be back, and then one by one they entered his patch of forest. Charred remains of his campfire were covered in one summer by new leaves and grass, and in the winter pine needles lay scattered on the whiteness of the snow in the small clearing. Deer came to nibble on the new growth of the baby apple trees that grew at the edge of the primeval forest, apple trees that had grown from seeds dropped from my hermit grandfather's apple core.

In the village where he had gone twice a year to trade his pelts, the storekeeper thought of him just once, in the spring.

"Where's that old trapper?" he asked his clerk assistant.

"The one with the beaver pelts?"

"Yeah. Isn't this about his time?"

They kept a lookout for my hermit grandfather for a week or so, expecting to see his deerskin jacket appear, his bowed head, the fringe on his pants dirtied by the spring mud. They listened for his voice, unused to words, his yes and his no, his lack of language. What they watched for, what they listened for, did not come.

And no one ever saw my hermit grandfather again.

The old man would have sat quietly with me and felt the sun pass overhead. At the end of the day he would have turned to me and said, "Well?" He would have held out his hand to me, and we would have gotten up together. Our muscles would have been cramped from a day of sitting and not moving, a day of pretending to be primeval animals. We would have walked out of the woods together. The old man would have understood that all I wanted was that one day, one day of seeing the place where my hermit grandfather had lived and breathed and thought his thoughts. One day of mourning. I would never have gone back.

I went back into the house through the garage door. Tamar was in the bathroom, the jar of artichoke hearts emptied and rinsed on the kitchen counter. In my bedroom upstairs I pressed my nose against the cold windowpane and looked out at the freak snow, blue in the darkness, and the light of the moon. Orange light flickered against the blue-white snow and the darkness of the woods. If you were a skier skiing through the foothills of the Adirondacks, on your way north to a patch of primeval forest near Vermont, you would be able to see where you were going by the light of the flames, their fierce heat burning up all the fake book reports I had ever written.

Certain trees need fierce heat to regenerate. Take the lodgepole pine, for example. Lodgepole pines do not grow in the Adirondacks. Even in a patch of primeval Adirondack forest, you would not find a lodgepole pine. They are high-altitude trees. They're huge. They can grow to be extremely old. But to reproduce, a lodgepole pine needs intense heat. Only then can a lodgepole pine dislodge its seeds. Baby lodgepole pines grow in the charred earth that is left after a forest fire. In order to have a chance at life, baby lodgepole pines must be born in flame. That's not the kind of tree that grows in the Adirondacks.

After I found the rusted pioneer pot, I washed it and dried it to prevent more rust, and I stored it with my metalworking tools. The old man had given me a pair of tin snips and a solder iron. He was going to train me in the art of welding, but we ran out of time. We didn't know that we would run out of time, but we did. I put the rusted metal pioneer pot in the back of my closet, in an old wooden apple crate that Tamar and I found once when we drove up north to Deeper Lake.

My hair is starting to grow in where the burned scalp was. I lift up my fingers sometimes to touch it and feel its featheriness. *It's dead*, I remind myself, but it feels alive and lovely despite its deadness.

In my twelfth year I learned the importance of usefulness as well as beauty. I began to see consistency among that which is inconsistent. I came to understand the art of possibility. Those were the ways that the old man had saved his life, and they are what he taught me. I was his apprentice, and he was the master.

The first night I ever saw the old man, black shapes moved through the trees, like shadows or bats flying low. I didn't see the old man at first. He moved behind light. Orange flame flickered in front of him. Something black behind the flame was what I stared at. The black shape bent and leaned, curved and straightened. I knew I was watching a metalworker. I knew that he was lighting lanterns.

The old man would be dead before the next winter was out. I didn't know that then. That's part of what being an apprentice means. An apprentice might be set loose at any time. She has to go on alone, remembering what the master taught her. She has to be able to see the world as separate but connected parts, joined not by letters and words but by relationships, and the possibility of beauty.

That first night all I knew was that someone in Nine Mile Woods was joining metal together, lighting up the forest. He was making something useful, something beautiful and full of possibility for the people passing by in the woods, something that I couldn't yet see or understand. But I was a child then.